P9-DTJ-948

REΠEWAL

How a
New Generation
of Faithful Priests and Bishops
Is Revitalizing
the Catholic
Church

*Anne Hendershott
& Christopher White*

Encounter Books
New York   London

The first author is grateful for permission to use the following previously copyrighted material: Anne Hendershott, *Status Envy: The Politics of Catholic Higher Education* (Copyright 2009) by Transaction Publishers. Reprinted by permission of the publisher.

First American edition published in 2013 by Encounter Books, an activity of Encounter for Culture and Education, Inc., a nonprofit, tax exempt corporation.
Encounter Books website address: www.encounterbooks.com

Manufactured in the United States and printed on acid-free paper. The paper used in this publication meets the minimum requirements of ANSI/NISO z39.48–1992 (R 1997) (*Permanence of Paper*).

FIRST AMERICAN EDITION

LIBRARY OF CONGRESS CATALOGING-IN-PUBLICATION DATA
Hendershott, Anne.
Renewal : how a new generation of faithful priests and bishops is revitalizing the Catholic Church / Anne Hendershott and Christopher White.
pages cm
Includes bibliographical references and index.
ISBN 978-1-59403-702-3 (alk. paper)—ISBN 978-1-59403-703-0 (ebook)
1. Church renewal—Catholic Church. 2. Priesthood—Catholic Church.
3. Christianity and culture. I. Title.
BX1746.H46 2013
282.09′051—dc23
2013003353

Never in history has modern man been in greater need of you . . . never has there been such loneliness in the midst of crowds, never such hunger in the face of satiation. Never has there been a more fertile ground for the seed and the harvest the Lord spoke of. All that is needed is a bearer of the Good News who speaks it with such authenticity that it can penetrate the most exhausted hearing, revive the most jaded language. With you lies the future and the hope. You and the Church you serve may be only a remnant, but it will be a saving remnant.—WALKER PERCY, ADDRESS TO SEMINARIANS AT ST. JOSEPH'S COLLEGE SEMINARY IN LOUISIANA (1983)

Contents

Acknowledgments

We began this project in late 2011—excited about the many signs of renewal we were witnessing in our Church and eager to share this good news with others (while also hoping to offer some correctives along the way). Since then, our enthusiasm has only increased, and we remain more excited than ever for both the present and future renewal of Catholicism throughout the world. Over the past few years, we've been encouraged by a number of individuals who deserve credit for their support of our work. In particular, we are grateful for The King's College, where the early seeds of this project were initially planted and whose faculty, staff, and students have greeted our collaboration with much excitement and kindness.

While doing research for this book we had the rich pleasure of meeting a number of priests who have responded to Pope John Paul II and Pope Benedict XVI's call to the New Evangelization. Their lives are models of sacrifice, holiness, and a living witness to the transformative power of the gospel. These men include Fr. Carter Griffin, Fr. Bill Miscamble, Fr. Luke Sweeney, Fr. Roger Landry, and Fr. Brian Welter—thank you for your service to our Church.

Finally, we wish to thank the good people at Encounter Books, who have shepherded this project from its early beginnings. In particular, we owe a great deal to Katherine Wong, Heather Ohle, and Roger Kimball, who deserve credit for their fine work in crafting this book to final form.

A word from Anne: I am grateful to my coauthor, Chris White, who helped to reframe this project from yet another depressing description of the culture wars into an optimistic look at the revitalization of the Church. I am also grateful to Carl Olson, editor of *Catholic World Report*, who provided a way for us to try out our ideas and theories in the initial stages of our project; and to Marvin Olasky, formerly the provost at The King's College, who has given me the opportunity to teach some of the best students I have ever encountered. And, thank you to Daniel Kempton, Vice President of Academic Affairs at Franciscan University at Steubenville, for finding a way to help me become a contributor to the commitment Franciscan has made to the New Evangelization.

A word from Chris: In my early months as a new Catholic, it was my coauthor, Anne Hendershott, who served as an endless source of encouragement to my young faith. I will remain forever grateful for her invitation to partner with her on this project, and I hope that my contributions in some small way can match the kindness and wisdom that she has imparted to me during this time. In addition, I've had the great privilege of interacting with a number of individuals—initially as professional contacts and now as personal friends. For their investment of their time and resources, I remain indebted to Francois and Therese Jacob, Jennifer Lahl, and the entire Center for Bioethics and Culture family, Maria McFadden Maffucci and Anne Conlon of the Human Life Foundation, Harry Bleattler, Mary Schwarz, Kate Monaghan, and Mary Eberstadt. Yet perhaps those who have been in the deepest trenches with me have been my reliable community of friends that support me in ways they will never fully understand. I cannot list all the names, but you know who you are. Finally, to my parents, thank you for first introducing me to the faith that sustains and motivates all of my endeavors—no matter how short I may fall of its teachings.

Introduction

In February 2013 when Pope Benedict XVI shocked the world with his surprise decision to abdicate the papacy, many critics seized the opportunity as further evidence of a Church in crisis. Some commentators were quick to speculate that this decision had little to do with Benedict's failing health and more to do with Church scandals. And during the conclave that elected his predecessor, much of the debate by those within and outside the Church focused on the need for reform of the Roman Curia, the Vatican's administrative body. Many wondered whether the pontiff would be an outside man or a Vatican insider. Would he be a conservative or a liberal? Could this new election bring about the possible changes so desperately sought after by progressive Catholics, such as women's ordination and an elimination of the celibacy requirement?

The election of Cardinal Jorge Mario Bergoglio from Argentina, now Pope Francis, was initially welcomed by most Catholics—including progressive media outlets that were quick to describe him as one of their own because of his concern for the plight of the poor. Yet the new pope is no liberation theologian, nor is he a political liberal. While serving as cardinal of Buenos Aires he clashed publicly with President Cristina Kirchner over her attempts to legalize same-sex marriage. In addition, he has issued some of the most strongly worded statements against abortion and euthanasia of all those issued by Church officials. At the same time, he has been a tireless advocate of the Church's duty to help the poor and serve as good stewards of the environment. All of this is motivated by what he sees as the truth of Catholicism that should influence every aspect of our lives. In a meeting with College of Cardinals just days after his election, Pope Francis offered these words to his brother Cardinals:

> Christian truth is attractive and persuasive because it responds to the profound need of human life, proclaiming convincingly that Christ is the one Saviour of the whole man and of all men. This proclamation remains as valid today as it was at the origin of Christianity, when the first great missionary expansion of the Gospel took place.[1]

And that same address also stressed the need for courage as essential to their ecclesial ministries and proclaiming the truths of Catholicism to a world hostile to its teaching. Having encountered his own resistance, both from those inside and outside of the Church, Pope Francis knows that courage and boldness—along with an uncompromising commitment to holiness—must be at the heart of a priest's identity. When these attributes are present, the Church is at her best and is able to succeed. When they are neglected, the Church fails in her mission.

Similarly, in an address inaugurating the "Year for Priests" in 2009, Pope Benedict XVI asked, "how can I not praise the courageous fidelity of so many priests who, even amid difficulties and incomprehension remain faithful to their vocation as friends of Christ, whom he has called by name, chosen and sent?"[2] The pope emeritus had reason to celebrate. After a long decade in the darkness surrounding the 2002 clergy abuse scandal—a time when progressive Catholics were predicting the end of the celibate male priesthood in books like *Full Pews and Empty Altars* and *The Death of Priesthood*—we are seeing steady increases in the numbers of priestly ordinations throughout the world.

According to the Vatican's Central Office of Church Statistics, there has been an increase of more than five thousand Catholic priests globally in 2009 than there were in 1999.[3] In the United States, many dioceses have had to build new seminaries or expand their facilities to accommodate the extraordinary increase in the numbers of men who want to be a part of a new evangelization in the Catholic Church. Similar increases are evident in Philadelphia and Chicago; Lincoln and Omaha, Nebraska; Newark, New Jersey; Bridgeport, Connecticut; and dozens of other dioceses. In a January 2012 interview published in the *National Catholic Register*, Boston's Cardinal Sean Patrick O'Malley said that when he arrived in 2003 to lead the Archdiocese—the epicenter of the sexual abuse crisis—"the priests were telling me to close the seminary because there were only 25 men."[4] Now seventy men are studying to be priests there, and they have had to turn men away from other dioceses because they just do not have room for them all.

This is welcome news for a growing Catholic population—one that has suffered through a real shortage of priests and a tumultuous recent history. The Pew Foundation recently revealed that half of the world's 2.2 billion Christians are Catholic, with 77.7 million here in the United States. In 1965, there was a Catholic priest for every 780 parishioners. In 1985 that number had increased to one priest for every nine hundred Catholics. But by 2011 the size of the gap had more than doubled, with only one priest for every two thousand Catholics. Catholics residing in places like Rochester and Albany, New York—where there are few priestly ordinations and many closed parishes—understand this shortage firsthand.[5]

Still, the data on the future of the priesthood are encouraging, and Catholics should have hope that this trend can be reversed. The 2012 Survey of Ordinands to the Priesthood by the Center for Applied Research in the Apostolate at Georgetown University (CARA) reveals that there were 487 new priestly ordinations in the United States in 2012—a number that has continued to climb since 2000. In addition, last year's class is slightly younger than the previous year's—following a pattern of lowering the age of ordination from a decade ago.[6] At a time when the teachings of the Catholic faith seem countercultural and the priesthood is facing severe attacks, it appears that the priesthood is once again becoming more attractive to young men.

This is not a surprise to those who have been following the remarkable success of World Youth Days. Attendance at these events is well into the millions, and the vocation fairs are one of the most popular attractions. Increasingly, young women are rediscovering a calling to the religious life, and young men are again attracted to a life of sacramental calling and an opportunity to defend the Church's teachings in their parishes and the public square. All of this stands in contrast with the dire predictions of a priesthood in decline offered by an earlier generation of progressive Catholic theologians and historians. Many of these aging Catholics were shaped by what they believed was an "unfulfilled promise" of Vatican II to embrace modernity. Claiming that the only salvation for the Church would be to ordain women and remove the celibacy requirement, some progressives have demanded that much of the teaching and administrative authority of the bishops and priests be transferred to the laity.

In fact, at the same time faithful Catholics were celebrating the Year for Priests, a coalition of progressive Catholic organizations—united in their four-decade-long desire to transform the teachings and structure of the Church—began making plans for their own national conference dedicated to changing Catholic Church teachings on such issues as women's ordination, priestly celibacy, and access to the priesthood for gay and lesbian Catholics. Toward this goal, the progressives created the American Catholic Council promising to build what they have called a "non-clerical Catholic Church in which the laity reclaims their baptismal priesthood." The group held a conference in Detroit in 2011 in an effort to encourage the laity to "remove the two-tiered system that separates the ordained from the non-ordained."[7]

Although we can never fully know another's motivation for this kind of spiritual quest, we have observed that once you scratch the surface of many of the progressive organizers and participants in the movement to remove what they see as the elite status of the clergy, you find individuals who seem to be drawn to the dissident movement out of sadness or anger over feeling left out. From women who want to be ordained, to gay men and lesbian women who want the Church to recognize the goodness of their sexual relationships, or married ex-priests who long to celebrate the Eucharist again, the desire for an inclusive Church that welcomes their ministerial gifts is what unites them. As progressives, they have long embraced a Church open to experimentation and adaptation to the world—willing to change with the changing culture. And, most important, tolerant and welcoming of all—regardless of Church teachings.

One of the earliest endorsers of the American Catholic Council is Paul Lakeland, a Professor of Catholic Thought at Fairfield University, and honored speaker at the annual meeting of CORPUS—a progressive organization of former priests, mostly married, who continue to lobby the Church for an end to celibacy. Writing that "the laity must reclaim their baptismal priesthood," his book *Catholicism at the Crossroads: How the Laity Can Save the Church* proposes a new and improved priesthood that welcomes noncelibate, heterosexual and homosexual, and married women and men. He writes: "some will be called to a ministry of leadership, including Eucharistic presidency, while others will be called to minister to the local community in a variety of different ways." On the surface, Lakeland's proposed Catholic Church is an egalitarian Church that is open to all. But, for Lakeland, and many of the participants in the American Catholic Council, some Catholics are more equal than others. Claiming that only some lay Catholics would be qualified to function as priests in his new "non-clerical" Church, he writes: "I am not so sure that someone who is also a plumber or an accountant is necessarily adding to the skills valuable to an ordained minister."[8] Rather, Lakeland, a former Jesuit priest who left the priesthood to marry, suggests that educators (especially theology professors, like himself) would be the most logical choice for ministerial leadership once the celibacy requirement is lifted.

For Lakeland and many Catholic theologians teaching on Catholic campuses, the role of lay theologians is to "engage in the process of the conscientization of the Catholic laity." Lakeland writes: "helping the laity to name their oppression is probably the most important thing the theologian can currently do for the Church, and the lot falls on lay theologians because only they share the experience of being lay that is a prerequisite for the effective solidarity that must emerge." In his book *The Liberation of the Laity*, Lakeland asserts that it is time for the Church to begin to democratize many of its processes.[9]

The problem of democratization and the blurring of the distinction between the ordained and the non-ordained was predicted more than two decades ago by Pope John Paul II when he articulated his concerns during his visit to the United States in 1987. In a discussion on the dangers of confusing the role of the clergy with that of the laity, the Pope spoke supportively of the role of lay participation in parish life but warned that in the movement of empowering the laity in ministry activities, "we run the risk of clericalizing the laity or laicizing the clergy." In the dissident culture that proposes to diminish the authority of the clergy, we can see how prescient the pontiff was.

In his 2013 book, *Why Priests? A Failed Tradition*, former Jesuit seminarian Gary Wills admits that he has effectively given up his faith, now denying the Real Presence in the Eucharist, the sacrificial interpretation of the Mass, and the salvific mission of Christ. In his new work, he argues for a "reenvisioning" of the Church that removes the distinction between the ordained and the laity. Yet rather than lobbying for female priests, or gay priests, Wills chooses instead to do away entirely with apostolic succession and the God-given power of the priest to consecrate the Eucharist. While Wills's hatred for priests and the priesthood is palpable on nearly every page of his angry polemic, it culminates in a chapter titled "Killer Priests," in which Wills pronounces: "priests killed Jesus. That is what they do. They kill the prophets."[10] Appearing to see himself as one of the prophets/martyrs, Wills devotes his entire book to ridiculing the practices of the Church—including what he calls priestly imperialism and human sacrifice.

Both popes John Paul II and Benedict XVI understood well what could happen to the priesthood when the roles are blurred, the status diminished, and sacraments are forgotten. Likewise, in 1996, Archbishop Elden Curtiss, the now retired leader of the Diocese of Omaha, Nebraska, published an article, "Crisis in Vocations?," in which he dismissed concerns about "the crisis" of the priesthood and pointed to U.S. dioceses where vocations are flourishing. He wrote: "when dioceses and religious communities are unambiguous about the ordained priesthood and vowed religious life; when there is strong support for vocations, and a minimum of dissent about the male celibate priesthood and religious life, loyal to the Magisterium; when the bishop, priests, Religious and lay people are united in vocation ministry— then there are documented increases in the numbers of candidates who respond to the call."[11]

For Archbishop Curtiss, religious organizations are stronger to the degree that they impose significant costs in terms of sacrifice and even stigma on their members: "I am convinced that shortages of vocations in any part of the country can be reversed by people who share enthusiastically in the agenda of the Church. We have to learn from the dioceses and communities which are experiencing an increase in vocations. . . . Young people do not want to commit themselves to dioceses or communities that permit or simply ignore dissent from Church doctrine." The archbishop argued that the declines in the rate of ordination in the Church in the 1970s, 1980s, and early 1990s was precipitated and continued by people who want to change the Church's agenda, by people who do not support orthodox candidates loyal to the magisterial teaching of the Pope and bishops, and by people who actually discourage viable candidates from seeking priesthood and vowed religious life as the Church defines the ministries.

In some ways, Archbishop Curtiss was talking about the Catholic culture wars—the battles between the progressives, who assert that there are no truths, and the orthodox, who still believe that the Truth has been revealed and requires constant reading and application. It is a battle between the progressives, who are defined by the spirit of the modern age, a spirit of subjectivism, and the orthodox, who are committed to "an external, definable and transcendent authority."[12] For more than four decades there has been a war in the Church between those who believe that the Church is a site of oppression for women, gay men, and lesbians and those who are faithful to the Church's teachings on abortion, sexual morality, and the male celibate priesthood—a war between those who are dedicated to the negation of the authority of scripture and a leveling of all verticals in authority in the Church and those who are proposing a renaissance of the Catholic intellectual tradition and a renewed appreciation for the Magisterium.

We decided to test Archbishop Curtiss's hypothesis, and the following chapters will describe the research we did to assess his contention that faithfulness and orthodoxy contribute to increasing rates of ordination. We were already familiar with a growing body of sociological literature that indicates that the more a religious organization compromises with society and the world, blurring its identity and modifying its teaching and ethics to conform with the world, the more it will decline. We believed that this relationship might also hold when looking at an individual's commitment to the priesthood. As Archbishop Curtiss postulated, we wanted to determine whether the bishop and the culture he creates in his diocese matters.

Drawing from theories on leadership from the business world, we began our research with the idea that it is likely that bishops may indeed make a difference. Large business institutions know that transformative leadership can bring a company from obscurity to great success. Effective business leaders create a corporate culture that inspires others to flourish. There is reason to believe that this is true for religious institutions also. We hypothesized that the more faithful the bishop, the greater the rate of ordinations in his diocese. But we also knew that we were unable to make such a statement without empirical data beyond anecdotal assumptions. Besides, there are so many other possible explanatory variables that must be measured before we could say that bishops play an important role in the rate of ordinations in their dioceses. There are several alternative explanations as to why some dioceses have many vocations and others none—and these variables must be ruled out in order to isolate the role of the bishop. Then, there was the challenge of determining how the "faithfulness" or the "orthodoxy" of the bishop could be defined and measured. The bishops who lead our dioceses are faithful and holy men—this is why our Holy Father called them to become bishops. Still, there are additional variables beyond simple faithfulness and holiness that may be contributing to the great disparity in the rates of vocations by diocese. These variables go far beyond simple "personality" factors. We needed to identify these variables.

We chose to study the characteristics of the bishops who are leading the ordination-rich dioceses and compare their characteristics with those whose dioceses are not producing priests. We already know that some bishops have been more outspoken than others in their support for Catholic teachings on the sanctity of life, traditional marriage, and social justice. An increasing number of them have been more willing than others to directly confront attacks on the Church and her teachings. Some have openly criticized Catholic politicians who have voted to expand abortion rights or change the definition of marriage. This has taken real courage, and those who have done so have been attacked by progressive Catholic media outlets like the *National Catholic Reporter* and *Commonweal,* denigrating their efforts. Some have called these bishops the "culture war bishops," claiming that they are violating the separation of church and state.

We were curious whether these outspoken bishops were inspiring others to follow them, or if the criticisms of their actions would dissuade potential priests. What we do know is that the new generation of priests and bishops show a dramatic difference from the older ones in terms of finding joy in their identity as priests. In a study on priestly identity by Dean Hoge, a now-deceased Catholic University sociologist, the generational divide is quite apparent. Hoge found that 30 percent of priests aged fifty-six to sixty-five saw the notion of a priest as a "man set apart" from the laity as a barrier to Christian community, whereas only 15 percent of priests aged twenty-five to thirty-five saw the differences between the laity and the clergy as necessary for the role of priest. And, while 70 percent of the older priests would welcome optional celibacy and a married priesthood, only 30 percent of the younger priests said that they would welcome such a priesthood. These are dramatic differences.[13] In two newly published books, *Why Priests are Happy* and *The Joy of Priesthood,* author Father Stephen Rossetti presents the results of the most comprehensive survey of American priests ever conducted. Father Rosetti finds that priests enjoy an extraordinarily high rate of happiness and satisfaction—among the highest of any profession.[14]

There is a sadness that one cannot help but experience when reading the books by the married former priests and the women who want to be ordained. It is clear that they genuinely believe that they have been called to the priesthood, but they seem to have forgotten that a genuine calling to the Catholic priesthood cannot involve women and married men. The priesthood is a special calling, and most of those who are priests are grateful for this calling. Ninety-seven percent of all priests said administering the sacraments and presiding over liturgies was their greatest source of satisfaction. Catholic priests are part of the mystery that the Catholic faithful still view with awe and honor. Priests make the transcendent real for us. And this is something that the laity can never hope to do—no matter how much they want to.

The following chapters will explore the reasons for this. The infighting continues as the aging generations of progressive Catholics continue to lobby the Church's leaders to change her teachings on reproductive rights, same-sex marriage, and women's ordination. Yet they are being replaced with a new generation of young faithful Catholics who are attracted to the Church because of the very timelessness of these teachings. These younger Catholics are attracted to orthodoxy. But it is not a reactionary or backward-looking orthodoxy. Rather, it is an orthodoxy that longs for the noblest ideals and achievements of the Church—the philosophy, the art, the literature, and the theology that make Catholicism countercultural. The new orthodox Catholics have found themselves drawn to the beauty of the liturgy and inspired by the commitment to the dignity of the individual that the Church has made.

An increasing number of young men are being called to be contributors to that commitment—alongside faithful and courageous shepherds who ask them to make sacrifices. We introduce these men in the following chapters. We expose the challenges they experience and the obstacles they face from those still working within the Church and her institutions who attempted to dissuade them from answering the call. Most important, we introduce the courageous and faithful bishops who continue to inspire them.

The Struggle for Catholic Identity

More than a decade ago, during a Mass for the members of the National Center for the Laity, Chicago's Cardinal Francis George gave a homily that startled the faithful by pronouncing liberal Catholicism "an exhausted project . . . parasitical on a substance that no longer exists." Declaring that Catholics are at a "turning point" in the life of the Church in this country, the cardinal concluded that liberal Catholicism had shown itself "unable to pass on the faith in its integrity and inadequate to foster the joyful self-surrender called for in Christian marriage, in consecrated life, in ordained priesthood." Cardinal George concluded that liberal Catholicism "no longer gives life."[1]

While shocking to some of the attendees, this was hardly a revelation to faithful Catholics. Orthodox Catholics have been complaining for more than forty years about what they saw as an attempted coup by progressive Catholics—wondering if their bishops had noticed, or worse, whether their bishops shared the sentiments of the liberals. But for the faithful listening to Cardinal George's homily, there were only a few moments of silent celebration before he moved on to anger some of them when he said that the answers to the problems in the Church "are not to be found in a type of conservative Catholicism obsessed with particular practices and so sectarian in its outlook that it cannot serve as a sign of unity in all peoples in Christ."[2]

For Cardinal George, neither radical liberal nor radical

conservative Catholics can help the Church to flourish. He believes that neither side can do the work of evangelization that all Catholics must do. Rather, Cardinal George believes, the answer is "simply Catholic." Simply Catholic embodies a faith that is able to distinguish itself from any cultures and able to engage and transform them all. It is a faith that is joyful in all the gifts Christ wants to give us and open to the world he died to save. Cardinal George believes that the Catholic faith shapes a Church with a lot of room for differences in pastoral approach, and for discussion and debate. Faithful Catholics believe that Christ cannot be adequately known except from within his Body, the Church. And, within the Church, the bishops are what Cardinal George calls the "reality check for the apostolic faith." The bishops are not free to change established dogma or create new doctrines—no matter how much liberal Catholics may want them to—because the Catholic Church locates power in Christ and in his gift of authority to the Twelve. Catholics who are "simply Catholic" accept these teachings.

Similarly, in his recent work *Evangelical Catholicism*, Catholic commentator George Weigel argues for a new understanding of the role of the Church in the world today, which, as his title suggests, he labels an evangelical Catholicism. Rejecting the divides of progressive Catholics or traditional Catholics, Weigel advocates for a Church that is both known and understood as a mission, anchored in a deep and personal friendship with Jesus Christ. Only through an embrace of this type of Catholicism will Catholics assent to the truths and teachings—even the difficult ones—that Christ has established for his Church.[3]

Understanding this helps explain the reason for the struggle over Catholic identity, both internally and externally. Faithful Catholics want to preserve the unchangeable doctrines and dogma of the faith. Although they understand Cardinal George's concerns about conservatives who "take refuge in earlier cultural forms of faith expression and absolutize them for all times and all places," they recognize a much greater threat from the liberal or progressive Catholics who want the Church to change her infallible teachings on what faithful Catholics know are impossible to change. Denying the legitimate authority of the bishops as the successors of the apostles, progressive Catholics want a church whose priestly ministry is open to any of the baptized—including women and noncelibate men. They want the Church to deny that homosexual acts are morally wrong; a church that celebrates a woman's right to choose abortion and artificial contraception; and a church that only views marriage as a secular union—not a sacrament that is meant to last for a lifetime.

We believe that Cardinal George was correct when he described the motivations and the behaviors of both sides of this struggle. As members of what we believe to be the side that is faithful to the non-negotiable teachings of the Church on faith and morals, we are grateful that the cardinal was willing to speak these words out loud. Had we been at that Mass on that cold January day in 1998, we too would have celebrated the courage of the cardinal. However, we would go a step further. In the following pages, we argue that the reason the Catholic Church is as strong as she is today lies in her response to the warring factions within. For more than two centuries, the Church has battled enemies both within and outside her gates. We maintain that the battles have not just helped her to survive; we believe that she is at her best when she holds steadfast to the bold commitments that have sustained her throughout the years.

Certainly, we understand Cardinal George's desire to end the battles, and we understand that most bishops would welcome a unified congregation in which all followers agreed on everything. But no institution—especially a cultural institution like the Catholic Church—can exist without conflict. The late sociologist Philip Rieff, author of *Triumph of the Therapeutic* and *Sacred Order, Holy Order: My Life among the Deathworks,* has written about this battle for identity. He has pronounced: "where there is culture, there is struggle . . . culture is the form of fighting before the firing actually begins."[4] For Rieff, culture is the continuation of war by other—normative—means. By its very nature, the work of culture is "the matter and manner of disarming competing cultures," something that always threatens sacred order. Rieff also reminded us that no culture in history has sustained itself merely as a culture: cultures—including Catholic culture—are dependent on their predicative sacred orders and will break into mere residues whenever their predicates are broken. What Rieff calls "verticals in authority" are absolutely necessary.

This is not to say that the Church must be resistant to all change. Change is inevitable, and through conflict, there will always be change. Conflict is inherent to culture. The Church, like all institutions, is constantly being "re-created." But this re-creation must be guided by the ultimate authority. It cannot be guided by the changing values of a given culture at a given time. The Church can never change the infallible teachings of the Magisterium, including the dignity of the human person, the sacredness of the family, and the institution of the priesthood. These are not just "values"—they are definitive teachings. For Rieff, "values give no stability—they fluctuate in the values market."[5] Yet progressive Catholics believe the Church should change as the culture changes. In contrast, orthodox Catholics believe that God—the ultimate authority—is active in our lives, and it is through trust and obedience, with the guidance of the bishops and priests as teaching authorities, that the people of God will flourish. Consider just one example of this: in 1968 when Pope Paul VI resisted the widespread cultural embrace of contraception—a trend in which Protestant churches radically altered their long-held positions—he predicted that in the long run, this embrace of contraception would be bad for society. In the encyclical *Humanae Vitae*, he noted that this would lead to four resulting trends: conjugal infidelity, a lowering of moral standards, a loss of respect for women on the part of men, and increased governmental coercion.[6] Now, almost fifty years later, we are seeing just how prescient Pope Paul VI was. This is precisely the type of long-term wisdom that the Church has to offer—the ability to resist cultural fads and influences in favor of ultimate truth and human flourishing. Yet this role—and mission—of authority is one that is constantly under assault from the liberal wing of the Catholic Church.

We must acknowledge that all Catholics, both progressive and orthodox, like to think of themselves as good people—acting with compassion, and treating others fairly and with respect. But in some ways, this is where the battle lines are drawn. All Catholics want their Church to reflect the same standards or definitions of "goodness" that they hold for themselves. And for the past four decades, Catholics have been battling over opposing visions of what constitutes the good. As liberal or progressive Catholics believe that the only way to respect the dignity of all is to ordain women to the priesthood, traditional or orthodox Catholics maintain that women can never be called to the priesthood, as the priests are not simply leaders, they are a representative of Christ himself. While most progressive Catholics believe that the only way to show respect to gay and lesbian Catholics is to support committed sexual relationships by providing access to marriage, the other side maintains that although gay men and lesbian women should always be treated with dignity, the very essence of marriage is—and only can ever be—the permanent union between one man and one woman. And in the debates over abortion, most progressive Catholics maintain that they can still be good Catholics at the same time they respect a woman's right to control her reproductive decisions. Pro-life Catholics maintain that sacrificing the life of an unborn child for a distorted definition of women's equality is always wrong.

There are many issues that divide Catholics—and both sides in the Catholic culture wars claim that theirs is the side that truly respects the dignity of the individual. Orthodox Catholics assert that Revealed Truth is on their side. They point to scripture, as it comes to us through the Magisterium—the official teachings of the Church—as what we need to rely on when we are speaking of the sinfulness of abortion, the impossibility of women's ordination, and the disordered nature of homosexual acts. Adopting the language of postmodernism, progressive Catholics deny the possibility of Truth—claiming that there are many truths—all based on the "lived" experiences of individual Catholics. For example, in *The Idea of a Catholic University*, George Dennis O'Brien, a progressive Catholic, claims that the hierarchical authority model used by the Vatican is "improper both to faith and academic freedom" and argues for a model that "respects different kinds of truth."[7] More recently, O'Brien published *The Church and Abortion: A Catholic Dissent*, which continues his assault on the Magisterium and argues that the Church should stay out of the debate on abortion.[8] Claiming that "there is a level of irrationality in the unbending condemnation of abortion that has created a silence in the Church akin to the silence of a dysfunctional family," O'Brien is critical of the "absolutism of Catholic anti-abortion" and says he is "disturbed by the harshness of anti-abortion rhetoric and the tendency of abortion to become the single issue for Catholics in the public square."[9]

Progressives like O'Brien believe that the only way we can truly respect the dignity of the individual is to "look to the subject," or look to the experiences of individual Catholics. They privilege the experiences of gay men or lesbian women who want the Church to recognize their loving relationships through marriage; women who are desperate to end an unwanted pregnancy; and women and noncelibate men who claim that God himself has called them to the priesthood. They negate the sacred teaching authority of the bishops and instead propose to build a Church in which there is no truth and no sacred order.

Beyond the moral issues of abortion and homosexuality, some of the greatest internal struggles in the Catholic Church focus on the priesthood and the requirements for ordination. In his article on the need for orthodoxy, Archbishop Elden Curtiss wrote that he was "personally aware" of progressive Catholic vocation directors, vocation teams, and evaluation boards who have turned away orthodox candidates for the priesthood who do not support the possibility of ordaining women, who defend the church's teachings about artificial birth control, or who exhibit a strong piety toward certain devotions, such as the Rosary. He also suggested that the priesthood has been damaged by those who do not support faithful priestly candidates who are loyal to the magisterial teaching of the pope and bishops. And he charges that these same people have discouraged excellent candidates from seeking priesthood and vowed religious life as the Church defines these ministries.[10] Then, once they have discouraged such candidates, those progressives who precipitated the decline in vocations by their negative actions or their writings called for the ordination of married men and women to replace the vocations they have discouraged.

The shortage of priests is actually celebrated by many Catholic progressives and is especially attractive to people like the aforementioned Gary Wills and the late Richard Schoenherr, a former priest and coauthor of *Full Pews, Empty Altars*, who advised the bishops that there was nothing they could do to address the decline in priests—except ordain women and married priests.[11] And more than two decades ago, former Jesuit priest Bernard Cooke predicted that "liturgical starvation" would lead the Church to ordain women and married men.[12] Claiming that although a liturgical leader may preside, "it is the community that celebrates the Eucharist," Cooke told a gathering on the University of San Diego campus that "the existence of a socially privileged group (priests) within the Church is not meant to be. . . . I hope that in a relatively short time, the inappropriate division between clergy and laity will vanish."[13] Many progressives view the shortage of priests as an opportunity to demand structural changes in the Church—including the ordination of women and married men.

Unfortunately, the case for the structural changes that Wills, Lakeland, Cooke, and Schoenherr have been making has, at times, been aided by a number of priests and even bishops who seem to have become conscripts for the progressive side of debates over Catholic identity. Three decades ago, Albany's Bishop Hubbard wrote to his priests that rather than clinging to "one's own identity or vested interest" one needed to work to empower the laity in ministry. Appearing to refocus the role of the priest away from the primacy of his sacramental role, Bishop Hubbard wrote: "I envision your role to be initiators, coordinators and facilitators of ministries."[14] Bishop Hubbard's admonishment to priests that they should not cling to their identity as priests was prescient. It is difficult today to avoid thinking that this has been a major problem in many dioceses as the line between the laity and the ordained became increasingly blurred—as some seem to have forgotten the divine origins of the priesthood. Hierarchical structures are problematic for progressives who believe that these authority structures infringe on the rights of the individual. In the past, some bishops appeared to have become swept up in the quest for social equality and egalitarianism that permeated even the priesthood and the United States Catholic Conference of Bishops (USCCB) in the past four decades.

But times have changed, as a new generation of priests and bishops have emerged. This new generation, appointed by Pope John Paul II and Pope Benedict XVI, is no longer willing to compromise with progressives on the infallible teachings of the Church. Progressive pundits have been calling these more orthodox bishops the "culture war bishops" because they are here for the fight—no longer willing to back down from battles over federal funding for abortion and threats to religious liberty. Courageous bishops like New York's Cardinal Dolan, Chicago's Cardinal George, Philadelphia's Archbishop Chaput, Phoenix's Bishop Olmsted, Newark's Archbishop Meyers, and Baltimore's Archbishop William Lori are no longer willing to allow State or Federal interference in Church matters as was recently attempted by the legislature in the state of Connecticut, and by the Health and Human Services attempt to mandate coverage for contraceptives—including abortifacients—by Catholic institutions.

All of this has angered the progressive side. Blogger John Gehring, a former employee of the USCCB, laments the renewed activism by the bishops. Working now at the George Soros–funded progressive advocacy organization, Faith in Public Life, Gehring longs for the days when "social justice" was the primary goal of the bishops' directives. He quotes someone he calls a "widely respected, now retired Church official," who served for several decades in his diocese's social justice office, who complained:

I am concerned about the tone of the bishops. What is missing today is the conciliatory, collaborative, politically astute leadership of the bishops of the '80s and '90s. To compromise is considered weak by this crowd. The bishops have become captives of the corporate elites, the National Right to Life, and conservative lay organizations. They have access and influence that eclipse that of progressive Catholics.[15]

The retired diocesan official also bemoaned the fact that "the church's social justice work is increasingly being drowned out by abortion politics, the fight against same-sex marriage and deep animus against the Democratic Party."[16] Many orthodox Catholics would counter that the USCCB, which has historically been staffed by progressives like John Gehring, has spent much of its institutional life since the 1960s as an adjunct of the Democratic Party—refusing to acknowledge the culture of death that has permeated the radically pro-choice political party.

Progressives like Gehring suggest that the bishops need to be more "conciliatory." They suggest that we all should try to ignore our differences, resigning ourselves to their incompatibility. They say that the two sides just need to agree not to argue about our differences anymore. But, as any sociologist knows—and certainly, Philip Rieff knew well—there are strong institutional pressures within the Church that drive members to a kind of uniformity of culture. These institutional dynamics operate whether Catholics like them or not, and they shape the ways in which young Catholics are taught; they shape the ways in which seminarians are formed; and they shape the everyday experience of the Catholics in the pews. The "taken for granted" dynamics then become an invisible part of the culture. Until recently, it has seemed to most conservatives that liberal Catholicism was the default position at the national bishops' conference. With their highly touted and most visible statements centering on nuclear disarmament, environmental sustainability, and community organizing, it was understandable when faithful Catholics were dismayed when Catholic politicians like former Speaker of the House Nancy Pelosi, with her 100 percent proabortion voting record, appeared to be in the "good graces" of the Catholic Church. When Pelosi assumed the leadership of the House in 2007, she was honored with a Mass presided over by the late Father Robert Drinan, a former pro-choice senator from Massachusetts.

Still, as a result of the inevitable conflict that accompanies all cultures—including the Church—change has arrived. Many bishops are beginning to recognize the problems of the past and have made a dramatic overhaul in the catechesis of children, strengthening the role of scripture and reintroducing the concept of sin and redemption. Faithful Catholics are grateful to the bishops for their renewed attention to catechesis, their robust defense of religious liberty, and their commitment to the priesthood. Unlike progressives, these Catholics know that one of the most important signs of a healthy Church is whether young men continue to be called to the priesthood.

Data on Vocations Trending Upward

According to the Official Catholic Directory, in 2010 there were 467 priestly ordinations.[17] In 2011 and 2012, the number of ordinations rose to 480 and 487, respectively. This is a steady increase from 2002, when there were 442 men ordained to the priesthood in the United States. Some dioceses experienced much greater increases, while other dioceses are still experiencing a stagnation or even a decline in ordination rates. One might be tempted to look for the easy answers to the disparity by simply looking at the percentage of Catholics living in a diocese and conclude that those with large numbers of Catholics would have large numbers of ordinations. This would be wrong. In fact, some researchers have found that when there is a greater percentage of Catholics living within a diocese as compared with the total population in the diocese, there are fewer ordinations.

This counterintuitive finding is given more meaning in the work of sociologist Rodney Stark. In his article "Market Forces and Catholic Commitment," published in the *Journal for the Scientific Study of Religion*, Stark and his coauthors suggest that the lower ordination rates in dioceses with a high percentage of Catholics stems from a lack of competitive pressure from other religions.[18] According to this theory, competition from other denominations for church membership forces a diocese to be more innovative and results in a more vigorous local

Church. They propose that in those dioceses where there are a greater proportion of Catholics there is less competition for Church membership and fewer signs of institutional health like ordinations. As Rieff might suggest, where there is no struggle for the faith, the faith can sometimes be taken for granted—and forgotten.

There is some anecdotal evidence for this market view of ordinations. For example, in 2009, there were no ordinations in El Paso, Texas, where there is a Catholic majority of 649,648 Catholics (79 percent) living in a diocese with a total population of 825,611. In contrast, there were four priestly ordinations in 2009 in the Diocese of Lincoln, Nebraska, where Catholics are a much smaller percentage of the total number of people living in the diocese. In Lincoln there are only 95,445 Catholics (17 percent) living in a diocese with a total population of 580,275. And, in the Portland, Oregon, diocese in 2009, there were six ordinations to the priesthood in a diocese where Catholics number only 409,864 (16 percent) out of a total population of 3,269,195.

Even so, the Stark theory of competition may not be adequate to explain the great variation by diocese because there are also dioceses with large numbers of Catholics as a percentage of the total population that also had large numbers of ordinations. In 2011, the Diocese of Newark, New Jersey, had 18 men ordained to the priesthood, and this diocese has 1,318,557 (47 percent) Catholics out of a total population of 2,784,183. Likewise, the Diocese of Paterson, New Jersey, had nine priestly ordinations in 2011, and this diocese has 424,722 Catholics (38 percent) out of a total population of 1,129,405.

Some researchers have suggested that rather than looking simply at population differences, the real explanatory variables for the disparity by diocese in ordinations are socioeconomic and demographic—including ethnicity. In *Full Pews and Empty Altars,* Richard Schoenherr and Lawrence Young suggest that dioceses with large percentages of Hispanic residents report significantly lower rates of ordinations. There is some support for that assertion in the most recently released *2012 Survey of Ordinands to the Priesthood,* by CARA. Commissioned by the USCCB, this survey found that although Hispanics/Latinos constitute approximately 34 percent of U.S. adult Catholics, they were only 15 percent of ordinands in 2012. In contrast, Caucasian/European American/Whites made up 71 percent of those ordained in 2012 and only 58 percent of adult Catholics nationally. Asians/Pacific Islanders constituted only 4 percent of United States Catholics overall but were

9 percent of those ordained in 2012, and African/African American/ Blacks constituted 3 percent of all adult Catholics nationally and made up 3 percent of ordinands in 2012.

The lower rates of ordination of Hispanics might help us understand the low rates of ordinations in El Paso, Texas. But when looking at the rates of ordinations throughout the dioceses in the United States, there are some dioceses with large numbers of Hispanics in the population and large numbers of ordinations. In the Corpus Christi, Texas, diocese, there were three ordinations to the priesthood in 2011. Corpus Christi is a diocese where Catholics—the majority of them Hispanic Catholics—constitute more than half of the total population of 558,831 (70 percent).

It is clear that the disparity in ordinations by diocese has a more complex cause than ethnicity. Some researchers, like Schoenherr and Young, have tried to contribute to the explanation for diocesan disparities by suggesting that higher levels of educational attainment and socioeconomic status by potential ordinands within dioceses would contribute to declines in rates of ordination. Implying that the seminary is a solution for those who have fewer choices, these researchers predicted that dioceses that are more affluent and have a more highly educated population will experience lower ordination rates. However, the most recent diocesan data on priestly ordination contradicts their 1993 predictions, as some of the most affluent dioceses have experienced some of the highest rates of ordination.

Although the USCCB study of the class of 2012 ordinands found that their education level prior to entering the seminary is somewhat lower than the education level reported a decade ago, there are other explanations for this disparity. Educational differences are more likely due to the fact that a larger number of 2012 ordinands had entered the seminary at the college level—at a younger age—instead of waiting until they completed their undergraduate studies. In 1999, 25 percent of responding ordinands had less than a college degree before entering seminary, compared to 61 percent of ordinands in 2012. Forty-three percent of all those who were ordained as diocesan priests in 2012 are age twenty-five to twenty-nine. Overall, the ordination class of 2012 is slightly younger than in 2011, following a trend in recent years of lower ordination age than a decade ago.

One sociological variable that seems to provide some explanatory power in helping us understand the disparity in diocesan ordination rates is the level of urbanization of a diocese. Given the sociological fact that residents of urban areas demonstrate weaker attachments to religion, one might expect that urban areas would produce fewer ordinations. But the opposite is true. As other researchers have found in the past, a contemporary review of ordination rates for the past few years reveals that the more urban the diocese, the higher the rates of ordination. In 2012, the dioceses with some of the highest rates of ordinations included the urban areas of Atlanta, Austin, Boston, Bridgeport, Chicago, Cleveland, Detroit, Indianapolis, Los Angeles, Newark, New York, Philadelphia, Portland, Oregon, St. Louis, San Francisco, Seattle, and Washington, D.C. Still, this theory of urbanization and ordination rates cannot explain why a rural diocese like Lincoln, Nebraska has experienced such high rates of ordination.

Moving beyond Demographic Variables: Bishops Matter

In his now classic article, Archbishop Curtiss asserted: "when dioceses and religious communities are unambiguous about the ordained priesthood and vowed religious life as the Church defines these calls; when there is strong support for vocations, and a minimum of dissent about the male celibate priesthood and religious life, loyal to the Magisterium; when the bishop, priests, Religious and lay people are united in vocation ministry—then there are documented increases in the numbers of candidates who respond to the call." Archbishop Curtiss cited "The Churching of America, 1776–1990," a sociological study published by Roger Finke and Rodney Stark, which points out that the more a religious organization compromises with society and the world, blurring its identity and modifying its teaching and ethics, the more it will decline.[19] Curtiss concluded: "Religious organizations are stronger to the degree that they impose significant costs in terms of sacrifice and even stigma upon their members. . . . I am convinced that shortages of vocations in any part of the country can be reversed by people who share enthusiastically in the agenda of the Church. We have to learn from the dioceses and communities which are experiencing an increase in vocations. . . . Young people do not want to commit themselves to dioceses or communities that permit or simply ignore dissent from Church doctrine."[20]

In 2001, Andrew Yuengert, a Pepperdine University professor, attempted to quantify Archbishop Curtiss's observations that the disparity in diocesan ordination rates is due not to changes in the socio-logical characteristics of the dioceses but to the characteristics of the diocesan staff—including what he calls the "theological attitude" of the bishops.[21] In a study titled "Do Bishops Matter?" Yuengert drew on theories of motivational leadership from the business management literature to explore the role of the bishop in fostering vocations. Us-ing diocesan ordination data collected from the years 1986–1997, Yuen-gert investigated the extent to which the characteristics of diocesan bishops can explain the variation in ordination rates across dioceses. Statistically controlling for population density and the socioeconomic characteristics of the diocese, Yuengert found that the year of ordina-tion to the episcopate had a large effect on ordination rates.

Yuengert found that bishops ordained and installed as bishops in the 1960s and 1980s had significantly higher priestly ordination rates in their dioceses during the years 1986–1997 than bishops ordained in the 1970s. Yuengert used this variable to "capture any differences across time in the criteria for bishop selection, and differences in the priestly training of bishops across generations." Of course, it must be acknowl-edged that Yuengert published his article more than a decade ago and drew on ordination data that is more than twenty years old. The date of Episcopal ordination and installation of most of today's bishops is in the 1990s—with many recently installed since 2000. In looking at the Episcopal ordination of today's diocesan leaders, there are far fewer members of the cohort of bishops of the 1970s.

In an attempt to quantify the effect that "theological attitude" may have on priestly ordination rates, Yuengert attempted to define ortho-doxy and progressivism by identifying the places where bishops pub-lished articles (for example, whether they published in the progressive *America* versus the orthodox *Catholic Answer*). However, trying to use the places that bishops published as an indicator of the theological at-titude of bishops may not have captured the bishops' characteristics as well as Yuengert would have liked. A more comprehensive analy-sis of "theological attitude" would require going beyond a review of the places bishops publish their articles to an analysis of their actual writings, including their letters to the faithful, and their public pro-nouncements. We have begun such a study. The following chapters will begin to provide support for our belief that the theological atti-tude of the bishop, along with his concern for new priestly vocations, has a significant impact on ordination rates. While we do not claim to have provided an exhaustive study of all of the writings of all of the bishops, we provide evidence that the more forcefully the teachings of the Church are defended by a given bishop, the greater the yield in vocations to the priesthood in the diocese led by that bishop.

This would not surprise Catholic novelist Walker Percy. In a speech to the graduating seminarians at St. Joseph's College nearly thirty years ago, Percy predicted a time when the Catholic Church and the faithful Catholic people—both priests and laity—will have become "a remnant, a saving remnant." He believed that the familiar comfort of the parish staffed by several priests may be changed, but in its place will be a pilgrim Church, "a sign of contradiction witnessing to a world in trouble."[22] Percy knew then—back in 1983—that the seminarians of St. Joseph's would be practicing their priestly ministry in a very different world. He knew that their priestly ministry would eventually become no longer coextensive with the greater culture. Percy understood that "hostility is no stranger to the Church," and he also understood that struggle is a necessary part of culture. Yet Percy assured the graduating seminarians that

> never in history has modern man been in greater need of you
> . . . never has there been such loneliness in the midst of crowds,
> never such hunger in the face of satiation. Never has there been
> a more fertile ground for the seed and the harvest the Lord
> spoke of. All that is needed is a bearer of the Good News who
> speaks it with such authenticity that it can penetrate the most
> exhausted hearing, revive the most jaded language. With you
> lies the future and the hope. You and the Church you serve may
> be only a remnant, but it will be a saving remnant.[23]

Percy knew that the shortage of priests was a problem—but it would not cause the end of the Church as we know it. Christ has promised us priests. Percy knew that even if there were few faithful priests left, those who remained would make the Church stronger. He would be happy to learn that the current data on the increasing numbers of ordinations to the priesthood are very encouraging.

2   Building Better Seminaries

In October 2010, Cardinal Donald Wuerl of Washington, D.C., announced that his archdiocese would be opening a new seminary to accommodate the increased numbers of young men responding to the call to the priesthood. In making his announcement, Cardinal Wuerl said: "at a time when the teachings of the Catholic faith seem counter-cultural, we are seeing an increased interest in the priesthood, particularly among younger men who want to be a part of a new evangelization in society." Blessed John Paul II Seminary, the new Washington, D.C., seminary, is the physical manifestation of the late pontiff's push for a new evangelization. Opened in the fall of 2011, the new seminary has the capacity for thirty seminarians. There were nineteen seminarians in the inaugural class, and in a January 2012 interview, Father Carter Griffin, the director of vocations for the Archdiocese of D.C., revealed that their seminary would soon be full: "the biggest challenge we face right now is a space issue," noted Griffin.[1]

Just a few blocks away from Blessed John Paul II Seminary is the Theological College, the national seminary of Catholic University of America (CUA). While Theological College serves as a training house for future priests throughout the United States, it is also experiencing similar expansion. Following the recent installation of Father Phillip J. Brown in March 2011 as the new rector of the seminary, Brown wrote a letter to friends of the seminary reflecting on both the blessings of its growth and the challenges it presents: "I am especially gratified that TC will have a full house this year. In fact, we were not able to accept all of the suitable candidates who wanted to come to TC this year and whose bishops wanted to send them here. . . . We have to take a serious look at how we might be able to provide more space for them."[2] Washington, D.C. is not alone in the tremendous growth in priestly candidates. There are other seminaries also enjoying full occupancy. In fall of 2011, the Archdiocese of Baltimore's Mount St. Mary Seminary—the second oldest in the United States—surpassed Chicago's Mundelein Seminary to become the largest seminary in the United States. Baltimore has served as the cradle of Catholicism in the United States, and Mount St. Mary's has long been held in high regard for its orthodox faculty and seminarians. The entering class was the largest in over ten years—currently housing more than 170 seminarians in training for the priesthood—placing the seminary at maximum capacity.

In Boston, there are currently seventy men training for the priesthood at St. John's Seminary. This is an increase from a low of twenty-five men in the Boston seminary in 2003, when Cardinal Sean O'Malley was appointed archbishop.[3] In North Carolina, the *Te Deum* Foundation acquired 484 acres of land to build a new seminary in Mooresboro. In making their announcement, the Foundation proclaimed on their website: "most seminaries only teach how to close parishes, cluster parishes, and how to administer to several parishes in light of dwindling numbers of Catholics. Praise be to God that this is not a problem in the South!"[4]

In a November 2011 news briefing, the Catholic News Service reported that this trend is replicated in seminaries throughout the United States:

> At the Pontifical College Josephinum in Columbus, Ohio, 40 new seminarians arrived this year, bringing total enrollment to 186, the highest level since the 1970s. St. Paul Seminary School of Divinity at the University of St. Thomas in St. Paul, Minn., welcomed 30 new graduate-level seminarians, making its class of 100 seminarians the largest since 1980. The influx forced 24 seminarians and two priests off campus into leased space at a former convent. In the Diocese of Scranton, PA., where the St. Pius X diocesan seminary closed in 2004 because of declining

enrollment, the number of seminarians has more than doubled from eight to 17 in the past two years.[5]

In addition to this latest surge in seminarians, there are still dioceses like the Diocese of Lincoln, Nebraska, which have had strong enrollments in their seminary for several decades. But, even in Lincoln, where vocations have continued to flourish throughout even the dark years for vocations elsewhere, recent increases in priestly candidates have moved the Diocese of Lincoln to expand its facilities. In 1997, Bishop Fabian W. Bruskewitz (now retired) acquired the land to build a full seminary for the Diocese of Lincoln, St. Gregory the Great. In 1999, the seminary graduated its first class, and today the seminary is viewed as model seminary—both in terms of its growth and formation of priests. During a February 2012 interview with the *National Catholic Register,* the now-retired Bishop Bruskewitz reflected on the great success that Lincoln has experienced: "We have a splendid clergy, and our religious life is flourishing. We have had many vocations, more than is adequate for a diocese of our size. In the last 20 years, I've ordained 67 priests for Lincoln and another 20 or 30 for other dioceses or religious orders. We have 38 seminarians studying for the priesthood. I've had the joy of constructing St. Gregory the Great Seminary, a college seminary, which opened 12 years ago. It instructs not only our students, but those from six other dioceses."[6] The success of St. Gregory the Great and the leadership of Bishop Bruskewitz has not only had a positive influence on diocesan priests but has also yielded success in religious life. Two years after St. Gregory the Great opened its doors, the U.S. branch of the Priestly Fraternity of St. Peter moved its seminary, Our Lady of Guadalupe Seminary, to the Diocese of Lincoln. This order of priests is dedicated specifically to preserving the extraordinary form of the Roman rite—a practice that many considered outdated and unnecessary but was welcomed by Bishop Bruskewitz as an opportunity to help in the preservation of the Church's great patrimony.

At the same time that St. Gregory the Great Seminary was opening in Nebraska, its neighboring state of Colorado was making preparations to reopen the seminary for the Archdiocese of Denver. When Archbishop Charles Chaput was appointed to lead the archdiocese in 1997, he made a commitment to expanding vocations and enhancing priestly formation. In his 2002 book *Goodbye Good Men,* Catholic journalist Michael Rose documented the seminary's transformation under Chaput's leadership. Rose points out that Archbishop Francis Stafford, Archbishop Chaput's predecessor, bought the forty-acre campus of St. Thomas Theological Seminary after the Vincentian-run institution closed in 1995. But serious moral and pedagogical problems emerged there. In 1999, Archbishop Chaput reopened the seminary—under a new name and with a new faculty:

> The new Saint John Vianney Theological Seminary is not only dedicated to the theology of Pope John Paul II and Joseph Cardinal Ratzinger, it is connected with the two-hundred-year-old Pontifical Lateran University. Officials at the Lateran, which is known as the Pope's University because it is directly under the Pope's authority, approved the Denver faculty and curriculum. . . . Its mission from inception is clearly to form holy and healthy priests for the "new evangelization." Rather than reading texts penned by dissidents who rose to notoriety in the 1960s, the Vianney curriculum emphasizes the philosophy of St. Thomas Aquinas and the "great books" of Western Civilization.[7]

Even prior to the 2002 sexual abuse revelations in Boston, Catholic commentators or the general media would hardly have predicted such staggering growth. The culture wars that defined the 1990s sought to label the Catholic Church as an outdated and archaic institution. Priests and bishops began to be viewed as men who could not relate with their own flock. How then did they manage to overcome this negative public opinion?

Orthodoxy and Orthopraxy

Both orthodoxy (right belief) and orthopraxy (right practice) are fundamental building blocks for successful seminaries. One trend that these seminaries all have in common—Washington, Boston, Lincoln, Denver, and others—is that they are all located in dioceses where the sitting bishop has prioritized fidelity to the Magisterium as a defining factor in his ministry and has made vocations a primary focus for the diocese. A recurring theme that emerges when we look at the data on ordinations and priestly candidates is that leadership matters. The data demonstrate that the Church is at her best when she is guided by leaders who are faithful to her teachings and who encourage others to exhibit the same level of faithfulness.

When Father John Folda, rector of St. Gregory the Great in Nebraska, was asked why the seminary was experiencing such growth in its number of seminarians, his response was simple yet revealing: "the love of the Church and the examples set by Pope John Paul II and Bishop Bruskewitz." Similarly, Father John Hilton, the former director of vocations for Denver, attributed the success of Denver to Archbishop Chaput and "his relentless efforts in promoting vocations." Francis X. Maier, former chancellor for the Archdiocese of Denver and now chancellor for the Archdiocese of Philadelphia, had similar praise to offer Archbishop Chaput: "what the archbishop does through his personal witness is to make the priesthood attractive to a lot of people . . . it's his highest priority."[8] Father Carter Griffin, vocations director for Washington, D.C., had similar words to say about Cardinal Wuerl in D.C.: "he has been instrumental in creating a culture of vocations through spending time with both the seminarians in prayer through retreats and celebrating Mass, but also through spending time with their families and supporting them through this process."

Likewise, in a 2005 interview published in *Catholic World Report*, a newly ordained priest of the Diocese of Yakima, Washington, described the personal attention of the now retired Bishop Sevilla to seminarians: "[Bishop Sevilla] takes time to visit our seminarians, most specially at the seminarian's year end evaluation, when there's a big celebration in the seminary, or simply when he's in the vicinity of the seminary. He phones the seminarian on his birthday, wishes him a happy birthday, assures him of this continued prayers, and most importantly, thanks him for studying for the priesthood in his diocese. He always reminds the seminarians that they should not hesitate to call him if they need anything."[9] In the same interview, a newly ordained priest spoke of similar involvement of then Bishop Kevin Boland (now retired) of the diocese of Savannah, Georgia: "At Christmas, Bishop Boland sends each of his seminarians a Christmas present, an orthodox book on some aspect of Catholic faith or spirituality. . . . Whereas some seminarians from other dioceses have never met their bishop, the seminarians of the Diocese of Savannah know their bishop, and Bishop Boland knows them long before the day he places his hands upon their heads."[10]

Similarly, when Father Brian Plate, then the vocations director of

Newark, was asked about the success of the archdiocese, which has consistently led the country in vocations, his response was on target with the others: "Newark's success to me seems to be leadership, orthodoxy, and vocations as a priority. We've been blessed with two back-to-back strong, unabashed Catholic archbishops, for whom vocations and priesthood are extremely important."[11]

Such concern from bishops, however, should not be uncommon. In *Apostolorum Successores*, the Directory of the Ministry and Life of Bishops, the Church teaches that "among diocesan institutions, the bishop should consider the seminary to have primacy of place, and he should make it the object of his most intense and assiduous pastoral care, because it is largely in seminaries that the continuity and fruitfulness of the Church's priestly ministry depends."[12] We have already pointed out in chapter 1 that bishops have tremendous influence in nurturing vocations. It is the strong leadership of Bishops Wuerl, Chaput, and Bruskewitz, among others, that consistently rank their dioceses as producing the highest number of vocations each year.

Creating a Culture Dedicated to Nurturing Vocations

Archbishop Carlson of Saint Louis has seen firsthand what happens when bishops become involved in the vocation discernment process. From 1995 to 2004, Carlson served as bishop of Sioux Falls and from 2004 to 2009 as bishop of Saginaw, Michigan; he was the chairman of the USCCB Committee on Vocations from 1992 to 1994. In a 2006 profile in the *National Catholic Register*, Bishop Carlson was described as placing all his energy on vocations: "when he was installed in Saginaw, he announced that he would 'personally work to build up the priesthood' in the diocese and named himself director of vocations." "That action convinces young men that vocations are a top priority," said seminarian Ben Moll.[13] In addition to personal recruitment, Carlson established the "Operation Andrew" program, which has spread to dioceses throughout the country. Named after the apostle Andrew, who was the first apostle to accept Christ's call to follow him, Operation Andrew is a series of dinners that provide a chance for men who are considering a vocation to the priesthood to have an informal dinner with the bishop—to ask questions and gain perspective on life within the priesthood. Typically these dinners are hosted by diocesan priests and are limited in size so that the bishop and the young men discerning vocations can have a relaxed and personal setting.

In addition to the Operation Andrew dinners, the Archdiocese of Chicago hosts a program titled InSearch, a weekly discernment group for men already out of college who are considering their vocation to the priesthood. During the weekly meetings, which are organized at Chicago's Holy Name Cathedral, these men gather together from throughout the archdiocese to hear various priests, and the bishop, candidly discuss aspects of the priesthood. In describing the program, Father Brian Welter, the current vocations director for the diocese, noted: "each week we invite a different priest from the Archdiocese to speak to the men about their own discernment of priesthood and to share about their priestly duties. We invite a cross-section of priests, so that the men in the program can see the variety of faces and ways that priesthood is lived out within the diocese. We invite parish priests, priests who are chaplains in the Army, or chaplain to the Chicago Police Department, seminary professors, etc. They are all Chicago diocesan priests, but have different duties within the diocese." According to Father Welter, typically the group averages ten men each year. From this group of ten, four to five men usually enroll in the local seminary. Currently, the Archdiocese of Chicago has recruited over thirty new priests from this program.

Meanwhile, in Washington, D.C., the archdiocese has launched the Blessed Teresa of Calcutta Vocation Society, which devotes special prayer for vocations within the diocese. According to Maris Moriarty, one of the founding members of the society, "the Society was founded in 2004 through the Office of Priest Vocations of the Archdiocese of Washington while then Reverend Robert Panke served as Director of Vocations." Moriarty was assisting with priestly vocation events at the time and was charged with the responsibility of organizing the Society. Reflecting on the founding, Maris recalled, "I believe that the beatification of Mother Teresa in 2003 brought a certain grace. Monsignor Panke, his family, me and my mother were in Rome for the occasion. During that time Monsignor Panke realized that prayer would be the primary tool for his work in priestly vocations." Today, the society boasts almost twelve hundred members—all committed to prayer and Eucharistic adoration for vocations to the priesthood and religious life.

Similarly, other dioceses are crafting their own strategies for a renewal of priestly vocations. Father Luke Sweeney, who served as vocations director for the Archdiocese of New York from 2007 to 2012, said that the archdiocese has set a goal of "40 candidates annually—in the hope that at least 20 will be ordained six to eight years later." In a January 2012 interview with the archdiocesan paper, *Catholic New York*, Father Sweeney outlined the four-part plan to reach that number: prayer, vocation promotion, the family, and priests. "the first element has to be prayer, especially Eucharistic adoration." This need for prayer, however, is not simply limited to those considering a vocation. Instead, he expects the entire Catholic community of an archdiocese to participate in a prayerful commitment for vocations to the priesthood. The second pillar of the program is a promotion of vocations. His job takes him to New York area colleges, high schools, and other events to simply ask young boys and men the question "Have you considered becoming a priest?"

In conversations in 2012, Father Sweeney expressed concern that in the past, the work of nurturing vocations to the priesthood was viewed to be the sole responsibility of the vocations office. Father Sweeney, however, rejects this categorization, believing it to be the responsibility of all Catholics—especially pastors and Catholic school teachers: "take Fr. George Rutler," noted Sweeney, "a popular pastor here in Manhattan. He frequently has seen his altar servers eventually entering the seminary . . . that's because he is providing them spiritual guidance and asking the right questions."[14]

The third element in New York's plan for vocations is to encourage families to create households with a healthy commitment to faith— and an openness to the priesthood. As he told *Catholic New York* reporter Claudia McDonnell, the Archdiocese of New York hopes that parents are open to the priesthood, and are able to "provide an environment where their children can be saints, and can come to know God's will and do it with all their hearts." Finally, Father Sweeney encourages priests to be recruiters of other priests. If priests are satisfied in their vocational calling, it will be evident to others, and this will attract others to pursue that same calling.[15]

"A False Sense of Freedom"

When asked about the theological formation that seminarians receive at Blessed John Paul II Seminary in Washington, Father Griffin was quick to note that "orthodoxy is a given."[16] While it would seem reasonable to expect that Catholic teaching is upheld and defended at Catholic seminaries, this has not always been the case in the past. Many Catholic seminaries throughout the country—like many Catholic colleges and universities—have been identified as places where dissenting professors are not only allowed to teach but are actually encouraged to dissent from Church teachings. Concerns about such dissidence within the seminaries led to a Vatican-initiated review of the moral and intellectual life of U.S. seminaries that occurred from September 2005 to July 2006. The report on the Apostolic Visitation, which was not completed and released until December 2008, found that the seminaries in the United States were generally healthy. Still, the recommendations of the visitation team specifically addressed areas in which faculty and seminarians needed to be faithful to the Church's teachings. In their report, they concluded that "a false sense of freedom was sometimes cultivated [in the seminaries], which led to the throwing off of centuries of acquired wisdom in priestly formation. . . . Often, the Visitation discovered one or more faculty members who, although not speaking openly against Church teaching, let the students understand—through hints, off-the-cuff remarks, etc.— their disapproval of some articles of Magisterial teaching. In a few institutes, one even found the occasional non-Catholic teaching the seminarians." The report labeled this a "lack of harmony" in priestly formation and noted that it is "almost always due to one or more educators being less than faithful to the Magisterium of the Church."[17] The report also lamented the lack of traditional Catholic piety and viewed it as a problem related to the lack of orthodoxy among seminary faculty:

> It is profoundly regrettable that many seminaries do not include traditional acts of piety in their *horarium*. Many make the excuse that they prefer to leave such acts of piety to the free choice of the students. Some institutes even have an atmosphere that discourages traditional acts of Catholic piety— which begs the question as to whether the faculty's ideas of spirituality are consonant with Church teaching and tradition. Unless a great many seminaries introduce regular recitation of the rosary, novenas, litanies, Stations of the Cross, and so on, the seminarians will lack an education in the sacramentals and

will be unprepared for ministry in the Church, which greatly treasures these practices.[18]

Suitability for the Priesthood

In the aftermath of the priestly abuse scandals, the issue of homosexual seminarians and priests has been one of the most scrutinized areas of the Church. Accounts of a "gay subculture" among seminarians and priests alike filled pages of books and news articles in the first several years of the new century. Not only was this environment toxic for producing Godly men and future priests, it also discouraged heterosexual men from pursuing their own possible vocations to the priesthood. While the Church has always taught that persons who struggle with homosexual tendencies should be accepted with respect and sensitivity, it has also made clear that they should not be accepted as candidates to the priesthood. In its 2005 document *Instruction concerning the Criteria for the Discernment of Vocations with Regard to Persons with Homosexual Tendencies in View of Their Admission to the Seminary and to Holy Orders*, the Church clearly states: "the Church, while profoundly respecting the persons in question, cannot admit to the seminary or to holy orders those who practice homosexuality, present deep-seated homosexual tendencies or support the so-called 'gay culture.'"[19]

In a 2002 article, "The Clergy Abuse Scandal: What Is Going on in the U.S.?," the author, John Burger, quotes from an interview with Father John Harvey, the founder of Courage, the Church's ministry for people with same-sex attractions: "In one seminary, which he declined to name, professors refer to Church teaching as 'the opinion of the Magisterium,' which gives the impression that the opinions of dissident theologians are as valid as Church teaching. If a moral theology professor teaches that it can be morally good for a Christian to have a homosexual relationship as long as he or she is monogamous, a student may very well apply that opinion to himself and feel free to act out on his inclinations."[20] Similar concerns were expressed by the report from the Apostolic Visitation—particularly among religious orders—though the prognosis is hopeful. The report stated: "nevertheless, in almost all the institutes where such problems existed, at least in the diocesan seminaries, the appointment of better superiors (especially rectors) has ensured that such difficulties have been overcome."

Lessons Learned from Cardinal Newman

Blessed John Henry Cardinal Newman converted to Catholicism and was ordained a Catholic priest in 1847 after a celebrated career—spanning twenty years—as an Anglican minister and a distinguished fellow at Oriel College. To convert to Catholicism in Victorian England was no small feat. It required personal courage and deep conviction. Newman was, in many respects, abandoned and even persecuted by family and friends after his conversion.

Yet Newman realized that his primary role as a Catholic priest was not to convert his fellow Englishmen to Catholicism—neither the political conditions of his country nor the theological attitude of Victorian Anglicans would allow for this. Instead, Newman understood that he must look at the Catholic Church herself. He knew that England's Catholic Church was not yet prepared to embrace converts from Anglicanism. Until the Church first understood herself from *within*, she could not live out her work publicly. As such, Cardinal Newman knew that both Catholic priests and laity alike needed a more comprehensive and uniform catechization.

For Newman, there are two defining elements of Catholicism—her unity and her obedience to authority. Both are essential to the Church's ability to fulfill her missionary role. Newman understood how best to address these defining elements through a strong episcopate and a unified, orthodox seminary: "a seminary is the only true guarantee for the creation of the ecclesiastical spirit. And this is the primary and true weapon for meeting the age, not controversy. Of course every Catholic should have an intelligent appreciation of his religion, as St. Peter says, but still, controversy is not the instrument by which the world is to be resisted and overcome." Quoting St. Peter's words on the priesthood, Cardinal Newman concludes: "you are a chosen generation, a kingly priesthood, a holy nation, a purchased people" (1 Peter 2:9).[21]

Newman knew that the eventual conversion of Anglicans—and other Protestants as well—would only be made possible through the strong formation of the young priests who are tasked with this purpose. For Newman, the seminary was critical in providing the consistent teachings of the Catholic faith. This unity would be necessary to reach England, where the Catholic faith had been misunderstood by many and intentionally perverted by others. Newman also recognized that the bishop needed to work closely with the seminarians in his diocese. The office of the bishop ensured continuity between Catholic flock throughout the world and provided unity with Rome. The seminary was, for Newman, an intertwined element of the unity and authority:

> Each circle of Christians has its own priest, who is the representative of the divine idea to that circle in its theological and ethical aspects. He teaches his people, he catechizes their children, bringing them one and all into that form of doctrine, which is his own. But the Church is made up of *many* such circles. How are we to secure that they may *all* speak one and the same doctrine? And that this doctrine is the doctrine of the Apostles? Thus: by the rule that their respective priests should in their turn all be taught from one and the same centre, viz., their common Father, the Bishop of the diocese.[22]

For Cardinal Newman, a strong episcopate was the only way to ensure unity in the education of seminarians: "They are educated in one school, that is, in one seminary; under the rule, by the voice and example of him who is the One Pastor of all those collections or circles of Christians, of whom they all in time to come are to be the teachers. Catholic doctrine, Catholic morals, Catholic worship and discipline, the Christian character, life, and conduct, all that is necessary for being a good priest, they learn one and all from this religious school, which is the appointed preparation for the ministerial offices."[23] While the experience of seminarians has certainly changed since Newman's day, we can see many parallels between his time and our own. Much like England at the time of Newman's writing, faithful Catholics in the United States today are often viewed with contempt by the world around them. The struggle for the Church to define itself has led to many exaggerations and distortions of Church teaching. Moreover, after Vatican II, many seminaries and houses of formation found themselves in an identity crisis, not knowing how to properly implement the reforms of the Council. As such, the unity of seminary training—one of the Church's best assets—was in many cases lost entirely. Many seminaries appeared to have lost their way. During the last decade, many have managed to correct their mistakes.

Responding to concerns about the shortage of priests throughout much of the Western world, Pope John Paul II issued his Apostolic

Exhortation *Pastores Dabo Vobis* ("I will give you Shepherds") in 1992. Calling bishops, priests, seminarians, and the laity to holiness in order to properly discern their vocations, Pope John Paul II charged the bishops with responsibility for creating a climate that would foster vocations and form faithful priests: "The responsibility of the bishop and, with him, of the presbyterate, is fundamental. The bishop's responsibility is based on the fact that priests receive their priesthood from him and share his pastoral solicitude for the People of God. He is responsible for ongoing formation, the purpose of which is to ensure that all his priests are generously faithful to the gift and ministry received, that they are priests such as the People of God wishes to have and has a 'right' to."[24]

During his papacy, John Paul II appointed a number of bishops who have made a commitment to living the truth of the teachings of the Church. These orthodox bishops have implemented the reforms of Vatican II in a faithful manner, and as a result, they are seeing strong growth in the numbers of young men called to the priesthood. Leadership is key to understanding the successful seminary experiences of priests in dioceses where vocations are flourishing. The defining difference between these ordination-rich dioceses and those that continue to suffer a shortage of priests is a commitment to bold orthodoxy and a focus on the renewal of the vocation ministry that begins with the bishop and extends to all of the People of God. As John Paul II noted, strong priestly formation is essential to evangelization and growth.

In response to *Pastores Dabo Vobis,* the USCCB spent the next decade restructuring their seminaries and training programs to reflect the pope's instructions. Releasing its *Basic Plan for the Ongoing Formation of Priests* in 2002, the USCCB intended this document to serve as a guide for priestly formation throughout all U.S. dioceses. Written primarily for bishops, as they lead their dioceses, the guide is also addressed to vocations directors to use as they assess the suitability of priestly candidates, and for helping seminarians inform their discernment. The guide is also intended to educate the laity as they encourage and pray for new vocations. Following the outline of Pope John Paul II's *Pastores Dabo Vobis* in developing four major dimensions in which a priest would need to be formed, the guide identifies the human, intellectual, spiritual, and pastoral dimensions that need to be addressed.

The *human dimension* primarily deals with the ways potential seminarians'relate to others. Here, the Church calls for helping candidates to develop specific skills in listening and speaking. The Church also calls on her priests to be formed in a way that teaches them to engage in the culture, through the arts, politics, and the sciences. It has often been said that "the Church is a school of humanity," and her priests should be able to emulate this in their personal ministry. But, as important, addressing the human dimension also includes the development of a proper understanding of one's sexuality through the Church's teaching on priestly celibacy.

The *intellectual formation* of priests is the second dimension that the USCCB's guide addresses. Here, the Church looks to the early Church Fathers as exemplars—men who were both pastors and intellectuals, thinking deeply and writing on matters of theology, philosophy, and history. This reflection on the holy mysteries is not something that the Church sees as outdated, but as an activity that priests should engage in on a regular basis to inform their ministry. In addition, the Church calls on greater intellectual formation in areas of the theology of marriage, medical-moral issues, the Church's social teaching, and the theology of suffering, illness, and death.

The guidelines to address the *pastoral formation* of priests mandates that they receive adequate training to properly serve their people. This includes ensuring that priests can deliver thoughtful, relevant and meaningful homilies—regularly engaging in the proclamation of preaching of the word of God. Pastoral formation also includes the priest's training in counseling and the provision of spiritual direction to his parishioners, as well as celebrating the Mass and presiding at the sacraments. In addition, this area of formation requires that priests be trained to adequately serve as pastors of parishes. Preparation in this realm requires that priests be given opportunities to learn practical skills in financial management, conflict resolution, and personnel management as well as general leadership principles. While many of these activities may seem mundane, vibrant parishes typically have pastors and priests who are able to accomplish these practical tasks well. Parishes that are forced to close or consolidate often lack priests who possess basic pastoral skills.

Spiritual formation is at the core of one's priestly vocation—it is developed throughout the course of a priest's lifetime. Still, the process of spiritual formation begins in the seminary, where priests are formed in the areas of priestly discipleship, pastoral charity, celibacy, obedience, and the simplicity of life. In addition, the Church has set the minimum requirements that priests receive 52 contact hours of education per year (one hour per week), one week of retreat, daily prayer, monthly celebration of the sacrament of reconciliation, and monthly contact with a priest group. Research by Father Stephen Rossetti has demonstrated clearly that priests with greater spiritual discipline and devotion are happier and healthier, and as a result, their ministries are enhanced.

Continuing his predecessor's focus on priestly formation, Pope Benedict devoted a substantial portion of his 2008 Papal Visit to the United States to meeting with seminarians. During his visit with the priestly candidates at New York's St. Joseph's Seminary, Pope Benedict celebrated the fact that the numbers of seminarians are increasing: "the People of God look to you to be holy priests, on a daily journey of conversion, inspiring in others the desire to enter more deeply into the ecclesial life of believers." One of the ways Pope Benedict advised seminarians to accomplish this is by "deepening your friendship with Jesus the Good Shepherd. Talk heart to heart with him. Reject any temptation to ostentation, careerism, or conceit. Strive for a pattern of life truly marked by charity, chastity and humility. . . . Dear seminarians, I pray for you daily."[25]

While it is impossible to gauge the direct effect of the Holy Father's visit to the United States in 2008, the prayerfully optimistic tone he set while speaking to the New York seminarians is one that cannot help but resonate with future seminarians and their leaders. At the core of his message was a call to holiness—a challenge to live a life of virtue and greatness. Pope Benedict reminded those gathered that holiness must become the defining mark of the Church's seminaries and must shape her instruction and formation. As each of the bishops continues to create a culture committed to holiness—involving himself personally and directly in the work of nurturing vocations—young men respond to that call.

3 | A Problem with Authority

In the midst of a resurgence in the number of priestly ordinations in many dioceses throughout the United States,
there has been a parallel movement promoted by progressive Catholics—critical of what they see as the privileged
status of the priesthood—that has attempted to diminish
the authority of the Catholic clergy. Numerous books demanding structural changes in the Church that would give
more authority to the laity and weaken the influence of
the bishops and priests evidence this. Some of these books
have launched a direct attack on the priesthood itself.

With titles like *Clericalism: The Death of the Priesthood,*
by George Wilson, S.J.; *Catholicism at the Crossroads: How
the Laity Can Save the Church,* by Paul Lakeland; *The Coming Catholic Church,* by David Gibson; *The Emerging Catholic
Church,* by Tom Roberts; and *Crisis of Authority in Catholic
Modernity,* a collection of critical essays authored by progressive Catholic theologians and historians, these books
promise a new and improved Catholic Church in which
the teaching and much of the administrative authority of
the bishops and priests is transferred to the laity.

One of the most recent releases, *In Search of the Emerging
Church,* published by Orbis Books, is also the most critical of the legitimate authority of priests and bishops. The
author, Tom Roberts, the editor-at-large of the *National
Catholic Reporter,* claims to have written this book because
he believes that a kind of corruption has taken hold within
the Catholic clergy—a corruption that he suggests is the

direct result of a "culture of isolated privilege and unlimited power."[1] Asserting that "Catholics want leaders who aligned more with the horizontal language of Vatican II than with the legalistic approach to belief," Roberts's book is a plea for a "new" Catholic Church—one in which the authority of the Catholic hierarchy is diminished.

On the basis of anecdotal data, primarily interviews with like-minded Catholics, Roberts concludes that Catholics are currently living through a time of tension due to what he believes is "the growing inadequacy of a hierarchical culture that owes more to royal constructs of the period of kings and princes than it does to the teachings of the Suffering Servant."[2] For Roberts, the clergy have created a kind of system not unlike that of ancient feudalism. But whereas feudalism's economy depended on the promise of land for protection, Roberts writes that "the church offers an economy of grace, promising salvation through the economy of the sacraments. . . . The Bishops grant benefices—parishes—to their priests, who promise obedience, homage and loyalty to the chief shepherd of the diocese."[3]

Roberts acknowledges that his was not a scientific study, and it is clear to the reader that his research data were not systematically collected. Rather, they involved anecdotal information gathered from those Catholics who seem to share his belief that the clerical/hierarchical culture can no longer be sustained. Of this, Roberts writes that this clerical culture has "maintained its superiority by claim of some ontological difference from the rest of humankind."[4] Seeing no difference between the laity and the ordained, Roberts, and those he cites throughout his book, offer a disparaging view of the authority of the Church and her priests and bishops.

At one point in his narrative, Roberts writes that today's bishops have become even more resistant to reform than those of the past. And, as a result of the pressure from progressives like himself, Roberts charges, these bishops have attempted to recapture a time in the Church when bishops had more authority. Denigrating attempts to revitalize the priesthood, Roberts enlists Donald Cozzens, writer-in-residence at John Carroll University, to support the conclusion that "the (clerical) culture is unraveling."[5] And, in what Roberts views as a feeble attempt by the bishops to regain their power, he alleges that they are attempting to reinstate the "appearance" of power:

We now see an increase in the accoutrements of royalty and of certain court behaviors. Websites that now refer to Bishops as "your grace" and the more familiar designation of "your excellency" and "your eminence" don't elicit the awkwardness they might have some decades ago. We see an increase in lace, and yards and yards more silk than has been the case since before the council. Capa magnas, long flowing capes suggestive of royalty of an earlier age, are making a comeback. The princes of the church who are so disposed, designate their own chapels where traditionalists gather to worship. The leaders sometimes process from rectory to church under canopies held aloft by young seminarians and priests, who are called on to attend to the trains of the prince's elaborate capes. In these ceremonies there is much vesting and de-vesting while sitting in "throne chairs," all done against a backdrop of murmured Latin.[6]

Mocking the signs and symbols of the timelessness of the teachings of the Church—symbols that are sacred to faithful Catholics—Roberts cites the even more contemptuous comments of Eugene Kennedy, a former priest, who calls the ceremonial behavior by the bishops "Civil War re-enactments" because of "the theatrical quality to it, as if someone has found a cache of props in a theater closet and set out to remake the past."[7]

The disparagement of the hierarchy of the Church by these reformers is especially offensive to faithful Catholics who know that the roots of the authority of the pope and the bishops are found in the Gospels and the writings of the apostles. These writings are based on the apostles' own experiences of Christ. The Gospel of Matthew 16:18 describes the granting of authority to Peter when Christ says: "You are Peter, and on this Rock (Peter) I will build my Church." In conferring this authority, Christ also delegated authority to the successors of Peter, the Church leaders who are called to govern his church on earth, under Christ's ultimate authority, through the application of his Word.

The authority that is given to the pope and to the bishops through apostolic succession manifests itself in the Catechism of the Catholic Church, the encyclical letters of the pope, and the writings and public statements of bishops. Faithful Catholics believe that the Church is God's creation, designed by him as a hierarchical institution, headed by the pope and guided by the bishops. Believers view the Church as infallible in her doctrines, with her leaders serving as the final interpreters of scripture and teachings. As one of the greatest Catholic writers of the twentieth century, Monsignor Ronald Knox, wrote: "the Church involves a hierarchy, not merely in the sense that one functionary is superior to another in dignity, but in the sense that each functionary derives from a superior, his commission to act in the Church's name. . . . When Catholics obey the Church, they obey the voice of God."[8]

Throughout the history of the Catholic Church, most Catholics would have agreed with Monsignor Knox. Catholics traditionally viewed papal pronouncements as the Word of God. This hierarchical view of the Church was taken for granted by faithful Catholics as bishops' letters were read at Mass and taken to heart by parishioners. But as the Enlightenment-era concept of egalitarianism has permeated all aspects of our lives, and calls for a democratic Church have emerged, the acceptance of the concept of an ecclesiastical hierarchy imbued with the authority to issue proclamations and rules to followers has become unacceptable to some Catholics. As a result, calls continue to grow for a democratic Church in which the laity get to choose their own leaders and determine their own doctrines.

Leading the call for what they call an "inclusive" and "adult" Church is a cadre of dissident scholars. Some of them, like Tom Roberts, work as editors and writers for progressive Catholic journals, but most of them are teaching on Catholic college campuses. For some contemporary theologians and historians, like Fairfield University's Paul Lakeland and David O'Brien of the University of Dayton, the hierarchical view of authority—with authority vested in the papacy and the clergy—is just one more sign of what Lakeland calls the "infantilization of the laity."[9] Refusing to be part of what they view as the subordination of the laity, they have called for a leveling of that authority. In their published works, O'Brien echoes Roberts's calls for a "more horizontal" relationship with the Magisterium, and Lakeland demands that the laity "grow up" to "create an adult Church" or an "open Church" in which the laity "reclaims its baptismal priesthood."[10]

In his book *From the Heart of the American Church*, David O'Brien writes that "Vatican II reintroduced an understanding of the divine human relationship that was more horizontal than vertical. God is less above the people, sending down messages through delegates, than abiding with them."[11] O'Brien denigrates the traditional position of the hierarchy and instead writes: "the more communitarian view leads to an ethical method that is anchored in the scriptures and in the experience of Christians, who necessarily must be consulted in moral formulations." For O'Brien, the more horizontal understanding "fastens the vision of the church beyond itself, in the historic liberation of the human family."[12]

Likewise Lakeland, in his book *The Liberation of the Laity*, argues for an "accountable church" with a "liberated laity." By this, Lakeland means liberated from the authority of the hierarchy. In fact, Lakeland identifies the task of the laity as working "to build a non-clerical church." He writes: "helping the laity to name their oppression is the most important thing the theologian can currently do for the church."[13] In his speeches, Lakeland has promised to "help our sisters and brothers exercise their baptismal priesthood." In an address to the 2007 Annual Meeting for the Core of Retired Priests United for Service (CORPUS), an organization of former priests—mostly married—who are still angry over the Church's priestly celibacy requirement, Lakeland's speech (available as an audiofile on the CORPUS website) is replete with his oft-used phrases, including his stated desire to "overcome the lay-clerical division" and address the "structural oppression of the laity" in the Catholic Church.

Marginalizing the bishops' teaching authority in favor of dissenting theologians and removing the distinction between the ordained and the followers are the real goals of organizations like CORPUS. Even the role of the deacon in the Catholic Church has come into criticism by Lakeland. In his 2007 CORPUS speech, he scathingly referred to the "monster species" of the deacon who belongs to a "lay-ecclesial minister species."[14] In a chapter of his book *Catholicism at the Crossroads* titled "An Open Church in an Open Society," Lakeland accuses the current Catholic Church as being "in the business of exclusion." To rectify this, Lakeland claims that "baptism leads inexorably to the restoration of the priesthood of all the baptized." He suggests that the "clergy need to see the laity as their equals, not just before God, but in the daily life of the Church. The laity need to abandon their fear of speaking out. They need to grow up."[15]

Recently, O'Brien and Lakeland were joined in their criticisms of clerical authority by several Catholic historians who are attempting to convince Catholics that the current claims to authority by the bishops are not in keeping with the true intentions of the Church itself. A new book has just been published by Oxford University Press that extends the criticism of the hierarchical structure of the Church by enlisting historians as well as theologians in the battle against the current hierarchical structure of the Church. With an enthusiastic endorsement on the back cover from Paul Lakeland, *The Crisis of Authority in Catholic Modernity* is a collection of essays—critical of the current hierarchy—by theologians and historians that promises to "focus on the tensions between authority asserted and authority observed."[16]

Edited by historian Michael Lacey, director emeritus of the American Program at the Woodrow Wilson International Center for Scholars in Washington, D.C., and Francis Oakley, president emeritus of Williams College, *The Crisis of Authority in Catholic Modernity* contains several essays that question the legitimacy of the authority within the Catholic Church. In the prologue, Lacey asks: "has the ultramontane papacy run its course?" With this question Lacey sets out the argument that since Vatican II, those who disagree with papal pronouncements "feel their claims to belonging, reservations and all, are rightful and cannot be trumped simply by appealing to formal authority or citing those passages in scripture that buttress the idea of divinely instituted apostolic succession and its claim to exclusive spiritual powers of discernment." For Lacey, "the children of the church have come haphazardly to feel like grown-ups and don't believe they have to abandon the family estate over differences in the family."[17]

An underlying theme in many of the chapters of Lacey and Oakley's new book is the call for a democratic Church in which the authority of the clergy is diminished and the laity are given a voice in all matters from the choice of bishops and pastors to doctrinal matters including homosexuality, abortion, birth control, and women's ordination. Lacey asks: "what is the point of the church's aloofness from the ideals and practices of democratic self government. . . . What is this feeling of lofty pride in its ecclesial structure all about?"[18]

In the opening pages of their book, Oakley pronounces: "the past is not what it used to be." Decrying what he called the "triumph of ultramontanism at the first Vatican Council with its twin definitions of papal infallibility and papal jurisdictional primacy throughout the universal Church," Oakley calls for the Church to "limit or balance papal authority."[19] Subsequent chapters continue the attack on magisterial authority. In his contribution to the collection, philosopher

Charles Taylor writes that "authoritative pronouncements on issues where contingent circumstances are crucial to our judgment cannot be taken as definitive, let alone infallible."[20] Like Lakeland, Taylor complains of the "infantilization of the laity" by the Catholic Church. For Taylor, the hierarchy of the Church has not always respected and provided for the inherent limits of its teachings. He believes that there has been a habit of oversimplifying its moral prescriptions, of not trusting the laity to deal with the complexities involved. He writes:

> The clergy cannot see the limits they are overstepping. . . . Let's look at the issue of abortion. Is there something wrong with abortion? Yes, should we try to reduce its incidence in our societies? Yes, but it doesn't follow (1) that outlawing it is the best way to achieve this latter goal (indeed, there is some evidence that the opposite is the case). And even if (1) were true, the issue remains (2) how much this should weigh in the overall decision to vote for X or Y. What if the candidate who would outlaw abortion is a superpatriot, burning to engage in ill-advised wars? This kind of all-in judgment is of the essence of moral decisions in politics and lies beyond the domain of magisterial authority."[21]

Taylor carries his criticism of Church teachings on abortion to Church teachings on women's ordination and homosexuality. Labeling such teachings as "false sacralization," Taylor charges that the Church has held a "too simple and direct reading of natural law, which accounts for the lapidary judgment that homosexual love is an objective disorder." And he questions whether we aren't "sacralizing certain historically based conceptions of gender identity when we conclude that women should not be ordained priests."[22]

Father John Beal's chapter continues the criticism of what he sees as paternalism and infantilization within the Church when he writes that "in the absence of genuine reciprocity between the governors and the governed, the latter are reduced in fact, if not in theory, to dependence on the paternal benevolence of the former." He sees the relationship as something he calls "benevolent despotism."[23] Complaining that "bishops, pastors and other officeholders are accountable for their stewardship to those who appointed them, not to those they serve," Father Beal calls for major reform in this relationship. In a chapter titled "A Teaching Church That Learns?," Gerard Mannion suggests that "dissent can be the most appropriate response when faced with the dilemma that a particular teaching or interpretation of a teaching is being afforded an authority and weight that it does not, or even should not, truly hold. . . . Truly authoritative teaching is that which is existentially liberating and empowering; it values and enhances human freedom and the wider participation of all in the church in the processes that constitute magisterium for such correctly refers only to the function and not the functionaries of authoritative teaching."[24]

Summarizing the chapters, Oakley's epilogue charges that the Church's "authoritarian willingness to impose all or nothing teachings on the faithful tends to be seen as in some measure analogous to King Canute's mythical attempt by royal fiat to prevent the tide from coming in." For Oakley, traditional Catholic thinking has focused "too exclusively on its divine dimension—eternal, stable, and unchanging—and underestimating the degree of confusion, variability, and sinfulness that goes along with its human embodiment as it forges its way onward amid the rocks and shoals of time."[25]

When Elden F. Curtiss, archbishop of Omaha, asserted that the "vocations crisis" was precipitated by people who wanted to change the Church's agenda, he may have anticipated the 2011 gathering of the American Catholic Council, a coalition of dissident Catholic organizations whose stated goal is to help build a nonclerical Catholic Church. With the promise of a way to help the laity reclaim their baptismal priesthood, participants in the American Catholic Conference gathered in Detroit during Pentecost to encourage Catholics to "remove the two-tiered system that separates the ordained from the non-ordained."[26]

Marketed as a kind of "off-site" Ecumenical Council, the Detroit gathering drew more than two thousand participants with the assurance that they would contribute to "thoughtful discussion of scholarly papers and presentations" by Catholic theologians and scholars with the goal of dramatic change in the structure and function of the Catholic Church. And although the organizers of the proposed national gathering appropriated the language and trappings of an authentic "Catholic council," the reality is that the American Catholic Council was conducted entirely outside the purview of the Church. Flouting canon law, organizers ignored concerns expressed by Detroit's archbishop, Alan Vigneron. In a letter posted on the archdiocesan website, Archbishop Vigneron asked the organizers to cancel their plans for their Detroit gathering, which, he said, "distorts the true Spirit of Vatican II." He also asked all Catholics "to pray for the guidance of the Holy Spirit so that we may embrace authentic development of faith and morals and shun efforts which threaten unity."[27]

Rejecting Archbishop Vigneron's request, conference organizers were determined to hold their conference in Detroit. Commemorating the fiftieth anniversary of what the organizers called the unfulfilled promise of the Second Vatican Council, they chose to meet in Detroit because it was the site of the 1976 Call to Action Conference—a conference that Joseph Bottum, the former editor of *First Things*, has described as the "low-point in post Vatican II American Catholic unity." Bottum recalled that the conference began by calling on the Church "to fight chronic racism, sexism, militarism, and poverty in modern society." But by the conclusion of the 1976 conference, Call to Action participants demanded that the Church change its positions on celibacy, women's ordination, homosexual relations, reproductive rights, and Communion for the divorced and remarried—with further decisions to be made by majority votes of lay people.[28]

Patterned after the Ecumenical Councils of the past, while mirroring the goals of the 1976 Call to Action Conference, the American Catholic Council has as its stated goal to "actualize the reforms of Vatican II for the United States Church." On its homepage, the American Catholic Council describes itself as "a coalition of organizations, communities and individuals calling for discussion at every level of the Catholic Church in the United States to consider the state and future of our Church."[29] All of the organizations and individuals involved are affiliated with reformist organizations—some of which have been officially censured by the Church for misleading the faithful.

The two cochairs of the American Catholic Council, Janet Hauter and John Hushon, are part of the leadership of Voice of the Faithful, a progressive organization that emerged in the wake of the clergy abuse scandal in 2002 with the goal of supporting victims. Since that time, it has expanded its goals dramatically to include major structural reform of the Church—including the ways bishops and priests are selected. Hauter has served as vice president of Voice of the Faithful, and Hushon has served as a trustee. Most of the organizations listed as endorsing the Declaration of the Council are well-known reformist organizations, including the Women's Ordination Conference, Dignity USA, New Ways Ministry, CORPUS, Voice of the Faithful, Future

Church, Americans for Rights in the Catholic Church, Call to Action, Take Back Our Church, the Catholic Diocese of One Spirit, the Women-Church Convergence, the National Association of American Nuns, Pax Christi, We Are Church, the European Network, Elephants in the Living Room, Sacred Quest, the Benedictine Monastery of the Holy Spirit, and the Society of Blessed John XXIII. Individual endorsers include Joseph O'Callaghan, Paul Lakeland, and Joanne Blair of Voice of the Faithful, Thomas Brooks of Celibacy Is the Issue, John Bammer of Spirited Lay Action Movement, and John Kinkel of Oakland University.

Promising that the national council will recapture the universal call to ministry, organizers promised to remove the two-tiered clerical system that separates the ordained from the nonordained and claimed to have launched the call for the national council in an effort to "create a more responsive, accountable Church that calls on the active participation of its people and more closely models the American experience." And while Council leaders have denied that they are attempting to create their own church apart from the Catholic Church, the American Catholic Council website homepage states their mission clearly: "we seek nothing short of a personal conversion of all to create a new Church, fully in tune with the authentic Gospel message, the teachings of our Church, and the American context in which we live."[30]

It was no surprise to orthodox Catholics to learn that the leaders of Voice of the Faithful were helping to launch the American Catholic Council. Since its founding in 2002, the goal of Voice of the Faithful has been "meaningful change in the Church." Encouraging systematic transformation and growth in the universal Church, Voice of the Faithful lists goals and objectives on its website that replicate the rhetoric of the American Catholic Council on what both organizations appear to view as the malevolence of the two-tiered clerical system or the separation of the laity from the ordained. Both organizations claim that Jesus envisioned a community that welcomed and encouraged the gifts of all, and both organizations lament that what they view as the promise of Vatican II—"the universal call to ministry"—has not yet been fulfilled.[31]

Although Voice of the Faithful slogan maintains that its goal is to "Change the Church, Not the Faith" and the organization claims that it organization "supports priests of integrity," Voice of the Faithful's organizational statements do not always match the sentiments of its leaders or members. This disconnect was especially evident in 2009, when individual members of Voice of the Faithful became strong, outspoken supporters of legislation introduced by two Connecticut legislators that would have allowed the state of Connecticut to control individual parishes' governance and financial affairs—relegating Catholic priests and bishops to an advisory role in their own parishes.

In March 2009, state senator Andrew J. McDonald and state representative Michael Lawlor, both Democrats, introduced Bill 1098, An Act Modifying Corporate Laws Relating to Certain Religious Corporations. Had this bill passed, it would have required the following.

- A corporation would have to be organized in connection with any Connecticut Roman Catholic Church or congregation in the state by filing in the office of the secretary of state.
- The Archbishop or bishop of the diocese would serve as an ex officio board member but could not vote on issues.
- The corporation would have a board of directors consisting of not fewer than seven and not more than thirteen lay members.
- The board members would be elected from among the lay persons of the congregation.[32]

According to Senator McDonald, the impetus behind the bill was what he called the worst case of financial mismanagement in a Connecticut Catholic parish. It involved Reverend Michael Jude Fay, a priest in Darien, who was convicted of stealing more than $1.4 million from donations by parishioners. In local press reports, McDonald claimed that his constituents asked for his help to address the priestly scandal. But there is much more to this story.

On the surface, the proposed bill looks like an unconstitutional takeover by state lawmakers in Connecticut. And while that is true, the motivation behind the legislation reflects a much bigger issue. The evidence surrounding this takeover points to yet another example of what sociologist Peter Berger calls the "secularization from within" the Church itself. The real force behind this bill is a small but well-organized group of Catholics—unhappy with Church teachings on moral and governance issues—attempting to enlist the state as a partner in radically transforming the Church from within.

To understand the real story behind the proposed legislation, one only has to look closely at some of those promoting the bill—including Paul Lakeland, who was on the front lines in leading the charge for the legislation. As a spokesman for the bill in media interviews, Lakeland has long lobbied for an end to what he calls the structural oppression of the laity by the clergy. Lakeland has been a presenter at conferences sponsored by Voice of the Faithful. At the spring 2009 Voice of the Faithful Conference at Fairfield University on April 26, Lakeland's speech, "Who Owns Our Church? A Theological Perspective," focused on many of the same themes of empowering the laity that are contained in his books.

The *National Catholic Register* reported that in June 2003, Lakeland was the keynote speaker at a conference for Voice of the Faithful affiliates in Newton, Massachusetts, where he told the gathering that lay Catholics were "suffocating from structural oppression." The newspaper also reported that Lakeland advocated the abolition of the College of Cardinals, the ordination of women, and lay participation in the election of bishops. He also predicted future priests would consist of "some married, some not, some straight, some gay, some women, some not."[33]

Criticism of the privileged status of priests and bishops in leading the faithful is at the basis of the 2009 Connecticut legislation. To understand the origins of the legislative attack on the Catholic Church, it is important to understand the agenda of Voice of the Faithful and some of its angriest members. While it was founded in the Boston area in 2002 to respond to the Catholic Church sex abuse scandals, the *agenda* for many of the members of the Voice of the Faithful now has expanded from protecting children to reducing the power of the Catholic hierarchy, eliminating the requirement for priestly celibacy, and supporting the ordination of women. Several Voice of the Faithful members mobilized to address what they viewed as yet another example of reckless clericalism when Father Fay was convicted of stealing parishioner donations to the Church in order to lead a luxurious lifestyle with his gay partner. According to press reports, Father Fay spent money donated by parishioners of St. John's Church on limousines, stays at New York hotels, elaborate meals in New York restaurants, jewelry, clothing, and a Florida condominium. The Fay case is most often cited by those promoting the legislative takeover of the Church in Connecticut.

The proposed Connecticut bill was promoted by those individuals who have had a powerful incentive to generalize from the Fay case in order to exaggerate claims of priestly sexual abuse and financial mismanagement. Catholic feminist theologians exploited the moral panic that surrounded the clergy abuse scandals of 2002 to criticize what they regard as the deviance of the Church's patriarchal hierarchy and the need for women's ordination. This tactic has been used since 2002, when in the midst of the clergy abuse scandal Lisa Sowle Cahill, professor of theology at Boston College, published an opinion piece in the *New York Times* asserting that the priestly abuse "exposes the weaknesses of a virtually all-male decision making structure."[34] Her proposed solution was to ordain women and encourage "all Catholics to withhold funds from all diocesan and Vatican collections and organizations" until the Church agrees to her proposed reforms.

While we cannot claim that Voice of the Faithful members had a hand in writing the actual legislation that was promoted in Connecticut, we must point out that many of the articles in the now-withdrawn Connecticut bill mirror those promoted by Voice of the Faithful's Bridgeport affiliate. In their *Annual Report* in 2005, Voice of the Faithful chairman Tony Wiggins reported that the Bridgeport Chapter's "Structural Change Committee identified five proposals for Structural Change for the Church." These five proposals were "overwhelmingly approved by the membership of the Voice of the Faithful Bridgeport Chapter." Voice of the Faithful's final document presenting these proposals to the state legislature advanced the idea of open election of bishops, parish priests, and parish and diocesan pastoral and finance councils and the ownership of church property by the people of the parish. The document supported these proposals with historical notations and argued that this was the model in the early Church. The necessary changes required in canon law were also noted. The document was then presented and approved by the Voice of the Faithful National Leadership meeting in Indianapolis in July 2005.[35]

Although the membership in groups like Voice of the Faithful continues to decline, and they have been plagued by financial troubles—coming close to declaring bankruptcy in 2010—this organization still reflects the beliefs and goals of a powerful minority within the Church who have been engaged in a 40-year battle with the hierarchy over issues including sexual morality, academic freedom on Catholic campuses, priestly celibacy, divorce and remarriage, and the ordination of women. Many of them work on Catholic college campuses, and some of them work within diocesan offices within the Church itself. They are able to wage battle effectively because some bishops have not always been willing to provide a robust defense of the Church's teachings. Sometimes bishops have actually put Church teachings in jeopardy by acquiescing to the state's demands.

In fact, just two years before the 2009 legislative proposal to take over the Church's governance, Hartford's archbishop reversed an earlier decision on emergency contraception by complying with the state's demands to provide the morning-after pill (also called Plan B) to victims of sexual assault at the four Catholic hospitals in the state. While the archbishop's statement on the Connecticut Catholic Conference website claimed that the administration of the morning-after pill after a pregnancy test is "in accordance with Catholic moral teaching," the Vatican statement on that pill, issued in 2000, condemns its use outright. The Pontifical Academy for Life states that "the absolute unlawfulness of abortifacient procedures also applies to distributing, prescribing, and taking the morning-after pill."[36]

One can conclude that the archbishop's decision on emergency contraception opened the door to state interference in Catholic hospital procedures. So it should be no surprise that lawmakers continue to ignore Catholic concerns about legislative decisions in other areas. Democratic congresswoman Rosa DeLauro, a Connecticut Catholic, was one of the sponsors of the Freedom of Choice Act. Within the state, Catholic lawmakers have passed some of the most permissive abortion laws in the nation. As a result, Connecticut continues to experience a significant rise in the number of abortions each year while national abortion rates continue to decline.

In the past it has seemed that many of the bishops have appeared to be reluctant to contribute to the conversations surrounding limits on late-stage abortion, parental notification laws, waiting periods, and other strategies that have been shown to reduce abortions in other states. But that seems to be changing. Beyond abortion, Catholic lawmakers have been especially eager to pass gay rights bills in the state. The sponsors of the now-dismissed Church governance bill, State Senator McDonald and State Representative Lawlor, both Catholics, are both openly gay men and outspoken same sex marriage advocates. Both have been tireless in their efforts to introduce same-sex marriage in the state, and both have been openly critical of the Catholic Church's opposition to laws dismantling the current definition of marriage as a union between a man and a woman. It appears that the Connecticut bishops paid a price for their defense of marriage. In fact, so convinced that the proposed state takeover of the governance of the Catholic Church was a form of "payback" for the Church's efforts to prevent the legalization of same sex marriage in the state, Bishop Lori told a newspaper reporter that he believed that "the proposed Church governance bill was an effort to silence the Church on important issues of the day—especially with regard to marriage." It appears that this may in fact be true, as the Church governance bill was proposed the day before the same sex marriage bill was to be heard.[37]

Despite the efforts of the supporters of the governance proposal, faithful Catholics and their leaders were gratified that the Democratic sponsors abruptly withdrew the controversial bill just a week after they proposed it. Responding to the thousands of phone calls, faxes, and emails from angry Catholic constituents, McDonald and Lawlor canceled a public hearing for the bill. Instead, the two lawmakers told newspaper reporters that they "plan to host a gathering of legal and religious scholars from throughout the state to discuss the issue." Despite the cancellation of the hearing, thousands of faithful Catholics traveled to the state Capitol to protest the takeover attempt. While Lawlor and McDonald were absent from the Capitol on the day of the protests, McDonald issued a published statement saying that the issue had "spun out of control." He acknowledged that "my attempt to create a forum for a group of concerned Catholic constituents offended a group of similarly devout Catholic parishioners."[38]

It is likely that the attempt to pass this legislation will continue in Connecticut—and elsewhere—not because of a perceived need by most Catholics for state oversight of their priests and parishes, but because there are so many within the Church who can gain so much by keeping this issue alive. For feminists lobbying for women's ordination, the image of the "problem priest" like Father Jude Fay points to the need for women to fill priestly roles. For angry former priests like Paul Lakeland and his counterparts in CORPUS, marginalizing the power of the bishops and elevating the power of theologians like themselves opens the door for them to return to the priesthood—especially if the parishioners are given the power to vote in favor of it. For gay rights activists intent on denouncing what they view as the Church's hypocrisy on homosexuality, the Fay case is often used to illustrate what can happen when gay men are not allowed to express their sexuality openly as priests. And for some of the members of organizations like Voice of the Faithful, which desire that the Church become a "democratic" institution, it became an opportunity to enlist the state as a partner in trying to create an egalitarian Church that reflects the will of the people rather than magisterial teaching.

Still Calling the Alternative Magisterium to Action

For the dissidents, the first Call to Action Conference in Detroit in 1976 is like a Catholic Woodstock that these now-aging revolutionaries all speak of as the most hopeful time of the Church—a time when the "promise of Vatican II" was most vivid to them. Today, Call to Action goes beyond most other dissenting Catholic groups in combining dissent against Church teaching with New Age and Wiccan spirituality. Membership draws heavily from former clergy and feminist nuns seeking to reform what they view as the "sinful structure" of the patriarchal Church.

A few years ago, the activities of Call to Action were deemed to be "so irreconcilable with a coherent living of the Catholic faith" that the Vatican publicly affirmed an Episcopal decree of excommunication for any member of the dissident organization. Claiming that Call to Action is "totally incompatible with the Catholic faith" and is "causing great damage to the Church of Christ," Cardinal Giovanni Battista confirmed the Episcopal decree that membership in Call to Action causes one to be automatically excommunicated from the Catholic Church. Despite this, many Catholic theologians teaching on Catholic campuses retain active membership in Call to Action—openly participating in meetings and conferences. One of the reasons theologians have confidently challenged the teaching authority of the Catholic Church is that many left-leaning theologians believe that they already form an "alternative magisterium" that interprets and implements the judgments of bishops and popes.[39]

Woven throughout the writings of liberal Catholic theologians remain questions about papal infallibility—and error. In *The Liberation of the Laity*, Lakeland makes the claim that the whole body of the faithful shares in the Holy Spirit guaranteed infallibility of the Church. Former *New York Times* religion writer Peter Steinfels goes even further by arguing that "it is possible for popes, despite the guidance of the

Holy Spirit, to fall into tragic error. . . . Many liberal Catholics believe that was probably the case in the 1968 issuance of *Humanae Vitae* and cannot be ruled out in the refusal of ordination to women." In an essay titled "Liberal Catholicism Reexamined," Peter Steinfels writes: "one definition of liberal Catholicism is simply papal teaching a hundred years too soon." Reflecting the sentiments of a small yet powerful number of angry Catholics who believe that their dissenting views on the path to salvation, apostolic succession, women's ordination, reproductive rights, and sexual morality are the views of the future of the Catholic Church, Steinfels argues that the possibility of "papal error" demands the continuing contribution of liberal Catholicism.[40]

Most of those calling for the "horizontal" Church that they believe was promised at Vatican II are senior citizens. The majority of the self-described "Revolutionaries in Rockports" who gathered in Detroit on Pentecost in 2011 were over sixty years old, leading some to suggest that we need not worry that they can continue to have a major influence on the people of the Church. But this neglects the fact that the students enrolled in undergraduate courses in moral theology, systematic theology, and ethics continue to be influenced by these dissident theology professors. Their students will be encouraged to participate in the formation of an alternative magisterium of the future as they too pursue graduate programs in theology and continue the cycle of disobedience on many Catholic college campuses.

The choice of Pentecost for the 2011 gathering of the American Catholic Council was no coincidence. Stressing the "emergent" message of the Holy Spirit working through the "people of God" to support a married priesthood and women's ordination is really the goal. Unfortunately, there have been bishops who support such views. Retired San Francisco archbishop John R. Quinn has supported these kinds of structural changes in his book *Papal Primacy and the Costly Call to Christian Unity*. Quinn's book argues for decreased papal authority with more control granted to bishops and parishioner involvement in the selection of bishops. Quinn believes that the "reunification of Christendom cannot be achieved unless such changes are implemented."[41] In a lecture at Oxford University's Campion Hall in 1996, Quinn stated that the Vatican should reopen discussion of such issues as the ordination of women, birth control and married priests. For Quinn, the papacy is located within the college of bishops: "this means that the pope cannot be understood to be outside and above the episcopacy. . . . In other words, the normal exercise of the papal office must be collegial."[42]

In some ways, it seems that many within this older generation of bishops and priests have been embarrassed by their own authority. Coming of age in the egalitarian 1960s, when all authority—including Episcopal authority—was contested, it seems that many of these bishops are reluctant to even admit that they have authority. This is not just an American problem. During Pope Benedict's 2010 trip to Britain, Archbishop Bernard Longley responded to a question from the media about the vestments worn by priests and bishops in the papal ceremonies by minimizing the important role of the clergy. Rather than explaining that the vestments are an important signifier that the members of the clergy are about to do something that only an ordained priest can do (consecrating the Eucharist), Archbishop Longley said that "the cloaks and cassocks aren't used to set the clergy apart from the Catholic laity. They are symbols of service to God."[43] This is misleading. The distinctive chasubles and miters signify that when the priests and bishops wear these vestments they are doing something that is not "ordinary." They are doing something the laity cannot do—no matter how much they may want to. Regrettably, some bishops seem reluctant to remind others that the ordained are able to do something others cannot.

In an address titled "Sacred Duties, Episcopal Ministry," Bishop Robert Francis Vasa told listeners that "teachers who advocate a popular, ear tickling message are more likely to be admired and warmly received and accepted by our secular age. . . . Such an approach may lull the evildoer with an empty promise of safety."[44] Bishop Vasa cautioned: "there is prudent silence, but there is also imprudent silence. There is indiscreet speech, but there is also discreet and bold speech." Recognizing that people have lost a tolerance for sound teaching, Bishop Vasa said that too often pastoral documents tend to appeal without necessarily being too direct or critical. As a result, too often, the bishop is viewed as offering mere opinion on issues rather than authoritative teachings.

Yet finally it seems the bishops are responding to such challenges to their teaching authority. Most recently, the USCCB's Committee on Doctrine issued critical statements concerning *The Quest for the Living God*, a book by Fordham University theologian Sister Elizabeth A.

Johnson, and *The Sexual Person: Toward a Renewed Catholic Anthropology*, by Creighton University theology professors Todd A. Salzman and Michael G. Lawler. Regarding the latter book, the bishops reminded the writers that "the Catechism insists that the historicity of the natural law does not negate its universality. . . . The natural law remains as a rule that binds men among themselves and imposes on them, beyond the inevitable differences, common principles."[45]

When the Catholic Theological Society of America sent a formal letter to the bishops' Committee on Doctrine, complaining about what they called a lack of dialogue from the bishops in issuing their criticisms of Sister Johnson's book, Cardinal Donald Wuerl of Washington, chairman of the Committee on Doctrine, responded to them with a letter titled "Bishop as Teacher," which spoke authoritatively about the roles and responsibilities of bishops and theologians in the Church.[46]

Throughout his almost eight-year pontificate, Pope Benedict continually reminded the bishops of their individual responsibility when he said: "if we are to stay true to our solemn commitment as successors of the Apostles, we Pastors must be faithful servants of the word, eschewing any reductive or mistaken vision of the mission entrusted to us. . . . We must work with the Gospel in our hands and anchor ourselves in the authentic heritage of the Apostolic Tradition, free from any interpretations motivated by rationalistic ideologies. . . . It is the Bishop's responsibility to guard and interpret the word of God and to make authoritative judgments as to what is or is not in conformity with it." Pope Benedict continued: "it must once again become clear that in each diocese there is only one shepherd and teacher of the faith in communion with the other pastors and teachers and with the Vicar of Christ."[47]

Pope Benedict knows that there have been many times when the alternative magisterium has been used to defy the infallible teachings of the pope. Most recently in the case of an elective abortion that was performed in an Arizona Catholic hospital, the leaders of the Catholic hospital defended their actions by saying that they "received permission" to perform the abortion from a theologian at Marquette. Reverend Thomas Olmsted, bishop of Phoenix, rejected that explanation and upheld his excommunication of the hospital administrator who had provided permission for the abortion. In explaining his decision, Reverend Olmsted explicitly pointed to the role played by Catholic theologians in providing theological cover for a "litany of practices in direct conflict with Catholic teachings." In a courageous decision, the bishop severed all ties between the Catholic Church and St. Joseph's Hospital, the Phoenix hospital where the abortion was performed.[48]

The break began in 2010, when a Catholic nun and longtime administrator of St. Joseph's, Sister Margaret McBride gave permission for doctors to perform an abortion. She claimed the pregnancy was terminated to save the life of the mother. Her decision drew immediate criticism from Bishop Olmsted, who then turned his attention to the role of the hospital itself. In a letter to Lloyd H. Dean, president of Catholic Healthcare West, the hospital's parent company, Bishop Olmsted wrote that he would be moving to revoke the Catholic status of the hospital unless certain conditions were met by hospital administrators. Among other things, the bishop demanded that hospital officials acknowledge in writing that the abortion performed there was a violation of Catholic directives for health-care institutions.[49]

But hospital officials defied the bishop and refused to meet his conditions. Rather than acknowledge that an illicit abortion had been performed at his hospital, Dean attempted to support Sister McBride's decision by pointing out that "many knowledgeable moral theologians have reviewed this case and reached a range of conclusions." In a letter responding to Bishop Olmsted's concerns, Dean asserted: "this is a complex matter on which the best minds disagree." Citing the opinion of Marquette University professor M. Therese Lysaught on the permissibility of the abortion that was performed at St. Joseph's, Dean appeared to suggest that the teaching authority of the Phoenix bishop was just one more "opinion" on a "complex matter."[50]

This case points to the real problem in the Church. For too long, the authority of the bishops has been limited to issuing mere opinions. This is especially true at Catholic colleges and universities, where bishops have little effect on the culture and curriculum. In the recent debate over President Obama's health-care plan, it was these same Catholic theologians who joined Sister Carol Keehan, head of the Catholic Health Association, to defy the bishops over the legislation in Congress. Cardinal Francis George, then president of the USCCB, criticized Sister Keehan and her organization for supporting a bill that did not contain provisions to protect life. Still, President Obama was so grateful for Sister Keehan's help in shepherding the bill through Congress that he awarded her one of the 20 pens used in the law's signing ceremony at the White House.[51]

Many theologians, like Professor Nicholas Healy of St. John's University in New York, maintain that theologians constitute "an alternative magisterium" to the teaching authority of the bishops. And in cases like the one at St. Joseph's, the alternative magisterium often trumps the true Magisterium of the Church. Catholic colleges and hospital administrators now "shop" for theologians who will support their decisions.[52]

Bishop Olmsted has refused to allow this to continue. In his letter responding to Dean, the bishop wrote: "you have only provided opinions of ethicists that agree with your own opinion and disagree with mine." Concluding that there can be no tie so to speak in this debate," Bishop Olmsted said: "it is my duty as the chief shepherd in the diocese to interpret whether the actions at St. Joseph's, meet the criteria of fulfilling the parameters of the moral law as seen in the Ethical and Religious Directives."[53]

While faithful Catholics supported Bishop Olmsted's actions in this case, a recent article in the Jesuit journal *America* by Kevin O'Rourke, a professor of bioethics at Loyola University of Chicago Stritch School of Medicine, cautioned that bishops should not be making these kinds of statements: "in regard to a moral decision involving facts and challenges of contemporary society, it seems Bishops should not make statements based solely on their own experience and knowledge. The people immersed in a particular moral situation may have unmatched knowledge valuable for a sound decision. This is especially clear in regard to moral questions arising in modern health care." For O'Rourke, "the principle of subsidiarity opts for the right of people other than the Bishop to speak to moral issues."[54]

Bishop Olmsted personified Pope Benedict's view of the teaching authority of the bishop with this strong defense of Church teaching— and application. He reminded the hospital administrators, just as Pope Benedict reminded the bishops, that "as the diocesan Bishop it is my duty and obligation to authoritatively teach and interpret the moral law for Catholics in the Diocese of Phoenix."[55] As the following chapters will demonstrate, we are seeing a growing number of bishops who are willing to publicly and authoritatively teach on matters of faith and morals. These are the same bishops who lead the dioceses with the greatest increases in vocations.

4   Best Practices of Transformational Leaders

Concluding that bishops are just too far removed from the lives of potential candidates to influence their vocational choices, most researchers have ignored the characteristics of the bishops when trying to understand the great variations in ordination rates in dioceses in the United States. Relying entirely on the demographic characteristics of the potential pool of ordinands in a given diocese, researchers like Schoenherr and Young painted a pessimistic picture in which the bishops are helpless responders in the face of seemingly irreversible sociological changes.[1] Yet Schoenherr and Young were not alone in this. As the previous chapter described, the 1980s and 1990s were characterized by an ongoing campaign led by former priests, dissident theologians, angry feminists, and progressive Catholics lobbying the bishops to remove these structural impediments. There were times throughout these years when hostilities raged and the bishops were confronted directly and quite publicly. On more than a few occasions, verbal battles emerged in which the bishops were publicly ridiculed and denigrated simply for supporting historic Catholic teachings on the priesthood.

Highly quotable, Schoenherr used the media to warn that the Church, because of the impending priest shortage, will no longer be able to offer the sacraments to the faithful. At one point he asked "whether the Catholic tradition of Eucharistic worship should be sacrificed on the altar of mandatory celibacy."[2] His coauthor, Young, often echoed these same sentiments and in 1998 predicted: "the Church will need to jettison male celibate exclusivity in priestly ministry, first through the ordination of married men to the priesthood and later through the ordination of women."[3]

We argue here that these sentiments have led to a serious oversight, as we have come to believe that the bishops and the culture they create in their dioceses provide a better explanation than demographics for the disparities in ordination rates by diocese. In fact, the most recent ordination data suggest that the variation in ordination rates by diocese cannot be reduced to demographics. Our opening chapters have suggested that the bishops have been poorly served by some of the sociological researchers the bishops have employed to help them understand the declines in priestly ordinations in the 1980s and 1990s. Too often those who appeared to be unbiased sociological researchers have had their own personal agendas to promote. It appears to us—and others—that these personal agendas may have biased their conclusions and projections for the future.

Schoenherr and Young began studying the demographics of ordination rates and priestly resignations in the United States in the 1980s, employing a rigorous methodology of data collection and a statistically sophisticated analysis. Many Catholics and their bishops seemed to accept their account of a dismal future for the priesthood. Yet the conclusions the researchers reached on the reasons for the decline in the total number of priests had little relationship with the demographic data they were analyzing. They collected no survey data and conducted no interviews with current or former seminarians to inform their conclusion that the reason for the decline in priestly ordinations and the increase in resignations was due to "structural impediments" to the priesthood. Yet this did not keep them from drawing conclusions and making recommendations that suited their own agenda of creating an open priesthood that welcomed women and noncelibate men.

Looking closely at the researchers themselves reveals some of the reasons they may have reached these conclusions. Schoenherr was ordained a priest in the Detroit archdiocese in 1961 but left the priesthood nine years later to marry. After receiving a Ph.D. in sociology from the University of Chicago, Schoenherr devoted much of his career to lobbying for an end to priestly celibacy. Shortly before his death he coauthored *Goodbye Father: Celibacy and Patriarchy in the Catholic*

Church—a book that continued the demand to end the celibacy barrier to the priesthood that he first made in *Full Pews and Empty Altars*. The 1996 obituary of Schoenherr published in the *New York Times* described him as "outspoken in attributing the clergy shortage to the church's requirement of priestly celibacy."[4]

Schoenherr and Young's 1993 book *Full Pews and Empty Altars* is still used as an important resource by dissident Catholic groups. The progressive FutureChurch still posts laudatory reviews of the book on its website because it strengthens their argument that removing the celibacy requirement is key to the future of the Catholic Church. Most progressive Catholics share the conclusions of Schoenherr and Young that "the church is being confronted with a choice between its sacramental tradition and its commitment to an exclusively male celibate priesthood." They charge that the bishops have "failed to accept responsibility for the choice . . . focusing on stopgap solutions to the ever-worsening priest shortage while hoping for a dramatic increase in vocations."[5]

Unfortunately, the USCCB was complicit in providing credibility for Schoenherr and Young's conclusions, for the USCCB itself underwrote the research costs for gathering the ordination data, performing the analysis, and producing a report that actually indicted Catholic teachings themselves for the priest shortage.[6] Worse, it appears that some of the leaders of the USCCB itself may have partnered with Schoenherr and Young's conclusions, for in addition to providing the bishops with written reports on their longitudinal and predictive analysis of data on priestly ordinations, retirements, and resignations, the leadership of the USCCB invited the researchers to present a three-day workshop to the annual gathering of the bishops. The presentation included an overview of the data, as well as the researchers' conclusions and recommendations on how best to ameliorate the decline in priestly ordinations. The conclusions were actually an indictment of current Catholic teachings on ordination as the real cause of the shortage. The only real solution offered to the bishops by Schoenherr and Young was the removal of the celibacy requirement for ordination.

While it appears that many of the bishops seem to have accepted the report by Schoenherr and Young, at least one bishop was open in his criticism of bias in the researchers' conclusions. Archbishop Roger Cardinal Mahony wrote a strong response to the report: "I reject the study's pessimistic assessment and feel that the Catholic Church in our Country has been done a great disservice by the report.... The study presumes that the only factors at work are sociology and statistical research. That is nonsense. We are disciples of Jesus Christ, we live by God's grace and our future is shaped by God's design for his church—not by sociologists.... Had sociologists studied the life of Jesus up through his crucifixion and death, I can just imagine the projections that would have resulted. But the resurrection and God's grace are not the products of research and surveys."[7] It is in this culture of pessimism surrounding the future of the priesthood for the past three decades that the bishops have had to try and rebuild a culture of hopefulness and faithfulness that welcomes candidates for the priesthood and nurtures them throughout their lives of priestly service. Most Catholics were unaware of the progressive Catholics' continued attacks on the bishops throughout these years. But Pope John Paul II was well aware. In an effort to address this issue, the pope issued his apostolic exhortation *Pastores Dabo Vobis* (I Will Give You Shepherds).[8] Although the papal letter was welcomed by faithful Catholics who continued to remain hopeful that things would turn around for the priesthood, the reality remains that the brunt of the work to transform the culture of the Church from one of pessimism to one of optimism fell to the bishops of each diocese. It is the bishop who has the responsibility to meet the sacramental needs of the people of his diocese and to help to create a culture that inspires hopefulness and faithfulness for all. It is the bishop who has to respond to a secular media so intent on changing what many view as the antiquated structure of the celibate male priesthood that reporters issue alarmist headlines like a recent one published by the Associated Press that read: "Priest Shortage Leaves Faithful Alone on Sickbeds."[9]

Some bishops have been more successful in changing the culture than others. The aforementioned Archbishop Curtiss may have had Schoenherr and Young in mind when he criticized "those who precipitate a decline in vocations by their negative actions and call for the ordination of married men and women to replace the vocations they have discouraged.... They have a death wish for the ordained priesthood."[10] In some ways, Archbishop Curtiss was echoing the work in the sociology of religion of Roger Finke and Rodney Stark, which concludes that the more a religious organization compromises with society and the world, blurring its identity and modifying its teachings and ethics, the more it will decline. Affirming our belief that courageous bishops like Archbishop Curtiss make a difference, Finke and Stark write that "religious organizations are stronger to the degree that they impose significant costs in terms of sacrifice and even stigma upon their members."[11] Rather than making it "easier" to become a priest by opening priestly ordination to women, and noncelibate men, Finke and Stark's work would suggest that it may be better to make it even harder to enter the priesthood—much like the Marines, who denied admission to many men and all women in their quest for just a "few good men." Archbishop Curtiss echoes these sentiments when he says: "I am convinced that shortages of vocations in any part of the country can be reversed by people who share enthusiastically in the agenda of the Church."[12]

Theory on Transformational Leadership

While there is as of yet no theory of exactly how a diocese's leadership can affect the recruitment of priests, the research by Finke and Stark provides a helpful framework for such a theory when it is supplemented by a growing body of literature from the business leadership sector—especially theories on transformational leadership. As its name implies, transformational leadership is a process that changes or transforms people. In his text on theories of leadership, Peter Northouse writes that "transformational leadership is concerned with emotions, values, ethics, standards, and long-term goals. It includes assessing followers' motives, satisfying their needs, and treating them as full human beings. Transformational leadership involves an exceptional form of influence that moves its followers to accomplish more than what is usually expected of them."[13]

We believe that theory on transformational leadership is especially applicable here because it addresses the kind of charismatic and visionary leadership that a growing number of courageous bishops are providing to the people in their dioceses. The concept of transformational leadership was first introduced in a book published in 1973 titled *Rebel Leadership: Commitment and Charisma in a Revolutionary Process,* by J. V. Downton.[14] However, as Northouse points out, its emergence as an important approach to leadership began in 1978 with the publication of *Leadership*, a classic work by political sociologist James MacGregor Burns. Differentiating leadership from power, Burns defined successful leaders as those who are able to tap the motives of followers in order to better reach the goals of both leaders and followers.[15] For Burns, effective leadership is different from power because it takes into account the needs of followers as well as leaders. This appears to have direct application on the recruitment and retention of priests by bishops.

Northouse points out that Burns additionally distinguished between two types of leadership: transactional and transformational. Transactional leadership is the more common and focuses on the exchanges that occur between leaders and their followers. Managers who offer promotions to employees who surpass goals and objectives are exhibiting transactional leadership. Some critics of what they view as the already "elite" status of priests would say that most bishops are transactional leaders because they give better assignments and desirable parishes to those priests who do not question the status quo in the Church. But an analysis of the characteristics of the bishops who have shown the most success in nurturing vocations reveals that the bishops with the greatest success are those who exhibit transformational leadership.

Transformational leadership is the process in which a bishop engages with his priests and those working in his diocese to create a connection that raises the level of motivation and morality in both the bishop and his followers. They are the bishops who are outspoken in supporting Church teachings on all issues, including especially life and family issues, and they are interested in creating a climate that nurtures vocations and a call to holiness—providing a powerful role model for their priests.

Transformational theory predicts that the effective leader actually transforms the self-concept of each follower by trying to link the identity of followers into the collective identity of the organization. These leaders forge this link by emphasizing the intrinsic rewards of the work itself and deemphasizing the extrinsic rewards. Throughout the process, leaders express high expectations for followers and help them gain a sense of confidence and self-efficacy. The goal is that followers will view the work as an expression of themselves as it ties followers and their self-concepts to the organizational identity.[16]

This is exactly what Archbishop Curtiss was referring to when he wrote that he finds that "young people everywhere . . . want to know what the Church teaches through its magisterium. They want to be part of the unity of the Church and not caught up in dissent and disunity. They are willing to listen to the call of the priesthood . . . and they want to be supported by people in their response to that call."[17] Transformational leaders communicate high expectations for followers and exhibit confidence in their followers' abilities to meet these expectations.

Beyond Burns, further refinements on transformational leadership theory have focused on the role that charismatic leadership plays within the model itself. Some authors have used charismatic leadership as synonymous with transformational leadership.[18] And, for our purposes, the original meaning of the word *charisma* has relevance. As sociologist Philip Rieff wrote in *Charisma: The Gift of Grace and How It Has Been Taken from Us,* the origins of the word *charisma* denote a divine origin or a special gift given by God that certain individuals possess that gives them the capacity to remind others of the moral life. The true charismatic leader is one who can convey that there is evil in the world—and in oneself. Charisma describes the gift of what Rieff calls a "high" and "holy terror," which installs the power of divine command so deeply in the soul that we can bear the thought "of evil in oneself and in the world." Rieff points out (as the Catholic leaders of the past used to point out to us), holy terror is fear of oneself, fear of the evil in oneself and in the world. It is also fear of punishment. Without this necessary fear, charisma is not possible.

Rieff writes that "to live without this high fear is to be a terror oneself—a monster."[19] Transformative bishops remind us of this high and holy terror. This is not an easy task in a society in which there is no normative order—when deviance, and even sin itself, has been so dramatically defined down that it no longer exists in some people's minds. If we believe, as scripture tells us to believe, that priests are truly "called by God," then charisma has even more meaning. Unfortunately in a secularized society, words lose their meaning. Rieff points out the fact that classic sociologist Max Weber, author of *The Protestant Ethic and the Spirit of Capitalism,* redefined charisma by emptying the sacred dimension of the word and instead positioning it as a special personality characteristic that gives a person an exceptional ability to persuade others to follow. He writes that the Weberian conceptions of the charismatic in fact "lead toward a successor type—the therapeutic, and toward a transformation of transgressive motifs in a way that throws no shadow of normative order upon the future."[20] From this perspective "badness" or evil becomes redefined as "sickness" in a therapeutic redefinition. No longer in need of priests, we have developed a therapeutic culture in which evil no longer appears to exist. As contemporary definitions of charisma have lost their link to the divine, today we talk about politicians or movie stars—or even the recent winner of the Westminster Kennel Club's Best in Show—as "having charisma."

Cardinal Timothy Dolan of New York is often described as "charismatic" because of his dynamic personality and jovial manner. Yet these same media outlets chastise him when he acts charismatically in the traditional sense by issuing strong authoritative statements on the evil of abortion or same-sex marriage. *New York Times* columnist Maureen Dowd has been especially harsh in her criticism of the cardinal—while at the same time writing about what she calls the archbishop's "Irish affability."[21] Calling him the "Starchbishop," Dowd decries Cardinal Dolan's "ferociousness in fighting against marriage between same-sex couples, painting it as a perversity against nature." Charging the Church with hypocrisy because "it has become a haven for gay priests even though it declares homosexual sex a sin," Dowd adds that "if only his church had been as ferocious in fighting against the true perversity against nature: the unending horror of pedophile priests and the children who trusted them."[22]

It has become increasingly difficult for bishops to issue these kinds of public pronouncements, yet when Cardinal Dolan speaks on moral issues, he is just doing what he is required to do—teaching the faithful. Many Catholics have become so accustomed to their bishops' reluctance to publicly judge behaviors or practices that when they do, it is surprise to these same Catholics. A few years ago, when then Archbishop Dolan was leading a vespers service in a Greenwich Village church celebrating the anniversary of the birth of Dorothy Day, one of the great leaders of the Catholic social justice efforts, he applauded "Dorothy Day's loyalty to the Church." Scandalized by this, Marian Ronan, a journalist who had attended the vespers service wrote that "while Dolan said a number of things about Day in his sermon, he stressed above all Dorothy Day's loyalty to the Church. She was a faithful Catholic. He didn't use the word obedient, exactly, but clearly that's what he was getting at." Ronan concluded her article by warning readers that "Dolan has committed himself to continuing the approach of [then] outgoing USCCB president Cardinal George of Chicago who stressed that the bishops are the authorities on interpreting the faith for Catholics. 'We're the teachers,' Cardinal George said, 'and not just one set of teachers in the Catholic community, but *the* teachers.'"[23] It was clear that Ronan found this startling and a bit disturbing.

Further refinements of transformational theory in 1985 demonstrate that such leaders motivate followers to exceed expectations by raising followers' levels of consciousness about the importance and value of specified and idealized goals; by motivating followers to transcend their own self-interest for the sake of the organization; and by moving followers to address their own higher level needs.[24] Successful bishops are already doing this. And as we look at the "best practices" of these bishops, we can see that they have been able to inspire followers to accomplish more than even the followers themselves thought they would. These bishops are recognized by the priests and the people in their dioceses as "change agents" who are good role models who can create and articulate a clear vision for the Church. These bishops have empowered their priests to meet higher standards and to act in ways that make others want to trust them. They give meaning to church life. And for the laity, these bishops are recognized as men who can be trusted to do what is best for the Church and for the people of God. They are viewed as charismatics who are willing to remind us that there is evil in the world—but that we can overcome this evil.

While the 1990s saw a handful of courageous bishops publicly confronting those who wanted to destroy the priesthood, there is a growing list of today's bishops who have been willing to risk ridicule and ostracism to defend not only the priesthood but to be outspoken in defending the growing threats to human dignity that currently face us. Defending life at all stages from conception to natural death, defending traditional marriage as the union between one man and one woman, and defending the conscience rights of all are some of the major moral issues confronting today's bishops. Although we cannot list the "best practices" of all of these bishops, we chose to highlight just a few to demonstrate the value of the transformational leader.

While each of the bishops we introduce demonstrates different styles or personalities, they are all charismatic in the traditional biblical sense that they appear to many faithful Catholics to be divinely inspired and courageous enough to speak out on important yet controversial moral issues. Some, like Cardinal Timothy Dolan, are outgoing and gregarious, and others, like Arizona's Reverend Thomas Olmsted, bishop of the Diocese of Phoenix, have a quiet courage that cannot help but motivate the priests and the people in his diocese and beyond.[25]

The intervention by Bishop Olmsted is best understood by looking closely at the gospel meaning of charisma. In *Charisma*, Rieff reminds us that in the gospel, charisma is a particular and individual case of intervention by the ideal figure of authority, "a forgiving yet demanding one." From this perspective, charisma is the gift of the ability to help others do the right thing—helping others to choose the good rather than the evil. Grace, then, is the basis for right action. For Rieff, grace is "entirely a normative term, the particular expression of the interdictory form of the early Christian culture. . . . The receiving of this intervening ideal is related to the giver by the decision of the giver, Christ, who is himself preeminently the receiver of it, on behalf of all others. In its basic form for the history of our cultures, charisma derives from the dual nature of the messiah. Christ himself is charisma incarnate, the idealizing gift of man's practical capacities."[26] Charismatic bishops remind us of this every day by proclaiming what is good and what is evil. Although their styles—or their personalities—may differ, what unites these charismatic bishops is a strong faith, a faith that inspires others to follow them.

The Charismatic Archbishop of New York: Cardinal Dolan

While the true meaning of *charisma* has nothing to do with personality characteristics, a bishop with a charismatic style surely has an advantage. Media outlets—from the *New York Daily News* to *Irish Central* and the major network news stations—have called New York's newest cardinal, Most Reverend Timothy Dolan, the "rock star" of the Catholic faith.[27] *New York* magazine titled a 2009 feature story on Cardinal Timothy Dolan, then the new archbishop of New York, "The Archbishop of Charm" and opened the article with a good-natured portrayal of the archbishop as a "boisterous, tall, energetic portly Irish-Catholic lug who likes smoking cigars and sipping Jameson's." But the reader of *New York* is warned at the start of the article that the author of this piece sees New York's new bishop as one who will enforce Catholic teachings, as he subtitles his article ". . . There Are Only So Many Nice Ways to Say No."[28] Focusing on some of the most contested issues in the Church, the *New York* story reminded readers that as early as his first week in office, Archbishop Dolan "went on record saying that he believed the union between a man and woman was hardwired into us . . . now, with a smile, he anticipates the question of where that leaves gay men and lesbians." Later, in the article Dolan is described as having "silenced one priest who entertained the idea of ordaining women, and shutting down a group of priests who wanted to discuss making celibacy optional." The author warned readers that Cardinal Dolan has a way of letting others know that there are some areas that are not open for discussion.

Still, the overall tenor of the piece was positive, as the author seemed to genuinely like the archbishop and actually acknowledged his authority when he wrote that "the New York Archbishop position is akin to being American pope. . . . From their pulpits here, Cardinal Francis Joseph Spellman and Terence James Cooke shaped the national discourse." The article is especially respectful of Cardinal John Joseph O'Connor, who is described by the author as the "model" of a New York cardinal: "he sparred jovially with Ed Koch and spoke out against abortion and for the rights of immigrants and the homeless." The feature story accurately captured the role of the transformational or truly charismatic bishop. Certainly not as someone who says no to everything but someone who has been entrusted with the teaching role of the Catholic Church in the United States. And sometimes that means saying no to the nonnegotiable issues like abortion or same-sex marriage.

The *New York* piece concluded with accolades for Cardinal O'Connor—even though the cardinal was described as a "polarizing figure." Writing that the now-deceased cardinal "brought a sense of excitement to the Catholic experience here, helping his diverse and disparate flock believe they were part of something bigger than themselves," the author accurately portrays the essence of the true leader. The transformational leader, like Cardinal O'Connor, is someone who is willing to be conciliatory on some issues—but not on the nonnegotiable ones. This is a difficult role to play, and even the author concedes: "it can't be easy being leader of the Roman Catholic Archdiocese of New York, expected to play creative defense on every issue that offends the sensibilities of the Church, in a city closer to Sodom than to Eden."[29]

Playing "creative defense" is an excellent way to describe the role of the faithful bishop in any diocese. It is clear that when we look closely at the most successful ones, they are also the most courageous ones, willing to say unpopular things, sometimes with a smile, like Cardinal Dolan, but always giving the impression that they are only mindful of God's plan for the good of the people of God.

Cardinal Dolan often tells interviewers that as a priest he found inspiration in Pope John Paul II, who had no ambivalence about engaging the world at large—always expressing the joy he found in his faith. Cardinal Dolan's book *Priests for the Third Millennium* is required reading in many seminaries because it provides practical information and guidance for future priests and for lay Catholics who want to serve God as fully as possible. He opens the book by writing that "priesthood begins with God's invitation, but it develops out of man's response." Then he devotes the remainder of the book to helping readers understand what it is to "respond enthusiastically, wholeheartedly, and faithfully to the call to serve." Emphasizing the importance of faith, Cardinal Dolan draws on scripture to remind us: "faith, as the Epistle to the Hebrews instructs us, is the guarantee of the blessings that we hope for, the proof of the existence of the realities that at present remain unseen." Using exclamation points to punctuate his writing on faith, Cardinal Dolan writes: "Our faith allows us to cling to certain things with steadfastness: God exists! He loves us passionately! He has revealed truths to us! He has sent his Son as the way, the truth and the life. . . . His Son has saved us by his death and resurrection, and is still alive, powerful, with us! Our hearts are steadfast in this faith. *Firmum est cor meum.*"[30]

The importance of faith is demonstrated throughout all of Cardinal Dolan's books as he reminds us that we Catholics are "a people of strong faith or we are nothing." Although we cannot know the hearts of writers like Schoenherr or the *National Catholic Reporter*'s editor, Roberts, their writings suggest a very different kind of faith—one that depends on the individual more than God. Lamenting that "there is nothing more pitiable than a priest without faith—and there are many," Cardinal Dolan writes: "without faith, the sacraments are empty because we don't believe in them, preaching is boring because we don't believe what we are saying and we futilely seek meaning in bottles, or boys, or women, or golf clubs, or stocks, or cars, or travel, or promotion, or ambition."[31] To help priests keep their faith, Cardinal Dolan reminds them that prayer increases their faith, for at its core, faith is a gift that is ours for the asking. He also reminds them that they need the company, support, and encouragement of people who will sustain their faith. That is the rationale of the seminary.

Cardinal Dolan understands well the need for priestly prayer and discipline, and he will need both faith and courage in New York, where in 2011, Andrew M. Cuomo, the Catholic governor of New York, rejected Archbishop Dolan's repeated requests for reconsideration and, with great fanfare, signed into law access to "marriage" for same-sex couples and in 2013 proposed allowing easier access to abortion in the third trimester—a proposal so radical that even 70 percent of New Yorkers thought the legislation unnecessary.[32] Many of New York's faithful Catholics felt betrayed by their governor, and disappointed by their archbishop for not doing enough to prevent the same-sex marriage law from passing. A *New York Times* reporter acknowledged this disappointment and wrote that the Catholic Church in New York "seemed to shrink from the fight." Reporting that the archbishop was "missing in action" in the battle over redefining marriage, the *Times* claimed: "as the marriage bill hurtled toward a vote, the head of the Church in New York, Archbishop Timothy M. Dolan, left town to lead a meeting of bishops in Seattle. He did not travel to Albany or deliver a major speech in the final days of the session. And when he did issue a strongly worded critique of the legislation, calling it "immoral" and an "ominous threat," it was over the phone to an Albany-area radio show.[33] This was hardly the robust defense that many Catholics expected—and deserved. But these reports did not tell the whole story.

The reality is that Cardinal Dolan surely did not "shrink" from trying to prevent the same-sex "marriage" bill from passing. Just the week before it was passed, the cardinal wrote that "communist governments presume to redefine fundamental rights and basic social institutions like the family" and that New York would be importing that mentality by passing same-sex "marriage" legislation. He warned that "it was a perilous presumption for the state to reinvent a God-given institution, which has been the cornerstone of Western civilization." And the cardinal met personally with Governor Cuomo to tell him of his concerns about the same-sex marriage bill. Following that private meeting, the cardinal reported that it was an encouraging conversation, yet a few days later, Governor Cuomo still pledged his support for same-sex marriage for New York.

In looking back on the unsuccessful efforts by the Church to stop same-sex marriage in New York, Dennis Poust, of the New York State Catholic Conference, was quoted in *The New York Times* as saying that "we were outgunned. . . that is a lot to overcome."[34] It was indeed a lot to overcome, and Cardinal Dolan could not do it alone. Even the "archbishop of charm" was unable to convince an entire state legislature and its Catholic governor that redefining marriage was wrong. But it appeared to some Catholics that there was a sense of defeatism on the issue of same-sex marriage within the conference itself—and from some of Cardinal Dolan's own brother bishops in the state of New York. In his written reflections in the aftermath of the passage of the law allowing same-sex marriage, Cardinal Dolan recalls: "My brother bishops of New York were particularly prophetic. When I arrived here a little over two years ago, they told me realistically that we faced a looming battle over the defense of marriage. They advised me that the odds were not in our favor, and that some experts were even suggesting that we give in and not put up a fight." Still, the ever-patient Cardinal Dolan defended his bishops by adding that the New York bishops were "resolute in their conviction that such would have been a dereliction of duty."[35]

It is likely that no reporter will ever again describe the Church in New York as "shrinking from the fight," because Cardinal Dolan has been leading from the front in every battle since that same-sex marriage debacle. Most recently, he confronted even the president of the United States about the Obama administration's attempt to impose a Health and Human Services mandate that would require all Catholic institutions, including Catholic hospitals, universities, and social service providers, to provide contraceptives—including the abortifacient "morning-after" pill—to all employees. Cardinal Dolan issued a report on the "misinformation" that was emerging from the White House and has gone on the offensive, appearing regularly on television shows and speaking to the press to make clear the Church's opposition to such measures. In all of this, he has learned that when the stakes are this high, the bishop has to fight as hard as the opposition is fighting.

Protecting Marriage in California:
Archbishop Cordileone

A similar battle over the redefinition of marriage in New York raged in Oakland, California, in 2009. But in that case, Oakland's transformational bishop, Most Reverend Salvatore Cordileone, now archbishop of San Francisco, chose a very different strategy—one that succeeded through prayer, fasting, and forging alliances with people across all faiths to defend traditional marriage. Rather than taking a defensive posture, Archbishop Cordileone mounted a statewide offensive designed to garner support from voters to fight the redefinition of marriage. Today Archbishop Cordileone is credited by most Californians with leading opposition to same-sex marriage in the state of California. In 2009, Archbishop Cordileone led an effort to use the proposition system in the state to amend the state Constitution to define marriage in California as between one man and one woman. The amendment, proposed under Proposition 8, would not have passed without Archbishop Cordileone's leadership. In fact, most media reports allege that the proposition itself would never have even qualified for the ballot without his leadership. It was Archbishop Cordileone who encouraged key San Diego Catholics to step forward and make the first significant donations that started the process of getting enough signatures from California voters to put the proposition on the ballot. Archbishop Cordileone had made many faithful friends in San Diego when he served as the auxiliary bishop there prior to his appointment to lead Oakland's diocese.

In an interview published in the *National Catholic Register,* Archbishop Cordileone was reluctant to take credit for the success and would only concede that what he learned from the battle was "the importance of forming alliances with people across all faiths—Catholics, evangelicals, Mormons—all working together.... We couldn't have done this without their support. Everyone involved has to trust and to prove themselves trustworthy.... No one was doing this for their own glory. They didn't care who got credit for what.... We did it only for the glory of God, not our own, and for the sake of the common good of our society."[36]

This is the language of transformational leaders who encourage others to accomplish things that they may never have thought they could accomplish. As would be expected from the transformational leader, Archbishop Cordileone said that the most important lesson from the battle to defend marriage through an amendment to the state Constitution was that it was a "spiritual battle." Framing the battle in spiritual terms, he said: "that's something evangelicals and Catholics have in common: We understand this concept of spiritual warfare. So, prayer and fasting are critical." It was the evangelicals who were calling for a forty-day fast leading up to the election. They called for "serious fasting." In the lead-up to the contest, "a group of about 30 young people, from around the country came to San Diego to participate in this 'spiritual warfare.' They prayed all day long and ate soup at night and that was it—for 40 days. In our Catholic tradition, our way of fasting is one meal a day, and I encouraged Catholics to do that."[37]

The final lesson that was learned in the successful battle over the redefinition of marriage in California was described by Archbishop Cordileone as "educating people about what marriage really is and why marriage is important. We need to explain that this is not about passing judgment on anyone and how they live out their intimate relationships. It's about marriage, because marriage is so critical for the good of society. It is the basis on which everything else is built."[38]

At the conclusion of the successful Proposition 8 Campaign, there was much anger directed at those who supported the traditional marriage amendment—especially toward Archbishop Cordileone. But for faithful Catholics—and for those considering a call to the priesthood—Oakland's bishop is viewed as a "hero" because of the courage he showed in the face of the powerful proponents of same-sex marriage.

Fighting for Religious Liberty: Archbishop Lori

Most Reverend William Lori, formerly the bishop of the Bridgeport diocese and currently the Archbishop of Baltimore, drew national attention in early 2012 when he testified before Congress about the threat to religious liberty posed by the Obama administration's mandate requiring Catholic hospitals, colleges, universities, and social service agencies to provide insurance coverage for their employees that included contraception—including sterilization and the abortifacient morning-after pill. Under attack from Democratic lawmakers who claimed that the leaders of the Catholic Health Association were supportive of President Obama's attempt to require health plans to cover the contraceptive care services, Archbishop Lori responded that these groups were not the Church and could not represent its views: "The Catholic Health Association does not speak for the Church as a whole, the Catholic bishops speak for the Church as a whole." Dismissing the authority of the Catholic Health Association, Archbishop Lori simply said: "it is a lobbying group, it is a trade association." Comparing the mandate to provide contraceptive care to "forcing kosher delis to serve pork," Archbishop Lori called for the requirement to include contraception in preventive care coverage to be removed entirely.[39]

This was not the first time Archbishop Lori had appeared before Congress. Only three months before his 2012 testimony on the health-care mandate for contraception, Archbishop Lori, the chairman of the bishops' newly established committee on religious liberty, appeared before the subcommittee on the Constitution of the Judiciary Committee of the U.S. House. Archbishop Lori chronicled the long list of threats to religious liberty in states like Illinois and Massachusetts, and in the District of Columbia, where Catholic agencies that received state financing had been forced to stop offering adoption and foster care services because those states required them to help same sex couples to adopt just as they helped heterosexual couples.

In his testimony, Archbishop Lori decried the requirement of the U.S. Department of Health and Human Services that the USCCB's Migration and Refugee Services provide the "full range of reproductive services"—including contraception—to sex trafficking victims and unaccompanied minors in its cooperative agreements and government contracts. This position mirrors the position urged by the American Civil Liberties Union in the Church's ongoing lawsuit challenging the constitutionality of the contracts held by Migration and Refugee Services as a violation of religious liberty.

In addition to the contraception requirement, the adoption issue, and the Migration and Refugee Services issue, Archbishop Lori provided a long list of attacks on the religious liberty of the Catholic Church including a reduction of the ministerial exception exempting religious institutions from civil law involving hiring and firing. Archbishop Lori has consistently argued that religious liberty belongs to the Church and other religious institutions because religious liberty is an individual right. Although he has just recently attracted national attention for this cause, Connecticut's faithful Catholics have long appreciated his courage in confronting attempted state interference in religious matters in 2009, when Democratic lawmakers attempted to partner with a group of progressive Catholics in an effort to diminish the bishops' role in the diocese. In fact, it is likely that Archbishop Lori's appointment to chair the Bishop's Ad Hoc Committee for Religious Freedom was due in part to his success in overturning the government takeover attempt (described in the previous chapter) that would have removed control of the diocese from the bishop and placed it into the hands of the laity.

In addition to fighting for religious liberty, Archbishop Lori has been a leader within the Church in creating a new policy on how to deal with priests who have been charged with sexual abuse, known as the Dallas Policy because it was first presented at the bishops' meetings in Dallas in 2002. Archbishop Lori was one of seven members of the ad hoc bishops' committee tasked with writing the policy and was one of four bishops chosen to travel to the Vatican to present the policy to the pope.[40] Archbishop Lori has also served as one of nine bishops on the USCCB Committee on Doctrine, which is charged with evaluating works by Catholic theologians—a job that draws criticism from progressive theologians. Called "Archbishop Law and Order" in a headline published by the *Hartford Courant,* Archbishop Lori continues his commitment to defending the Church from unfair attacks from both within and outside the Church.[41]

Reclaiming Catholic Identity in Political Life: Archbishop Chaput

Most Reverend Charles J. Chaput, currently the archbishop of the Philadelphia diocese, has written often of the need for all priests to show courage in light of the growing threats to religious liberty. In the preface to a recently published book by Randall J. Meissen, L.C., on the legacy of Pope John Paul the Great, Archbishop Chaput draws on the language of the transformational leader when he calls on priests to be "heroes":

> God calls and the Church needs heroes: priests who love God more than themselves; who seek God's glory more than their own; who want to lead by serving others; who have a mercy and a humility born of a knowledge of their own sins; who

have the courage to preach the truth even in the face of contempt; who have a hunger for winning souls; priests who are faithful to the Church and her teachings; who are obedient to their vocation as Jesus Christ was obedient to his; who stand in *persona Christi*—modeling the person of Christ to their people.[42]

In his writing, Archbishop Chaput is really referring to the need for all priests to become transformational leaders, especially when he writes that "the priests we need are men who will turn away from comfort, who will listen for the voice of God, who will follow Jesus Christ into the storm, and in their failures, will turn to him. . . . We need priests who are men of prayer, men of courage, men for others, men anchored in the sacramental life of the Church. We need priests who spark not a new clericalism, but a new friendship, equality, co-operation, and fire from every vocation and form of discipleship in the Church."[43]

A transformational leader like Archbishop Chaput inspires the priests and the people in his diocese—and beyond—to be "more" than they thought possible. His writings and his public statements clearly demonstrate his faithfulness and his courage. As the longtime leader of the Denver diocese prior to his appointment as Philadelphia's leader, Archbishop Chaput has been bold in his defense of Catholic teachings on the sanctity of life. Most recently, the archbishop was one of the most outspoken bishops in decrying the passage of the federal health-care legislation—replete with federal funding for abortion—promoted by President Obama in 2010. Calling the legislation a "bad bill," the archbishop condemned the passage of the bill as a "failure of decent lawmaking" that "remains unethical and defective on all of the issues pressed by the U.S. bishops and prolife groups." The archbishop wrote that the executive order that President Obama proposed at the last minute to accompany the legislation to reassure the pro-life community that the health-care bill would ban the use of federal funds for abortion "does not solve the many problems with the bill." Archbishop Chaput was especially critical of the role that "self-described Catholic groups played in helping to pass the bill—claiming that these 'Catholic groups' have done a serious disservice to justice, to the church, and to the ethical needs of the American people by undercutting the leadership and witness of their own bishops." Pointing specifically to the role played by groups like Network and Catholics United, Archbishop Chaput was especially harsh in his criticism, saying: "in their effect, if not in formal intent, such groups exist to advance the interests of a particular political spectrum." Of Network, an organization of women religious who lobbied heavily for passage of the health-care legislation, the archbishop wrote that "whatever the nature of its good work, it has rarely shown much enthusiasm for a definition of social justice that includes the rights of the unborn child."[44]

In his book *Render unto Caesar*, Archbishop Chaput identifies the role that American Catholics—and their leaders—must play to combat the culture of death and develop a culture of life. In the first chapter, he tells readers that the reason he wrote the book was that he was tired of "the Church and her people being told to be quiet on public issues that urgently concern us." In an address following the publication of the book, the archbishop said, "frankly, I got tired of hearing outsiders and insiders tell Catholics to keep quiet about our religious and moral views in the big public debates that involve all of us as a society. That's a kind of bullying, and I don't think Catholics should accept it."[45] Archbishop Chaput said that he wrote the book to try to help Catholics "recover what it really means to be Catholic," and to try to encourage Catholics "to be Catholic Christians first—not in opposition to our country, but to serve its best ideals."[46]

As a transformational leader, Archbishop Chaput encourages all Catholics to work to change the culture. In a chapter titled "What Went Wrong," he notes that instead of transforming the secular culture in which they live, far too many Catholics—including Catholic politicians—have placed secular values above the truths central to the Catholic faith. Although he is especially critical of the "pro-choice" platform of the Democratic Party, he writes that neither political party's platforms nor policies are fully compatible with the truths of the faith. The final two chapters of his book focus on abortion and advise Catholics that "some acts are so evil that tolerating them becomes a poison that weakens the whole of society. . . . Deliberately killing the innocent is always, inexcusably wrong. It sets a pattern of contempt for every other aspect of human dignity."[47]

In an address delivered in October 2008, a few weeks before the election of President Barack Obama, Archbishop Chaput warned: "Senator Obama, whatever his other talents, is the most committed 'abortion rights' presidential candidate of either major party since the *Roe v. Wade* abortion decision in 1973." The archbishop was especially critical of the role played by Catholic professors like Douglas Kmiec, an Obama supporter who wrote a book suggesting that Catholics can indeed support Obama because there are "defensible motives" to support him. Arguing that Senator Obama would actually "reduce" the number of abortions because of his attention to the need to expand opportunities and welfare for the poor, Professor Kmiec's book asked Catholics to support Senator Obama for president rather than the candidate who promised to work to put an end to abortion. Yet in his address, Archbishop Chaput countered that by reminding Catholics that the party platform that Senator Obama ran on was "not only aggressively pro-choice, it has also removed any suggestion that killing an unborn child might be a regrettable thing." The archbishop concluded his address with a rejoinder to "Catholic" advocacy groups like Catholics United, and the George Soros–supported Catholics in Alliance for the Common Good, for "confusing the natural priorities of Catholic social teachings, undermining the progress pro-lifers have made, and providing an excuse for some Catholics to abandon the abortion issue instead of fighting within their parties and at the ballot box to protect the unborn."[48] In 2009, President Obama rewarded Professor Kmiec for his support with an appointment as ambassador to Malta.

For Archbishop Chaput, and for all of the transformational bishops we have studied, sanctity-of-life issues are foundational—"not just because of religious views about abortion, but because the act of dehumanizing and killing the unborn child attacks human dignity in a uniquely grave way."[49] Many of these bishops have been outspoken on the role that Catholic politicians have played in contributing to the culture of death through their votes designed to expand women's access to abortion here and abroad. In fact, this is where the transformational bishop distinguishes himself from the others, for it takes real courage to publicly confront the culture of death that has been promoted at the state and federal level by Catholic politicians who continue to believe that they can be "personally opposed to abortion" yet still vote in favor of legislation that expands the rate of abortion by making it more accessible to all—including minors.

When Archbishop Chaput was appointed to lead the Philadelphia archdiocese, David J. O'Brien, a Catholic professor of theology at the University of Dayton, published an angry op-ed in the *Philadelphia Inquirer* that suggested that the reason for Chaput's appointment was that he was willing to ignore the needs and desires of the "people of God" in favor of privileging the hierarchy and the pope:

his promotion most likely came about because of the support of Americans with influence at the Vatican. The most powerful of these is Raymond Burke, now head of the Vatican's highest court, who regularly makes the restorationist agenda clear. Chaput is cut from the same cloth as Burke, who launched the Church's continuing campaign to humiliate Catholic Democratic politicians when he denied Communion to a respected Catholic congressman, David Obey of Wisconsin, in 2003. Chaput thought it was a great idea, and he made it clear that then-presidential candidate John Kerry should not appear at the Communion rail in his jurisdiction. He wrote a book arguing that real Catholics would reject John Kennedy's famous distinction between his religion and his public service.[50]

Professor O'Brien joins several other Catholic college professors in decrying what they call the culture war bishops. In an article for *Commonweal*, University of Notre Dame law and theology professor Cathleen Kaveny expressed her exasperation with what she has called the "culture war bishops" because "their rhetoric is counterproductive. It leads many Americans to disengage from the public discussion of abortion, thus leaving the *status quo* intact. . . . We are beginning to see rhetoric from Chaput and others that looks less like a jeremiad and more like a lamentation—the predictable next rhetorical step of a disheartened Jeremiah."[51] Professor Kaveny served on Barack Obama's Catholic National Advisory Committee during his 2008 presidential campaign—along with eight other professors from Catholic colleges and universities.

Archbishop Chaput is mindful of the problems on Catholic campuses where professors like Kaveny and O'Brien remain in leadership positions. In an address at Assumption College in 2011, he acknowledged that Catholic institutions of higher learning have suffered greatly from the secularization that has taken place under the banner of academic freedom: "instead of Catholics converting the culture, the culture too often bleached out the apostolic zeal in Catholics while leaving the brand label intact." He suggested: "instead of seeking to impress the world on its own terms, Catholic schools must recapture the genius that once gave life to Western civilization with its harmony of reason and faith. . . . The vocation of a Catholic college is to feed the soul as well as the mind . . . to offer a vision of men and women made whole by the love of God, the knowledge of creation, and the reality of things unseen."[52]

The archbishop did not overlook the role that bishops and priests have played in neglecting the problems on these campuses though. In an address to the 129th Annual Convention of the Knights of Columbus in 2011, the archbishop acknowledged: "the clergy's leadership in the Church should always be marked with humility and service and never by a sense of entitlement. . . . Bishops, priests and deacons are too often weak and sinful. They need to be held to high standards. Some deserve to be chastised. . . . But men and women didn't found the Church, they don't own her, and they have no license to reinvent her."[53] Concluding his remarks by citing the importance of faith, Archbishop Chaput suggested to the gathered Knights of Columbus that the most important thing needed for any lasting Church reform is faith: "not faith as theology, or faith as a collection of doctrines and practices, but faith as a single minded confidence in God, and faith as the imprudence, the passion, the recklessness to give ourselves entirely to Jesus Christ. . . . That kind of faith changes people. That kind of faith shifts the world on its axis because nothing can stand against it."[54]

Simply Catholic: Cardinal George

This emphasis on faith is echoed by Cardinal Francis George, the bishop who served as Cardinal Dolan's predecessor as the head of the USCCB until 2010. In his recent book *God in Action: How Faith in God Can Address the Challenges of the World,* Cardinal George argues for what he calls "simply Catholicism." What he means by "simply Catholicism" is a clear sense of Catholic identity that is neither liberal nor conservative but something that "you see in the lives of ordinary Catholics who take for granted that we go to Mass, we say the rosary. . . . We contribute to Catholic charities and we take care of our neighbor in very spontaneous ways. You see it in family life a lot. . . . It's bolstered by Catholic practices, which are fewer now after the Council. That's unfortunate."[55]

In *God in Action,* Cardinal George decries the fact that faith in God has been reduced to personal spiritual convictions or peculiar ideas found only in churches. Rather, the cardinal argues that God is always and everywhere present in the unfolding of our lives—both the good and the bad. Far from being in what he calls the "deep background" of our lives, Cardinal George reminds readers that it is God who "makes all things new," because "only God can create something from nothing . . . he provides the very being of a human race that deserves respect in all circumstances but enjoys eternal life only when transformed by God's grace."[56] What sounds simple (or, in Cardinal George's words, "simply Catholic"), that God acts in our day to day lives, and in the life of our country, requires real faith because our natural inclination is to believe that things happen by chance or because we make them happen. But Cardinal George writes that "while natural agents are acting on their own steam and in their own order of creating being, God is acting all the while through them for his own purposes, in order to restore to them and all of us the freedom lost in sinning."[57] This takes faith, and there are many Catholics who continue to question that kind of faith. But the transformational bishop does not question it—faith is real to him, and the priests and the people of his diocese know this.

Like the "best practices" of the other transformational bishops we have studied, Cardinal George has been courageous in his stand to protect the unborn. Recently he said that "too many Americans have no recognition of the fact that children continue to be killed (by abortion) and we live therefore, in a country drenched in blood. This can't be something you start playing off pragmatically against other issues."[58] Even before President Obama took the oath of office for the presidency in 2009, Cardinal George warned: "if the election is misinterpreted ideologically as a referendum on abortion, the unity desired by President-elect Obama and all Americans at this moment of crisis would be impossible to achieve. Aggressively pro-abortion policies, legislation and executive orders will permanently alienate tens of millions of Americans and would be seen by many as an attack on the free exercise of their religion." According to church officials, and as was published in the Religion News Service, Cardinal George's statement on abortion and the president-elect was unanimously approved by nearly three hundred bishops in a closed-door session at the end of the bishops' semiannual meeting.[59]

In his farewell address to the bishops at their gathering in November 2010, Cardinal George thanked them for their fidelity—telling them that during his years in office, he had "come to a deep appreciation for the bishops' pastoral expertise and fidelity to our common vocation as bishops in the Church." Yet the cardinal also reminded his brother bishops that the country continues to struggle with "political and social divisions that have challenged us in our vocation to keep the Catholic people united visibly around Christ in his body, the church."[60] One of the bishops in the audience that day was Portland's new archbishop, Alexander Sample, who at the time of his Episcopal ordination as bishop of Marquette, Michigan, in 2006, was the youngest Catholic bishop in the United States and the first to be born in the 1960s. A truly transformational leader, Archbishop Sample, at fifty-two years old, is now the youngest archbishop in the Church in the United States.

Leading the Transformation and Renewal of the Priesthood: Archbishop Sample

Although a young bishop, Archbishop Sample has been courageous in confronting those—including his own brother bishops—who dissent from Catholic teachings on faith and morals. In 2009, for example, Archbishop Sample asked Bishop Thomas Gumbleton, retired auxiliary bishop of Detroit, not to speak in the Marquette diocese because of his dissenting views on homosexuality and the ordination of women. He also condemned the University of Notre Dame's decision to honor President Barack Obama, calling the move "unconscionable" and "completely out of step with Catholic Church's teaching."

In an interview for *Catholic World Report* in 2011, then-bishop Sample recalled his love for the priesthood—saying "I never doubted my call to the priesthood. From the time I decided to enter the seminary, I felt a great peace. There were those who opposed my decision, including my father and my college professors. And, since I was ordained a priest I have loved and enjoyed my life ever since."[61] Since his ordination, Archbishop Sample has devoted much of his life to renewing the priesthood. In 2002, as Marquette's chancellor and director of ministry personnel services, Archbishop Sample was the "point man" when it came to dealing with issues of clerical sexual abuse in the Marquette diocese. He recalls worrying that "this would be the death blow for vocations." But he found instead that he was "completely surprised. Many young men—wholesome, faith-filled, zealous men stepped forward to become part of the solution, to rebuild the Church. They wanted to be part of the renewal of the Church. That's remarkable, it's a work of the Holy Spirit."

Like several of our transformational leaders, Archbishop Sample describes himself as "a John Paul II priest and bishop. . . . He had great zeal and enthusiasm and spoke boldly on faith and morals in the face of a culture that rejected the very moral values that the Church had always upheld." In some ways, Archbishop Sample's newest assignment to lead the Diocese of Portland will present the same kind of challenge that Pope John Paul II faced in confronting a culture that rejects so much of what the Church teaches to be true about marriage and life issues. Priding itself on its support for issues like same-sex marriage, unlimited access to abortion, and assisted suicide, Portland is almost "missionary" territory for Archbishop Sample. But he brings the zeal of the true missionary priest—a recognition of the importance of the sacraments and prayer: "it's important that we learn to pray on a deep level, not just vocal but mental prayer and contemplation. . . . We need to be quiet and listen. We need to develop a personal, deep relationship with the Lord and pour our hearts out to him in prayer . . . being docile to the word of God and humbly accepting the teachings of the Church."

This is the essence of the transformational leader in the Church— one who engages with his priests and his people to create a connection that raises the level of motivation and morality in both the bishop and his followers. Outspoken in supporting Church teachings, Archbishop Sample has succeeded in creating a climate that nurtures vocations and a call to holiness—and a model of leadership for future generations of priests and bishops alike.

5   No Charisma without Creed

While the previous chapters have argued that candidates for the priesthood are drawn to dioceses led by bishops who personify the new evangelization within the Church by proclaiming the good news of the Gospel and consistently and courageously defending Church teachings on matters of faith and morals, we also must acknowledge that those bishops who have been publicly critical of Church teachings on issues like papal authority, women's ordination, priestly celibacy, reproductive rights, or homosexual unions, have been much less successful in encouraging vocations in their dioceses. In our research, we have seen dramatic increases in vocations in places with courageous leaders like Washington, D.C., Philadelphia, Chicago, Lincoln, and Newark. At the same time, there have been far fewer priestly ordinations in places like Arlington, Virginia; Milwaukee; Rochester, New York; Albany, New York; El Paso, Texas; and a number of dioceses throughout California and Florida.

Arlington, Virginia, provides an interesting case study on just how essential the role of the bishop is in the vocations process. From 1985 to 2000, the diocese was heralded as a model for producing new priests. The diocese, led by Bishop John Keating from 1983 to 1998, produced between eight and ten new priests a year during that time and was widely viewed as the golden standard for other dioceses to emulate. Leading Arlington's quest for vocations was Father James Gould, who began his service in

1985 under Bishop Thomas Welch and continued until 2000 (when he was reassigned). However, Arlington's fifteen years of consistent success came to an abrupt end at the turn of the century. In 1998, Bishop Keating died unexpectedly of a heart attack during his *ad limina* visit to Rome. Keating was replaced by Bishop Paul Loverde from Ogdensburg, New York. Hardly an example of courageous orthodoxy and bold conviction, Bishop Loverde has been immersed in a number of controversies during his years in Arlington—most specifically in his handling of a number of priests who have spoken out against their brother priests who are engaging in homosexual lifestyles, involved in embezzlement, and various other ways they have not been faithful to their priestly vows. Rather than siding with the priests who have raised concern about such matters, Bishop Loverde has engaged in reshuffling these priests to different parishes and in several documented cases removed them from their priestly duties. Meanwhile, this diocese, which used to lead the nation in vocations, has had a significant decrease in ordination rates—consistently averaging a total of three new ordinations a year over the past decade under Lovderde.[1]

Similarly, the dearth of vocations in Milwaukee from 1993 to 2002 is best understood in light of the revelations about its longtime leader, Archbishop Rembert Weakland. On May 23, 2002, Paul Marcoux, a former Marquette University student, appeared on ABC's news program *Good Morning America* and accused the longtime Milwaukee archbishop of sexual assault. Producing a number of handwritten letters from the archbishop as proof of the sexual relationship, Marcoux also revealed that in 1998, Weakland had paid him a sum of $450,000 to keep their sexual affair quiet. Marcoux claims that he had been a theology student at Marquette University in the 1980s when he approached the archbishop for advice on entering the priesthood. It was during this encounter that Marcoux alleges that the abuse took place.[2]

While Weakland denied the assault charges, he acknowledged the relationship and publicly apologized to the members of the Milwaukee diocese "for the scandal that has occurred because of [my] sinfulness." Claiming, however, that the $450,000 paid to Marcoux was taken from funds that he had "personally earned from articles and lectures over the years that far exceeded that amount," Weakland did not admit to embezzling the money from diocesan finances. This did not stop the U.S. attorney general's office from conducting an investigation into the source of the settlement. The investigation revealed that

Weakland had earned only a small portion of the amount he had paid to his former lover. The remainder came from Milwaukee parishioners' donations—which Weakland has promised to eventually repay.[3]

During most of his tenure as archbishop—for more than twenty years—faithful Catholics were concerned about Weakland's outspoken views on sexual morality and reproductive rights. As the Australian Journal *AD2000* noted in 1992, "Archbishop Weakland has led the push for a far more distinctively American Church, as independent as possible from Rome. Associated with this push have been Weakland's highly controversial policies and views on abortion, homosexuality, AIDS education, sex education, clerical pedophilia and feminism." The author concluded: "presumably these developments would make the American Church more American. That it would also be less Catholic is equally clear. Whether it would be Catholic at all remains an open question."[4]

A major problem with having a leader like Weakland is that the priests of his diocese cannot help but be affected by his heterodox beliefs. In Milwaukee, while orthodox priests were marginalized under Weakland, priests like Reverend Michael H. Crosby have built their entire careers on marketing their dissidence. A favorite speaker on Church reform at conferences for dissident Catholics like Call to Action, Crosby has marketed himself on his website as a "reformer"—publishing a number of articles critical of the celibacy requirement for the priesthood. In his article "Is Celibacy a Main Reason for the Lack of Vocation?" Crosby concludes that the reasons for celibacy are "less and less convincing." Predicting that fewer men will be attracted to the priesthood because of this, Crosby writes that this has not occurred "because religious congregations are too liberal or too questioning of the Vatican."[5] In an article titled "Beyond the Notre Dame Brouhaha: How Catholics Are Tuning Out Their Bishops," Crosby writes that "somehow some official Church leaders still seem to think that because of their 'teaching authority,' they speak de facto in the name of God. Whether or not this is so is up to them and theologians. What is clear however is that their communication is not being 'received.'"

Crosby concludes his article on the ways Catholics are "tuning out" their bishops by saying: "as I have written the Pope and said to bishops (with such thoughts falling on deaf ears), it is not an issue of the people's relativism as much as the relevance of the way the leaders are communicating . . . it's not what such bishops say, it is how they say it, and ultimately how they are heard."[6]

The Release of the *Catechism of the Catholic Church* and *Veritatis Splendor*

Concerned about what he called "the detachment of human freedom from its essential and constitutive relationship to truth," Pope John Paul II issued *Veritatis Splendor*, his 1993 encyclical on the foundations of moral theology.[7] In the introduction to the encyclical, the pope reminded followers: "no one can escape from the fundamental questions: What must I do? How do I distinguish good from evil?"[8] He opened his encyclical with a reminder that as a result of original sin, we are constantly tempted to turn our gaze away from the living and true God in order to direct it toward idols, exchanging "the truth about God for a lie" (Romans 1:25)—warning that the very foundations of moral theology are "being undermined by certain present day tendencies."

Pope John Paul II tied the release of *Veritatis Splendor* to the release the previous year of *The Catechism of the Catholic Church*, which contains a complete and systematic exposition of Christian moral teaching. For faithful Catholics, the Catechism presents a guide for living a moral life. The tendencies that so concerned Pope John Paul II were the erroneous moral teachings promoted by theologians—and some bishops. In fact, the pope was so concerned that he called on his "Brother Bishops" to draw attention to those elements of the Church's moral teaching that today "appear particularly exposed to error, ambiguity or neglect."[9] Unfortunately, some of these bishops have been reluctant to respond to what Pope John Paul II described as "the development of certain interpretations of Christian morality which are not consistent with sound teaching."[10] The pope acknowledged that although he respects the methods and requirements of the theological sciences, "there is a difference between the deposit or the truths of faith and the manner in which they are expressed." He called on the bishops to address this by counseling theologians to find ways to communicate the truth to the faithful.[11]

Pope John Paul II, both a theologian and philosopher by training, was consciously requesting collaboration with the bishops and the theologians in addressing the degradation of the culture. Sadly, most

Catholic theologians teaching at Catholic colleges and universities have been reluctant collaborators. In *Evangelical Catholicism*, George Weigel acutely critiques this widespread trend, nothing that "progressive Catholicism has no demographic traction in the world Church (although it is sustained in academic life by the tenure system)."[12] Caught up in the same wave of postmodernism and relativism that engulfed their colleagues on secular campuses, a large number of these Catholic theologians no longer look to the Gospel as the source for saving truth. Instead, these theologians echo the postmodern claim that there is no truth, only "truth claims." Indeed, it is within the theology departments of Catholic schools that faithful Catholics are meeting the most resistance.

Anticipating this move to relativism, *Veritatis Splendor* demonstrates that the root of the problem in identifying what is morally right and wrong is the detachment of human freedom from its essential and constitutive relationship to truth. Thus, the traditional doctrine regarding the natural law, and the universality and permanent validity of its precepts, is rejected. Certain elements of the Church's moral teachings are found simply unacceptable; and the Magisterium itself is considered capable of intervening in matters of morality only in order to "propose values in the light of which the individual will independently make his or her decisions and life choices."[13]

Still, *Veritatis Splendor* also reminds us that no darkness of error or sin can totally take away from man the light of God the Creator: "In the depths of his heart there always remains a yearning for absolute truth and a thirst to attain full knowledge of it." Sacred scripture remains the source of the Church's moral doctrine—"the source of all saving truth and moral teaching."

In his encyclical, Pope John Paul II deals with a common objection to moral norms, namely, that defending objective precepts is often seen as intolerant or not taking into account the complexity of an individual's particular situation. He noted that the bond between truth, the good, and freedom is often overlooked and warns that too often truth is not accepted and "freedom alone, uprooted from any objectivity, is left to decide by itself what is good and what is evil." For Pope John Paul II, in the depths of our hearts there always remains a yearning for absolute truth and a thirst to attain full knowledge of it.[14] Yet in a secular society, most maintain that there are no objective properties that all acts can be said to share—there are no moral absolutes.

Encouraging the Bishops to Respond
to Theological Error

In an effort to strengthen the bishops' ability to respond to theological error and the growing cultural relativism within the Catholic community, Pope John Paul II released *Ex Corde Ecclesiae,* his major document on Catholic higher education. Literally translated as "from the heart of the Church," *Ex Corde Ecclesiae* called for all Catholic colleges— some of them housing the seminaries that are training young men to be priests—to be accountable to local bishops. A key component of this accountability led to a requirement within the document that all theologians obtain a *mandatum,* or a certificate from the local bishop, attesting that their teaching was in communion or in keeping with official Church teachings.[15] Yet more than twenty years later, *Ex Corde* continues to be resisted because the faculty and administration on many of these Catholic campuses claimed to view it as a threat to their academic freedom and independent governance. In response, most of the bishops leading dioceses that house these Catholic colleges and universities appear to have been reluctant to publicly implement the mandatum.

In fairness, we must acknowledge that the bishops have met tremendous resistance to *Ex Corde* from the majority of Catholic theologians and administrators on Catholic campuses. When it was first released, a commentary published in the Jesuit magazine *America* by Notre Dame's then president, Father Malloy, and Father Donald Monan, chancellor of Boston College, warned of "havoc" if it were adopted and called the *mandatum* requirement "positively dangerous" to Catholic institutions in America. Describing the decree as "unworkable and dangerous," the editors of *America* warned that the impact of the norms of *Ex Corde* would be disastrous for Catholic colleges and universities.[16] In an especially hyperbolic article, one theologian likened the approval of *Ex Corde* to the "Doomsday Clock" for Catholic higher education. Drawing on the metaphor of the doomsday clock, a vestige of the Cold War, when the *Bulletin of Atomic Scientists* showed how close the world was to the midnight of mass nuclear annihilation, Jon Nilson, theology professor at Loyola University, Chicago, warned of a similar annihilation for Catholic colleges:

if there were a doomsday clock for Catholic higher education in the United States, its hands moved closer to midnight in November, 1999, when the U.S. bishops approved *Ex Corde Ecclesiae*. The hands moved still closer this past November when the bishops accepted draft procedures for implementing the Application's requirement of a mandatum for theologians. The hands are still moving, counting down to the moment when the American experience of independent but church related colleges and universities . . . will be terminated.[17]

Nilson was especially critical of "the Vatican's inability to appreciate a system of Catholic higher education independent of the church's juridical control" and described the document as an attempt by Rome to "put theologians on a short leash" in the application of the requirement of a mandatum for theologians.[18]

In response, the faculty senate at Notre Dame voted unanimously for the guidelines of *Ex Corde* to be ignored;[19] and Reverend Raymond Collins, dean of the Religious Studies Department at CUA, advised faculty members to "selectively dissent" from *Ex Corde* by refusing to implement the parts they disagreed with. In an attempt to avoid outright confrontation with Church authorities, Father Collins advised that theologians should "set aside Church teachings they found wanting, but without fuss, thus implementing the *Ex Corde* guidelines selectively—being faithful in their fashion."[20] The mandatum for theologians was never publicly implemented on most of these campuses. And if there was a private agreement made between the bishops and the presidents of these Catholic colleges and universities, the faithful Catholics teaching on these campuses were never aware of it—nor were the families of current or potential students. As a result, the requirements of *Ex Corde* appear to the faithful to have been ignored by most of the bishops and administrators of the Catholic colleges and universities they were supposed to oversee.

For those who have spent the past twenty years fighting for the implementation of *Ex Corde Ecclesiae*, there is great disappointment in those bishops who appear to have abandoned the fight. The contentious battles that once surrounded the release of the document have ended as the majority of college presidents quietly refused to implement it, and many of the bishops stayed silent. Even University of Notre Dame professor of law Gerard Bradley, a longtime proponent of the implementation of the document, has declared it "dead."[21] In a published interview for the *Chronicle of Higher Education*, the president of the University of San Diego called the controversies that surrounded *Ex Corde Ecclesiae* "so 90s."[22]

In January 2013, the Office of the Secretariat of Education at the USCCB released what they called *The Final Report for the Ten Year Review of the Application of "Ex Corde Ecclesiae" for the United States*. Unfortunately, the Ten Year Review provides almost no information about the progress that has been made in implementing the papal document on the 230 Catholic campuses throughout the country. Rather than providing facts about the implementation, the *Ten Year Review* is a one-page, self-congratulatory, platitudinous document that lauds "ongoing dialogue" and a "spirit of collaboration" but says almost nothing about what is really happening in Catholic higher education. In fact, any Catholic who has been paying attention to the culture and curricula on many of these campuses can be forgiven if he felt like he had stepped into a chapter of George Orwell's *1984* when reading a recent headline in the *National Catholic Reporter* that proclaimed: "Bishops, Colleges Find Good Collaboration in *Ex Corde* Review." That same Catholic must have been even more surprised to read a headline in *Our Sunday Visitor* that claimed: "Progress Seen in Boosting Catholic Identity on Campuses."

The USCCB provided a one-page report that claimed that the relationship between the U.S. bishops and Catholic colleges has led to "increased cooperation over the last decade." Bishop Joseph P. McFadden, current chairman of the Committee on Catholic Education of the USCCB, issued the report without any data—even anecdotal data—supporting its assertions. The report simply stated in almost Orwellian language: "bishops reported that they believe our institutions of Catholic higher education have made definite progress in advancing Catholic identity . . . the relationship between bishops and presidents on the local level can be characterized as positive and engaged, demonstrating progress on courtesy and cooperation in the last ten years. . . . Clarity about Catholic identity among college and university leadership has fostered substantive dialogues and cultivated greater mission-driven practices across the university."

Orwellian Doublespeak

In Orwell's dystopia, as the truth becomes uncomfortable, facts are redefined—or sometimes removed—by the Office of the Ministry of Truth. This new version of the "truth" is then disseminated by the Office of the Ministry of Propaganda. While this is not to suggest that the USCCB has become the Catholic Church's Ministry of Truth, it is difficult not to conclude that the Ten Year Review of the Implementation of *Ex Corde Ecclesiae* provides readers with absolutely no information about what is really happening at Catholic colleges and universities. In fact, the report says nothing about campus problems in the past except to claim that despite the progress that has been made, "there is still work to be done."

To understand how such a vacuous report could be disseminated by the USCCB, one has to go back to November 14, 2010, when the USCCB Committee on Catholic Education approved a ten-year review of the application of *Ex Corde Ecclesiae* for the United States. Headed by Most Reverend Thomas Curry, then an auxiliary bishop of Los Angeles, the Committee on Catholic Education set the goals and the guidelines for the ten-year review. (Curry recently resigned as bishop in the wake of the release of documents showing that he deliberately and knowingly took steps to conceal the abuse of children from law enforcement and to protect abusive priests.)

The guidelines for the ten-year review guaranteed that no data of substance would be collected or analyzed to determine effectiveness. Rather than collecting data to assess effectiveness and progress toward meeting the goals of *Ex Corde Ecclesiae*, the committee stated that the purpose of the review was to "provide a reference tool for both bishops and presidents of Catholic institutions." Rather than collecting specific information that could be quantified and analyzed, the review was to simply consist of a "conversation between a bishop and each university president within his diocese." In lieu of collecting facts to inform a report that would assess progress toward goals, the review was described by Bishop Curry and his committee as "not a report, but rather an opportunity for a bishop and a president to meet and discuss the application of *Ex Corde Ecclesiae* for the United States."[23]

It was anticipated that "this 10-year review, modeled on the five-year review of 2006, will occur in a spirit of ecclesial communion and will yield an appreciation of the positive developments and remaining challenges in our collaborative efforts to ensure the implementation of *Ex Corde Ecclesiae* in the United States." Rather than a real assessment, the purpose of the review was identified as simply providing an opportunity for the bishops and the presidents to talk with one another—to "dialogue." The words "dialogue" and "conversation" are used frequently in the one-page report on the 10-year review, as were "positive" and "progress." The reviewers also promise "continued dialogue . . . for greater cooperation in advancing the mission of the Church."[24]

What the original committee identified as a key element of the review was providing a way for bishops to "share their reflections with one another at USCCB regional meetings." Once these "reflections" were shared, the minutes of the discussions at all the regional meetings would be compiled by staff and presented to the president of the USCCB. Beyond that, a mechanism was never created to share any of the outcomes of these conversations with any other stakeholders—including donors, faculty, students, parents, and other Catholics interested in the progress that is being made on their Catholic campuses. The review was never intended to be disseminated beyond a one-page document that offers no specifics on the current state of Catholic colleges and universities.

In a February 2013 interview, Sister John Mary Fleming, the new executive director of the USCCB's Secretariat of Catholic Education, helped put the report into context by saying that the ten-year review was "never designed to be an attempt to assess the past." And although Sister Fleming acknowledged that "the relationship between the bishops and the college presidents was fractured in the past," she spoke optimistically about the future, lauding the bishops for "focusing on how they can reach out to create a culture of communion and support." Acknowledging that challenges do remain, Sister Fleming pointed to the one sentence within the report admitting that "there is still work to be done." Sister Fleming also pointed to the formation of a group of bishops and college presidents who will be working under Bishop Joseph P. McFadden, the current chairman of the Committee on Catholic Education. According to Bishop McFadden, the working group will "continue the dialogue about strategic subjects on a national level."[25]

According to the USCCB website, the working group will begin gathering "information on best practices, will offer suggestions for local conversation, and, as needed, develop resources."[26] Once again, the website says nothing about whether the review will involve collecting data to assess goals, objectives, or activities to meet the requirements of *Ex Corde Ecclesiae*. Yet any undergraduate student in public policy or social research knows that one cannot adequately assess the effectiveness of a program without systematically collecting and analyzing quantifiable data. Conversations alone will not do it.

Among faithful Catholics monitoring the situation, there has been great optimism that Sister Fleming, a member of the Dominican Sisters of St. Cecilia in Nashville, will begin to turn things around for Catholic education. Yet she will have to find out what is happening on these campuses through a real assessment that quantifies goals, objectives, and activities—not just through "dialogue" with those who will tell her what they want her to know.

For faithful faculty and students, the real losers in the struggle for Catholic identity, the campus itself stands as a sad reminder of what once was—and might have been. While the once hallowed ground still remains, the sacred symbols—the saintly statues and crucifixes that continue to adorn many of these campuses—have become hollow reminders of what has passed. For Father Wilson Miscamble, professor of history at Notre Dame, most Catholic campuses now possess "a certain Potemkin Village quality.... While their buildings are quite real, what goes on within them has increasingly lost its distinctive content.... Students emerge from Catholic schools unfamiliar with the riches of the Catholic intellectual tradition and with their imaginations untouched by a religious sensibility."[27] Like the fake "Potemkin villages" that were built to create an impression of prosperity during Catherine the Great's tours of Ukraine and the Crimea, the Catholic campuses of today create a false impression of a commitment to faithfulness to the truth of the Church that is presented in campus tours to potential students and their parents. And, as in the case of the Potemkin villages, Professor Miscamble predicts, for most Catholic colleges and universities "it will be increasingly difficult to maintain even a Catholic façade in the academic life of these institutions."[28]

"Bishops without Voices"

Some have suggested that the reason that so many of the bishops have been reluctant to speak out on these issues is that they are fearful of appearing judgmental—especially after suffering through the attacks on their leadership in the wake of the clergy abuse crisis. Pope John Paul II certainly anticipated this problem when he wrote that "upholding the truth on moral issues does not mean that the Church is lacking in compassion."

Still, in a culture that is controlled by relativism on issues surrounding marriage, sexual behavior, reproductive rights, and gender relations, it is difficult for faithful Catholics and their leaders to make moral judgments on these issues without being viewed as lacking in empathy. Although Pope John Paul II pointed out that concealing or weakening moral truth is not consistent with genuine understanding and compassion, the reality is that when Catholics—including their bishops—attempt to draw on Church teachings to pronounce activities like abortion or homosexual relations as morally wrong, these same Catholics are often stigmatized by those within their own Church.

Pope Benedict XVI regularly echoed his predecessor's concerns about the reluctance to defend Catholic teachings on issues of faith and morals, and he called on all Catholics—including the bishops—to resist what he has described as the "dictatorship of relativism."[29] Pope Benedict may have been referring to the diversity of opinion held by Catholics (and even some priests and bishops) on such issues as same-sex unions, women's ordination, and abortion. For these Catholics, doctrine is viewed as a social construct contingent on the specific historical, cultural, and institutional contexts in which it emerges. Rather than adherence to Catholic teachings as set forth by the Magisterium, this group of Catholics maintain that Catholicism is grounded in the view that interpretive authority is diffuse: "it is not located solely in the official hierarchical power structure, but is dispersed, seen in the everyday interpretive activities of ordinary Catholics."[30]

It is clear that those responsible for attacking the legitimate authority of the bishops and the pope knew the importance, and the benefits, of "disarming competing cultures." One of the most effective ways Catholic culture was disarmed on Catholic campuses was through attacking the legitimacy of authority within the Church—and in many cases, denying the existence of truth itself. In a postmodern appropriation of the title of Cardinal Newman's 1854 classic *Idea of a University,* George Dennis O'Brien, the former president of Bucknell University and president emeritus of the University of Rochester, dismisses the possibility of what he calls a "single truth." Rejecting the conventional institutional juridical hierarchical model used by the Vatican as "improper both to faith and academic freedom," O'Brien argues that "in an effort to preserve the integrity of both church and university," Catholic colleges must adapt a model that appreciates what he calls "different kinds of truth—each with its own proper warrant and method."[31]

With a strong endorsement on the book jacket from Charles Curran, one of a handful of dissident Catholic theologians to be publicly corrected by the Vatican for his erroneous writings, O'Brien promises that his book questions not only the ideology of the modern Catholic university but also "the way in which Catholic defenders of the truth of the Catholic faith construe truth."[32] O'Brien claims expertise and impartial outsider status as the former president of two highly ranked secular colleges to make a case for the futility of the kind of truth claims that have been made on a Catholic campus.[33] In a dismissal of the traditional truth claims of doctrine and dogma, O'Brien argues that on a Catholic campus, "one can uncover academic dogma and Christian freedom, university infallibility and dogmatic fallibility."[34]

On some Catholic campuses there has been an attempt to remove the bishop from the governing boards. In November 2007, the Board of Trustees at the University of St. Thomas in St. Paul, Minnesota, voted to remove the bylaw that maintained the sitting archbishop of St. Paul-Minneapolis as the vicar general and priest president of the university—effectively severing all ties to the archdiocese. The St. Thomas Board, which includes Father Edward Malloy, the retired president of the University of Notre Dame, voted unanimously to change the university's bylaws and install the soon-to-retire, longtime liberal Archbishop Harry Flynn as chairman for a five-year term. The move was denounced by orthodox Catholic publications as an effort by the university to override the authority of and possible reforms by Archbishop John Nienstedt, Flynn's more orthodox Catholic coadjutor bishop, who was scheduled to succeed him as head of the archdiocese in 2008.[35] Named by the Rainbow Sash Alliance, a gay advocacy organization, as one of the four most "gay friendly bishops" in the United States, Archbishop Flynn had been a favorite of the faculty.[36] With this historic move, St. Thomas University, which describes itself in its mission statement as "inspired by the Catholic intellectual tradition," has chosen to limit the influence of a new and faithful archbishop.

In *Catholic Identity: Balancing Reason, Faith and Power*, sociologist Michelle Dillon argues that those who belong to organizations like the proabortion Catholics for a Free Choice or the gay rights advocacy organization Dignity are simply engaged in pushing for the elimination of institutional impediments to diversity and the expansion of interpretive and participative equality in the Church.[37] Those Dillon calls "pro-change Catholics" believe that they are simply ahead of the curve of other Catholics. And for Dillon, conservative Catholics are those who desire to "restrict the intra-church participation of their coreligionists." For Dillon, "pro-change Catholics are committed to remodeling the Church as a more inclusively pluralistic community.... Pro-change Catholics seek not only to overturn official church teaching de-legitimating Catholics who are gay or lesbian, or advocates of women's ordination, or pro-choice on abortion," they also seek to "reconstruct an inclusive, egalitarian, and pluralist church wherein these identities are validated."[38] While Dillon believes that prochange Catholics can transform the Church into one that is inclusive in practice and validates as full members in communion with the Church even those Catholics who support abortion or gay marriage, she also believes that these same prochange Catholics can integrate this change with what they consider to be core aspects of Catholicism as their community of memory.[39]

Most faithful Catholics find Dillon's suggestion impossible, maintaining that the Church cannot allow those who deny authoritative teachings on the "nonnegotiable issues" or commanding truths like teachings on the evil of abortion to claim that they are maintaining "core aspects of Catholicism." Yet even the orthodox must acknowledge that the chaos within the Church itself that followed the Second Vatican Council might have led those change-seeking Catholics to think that the Church was indeed going to be more open to women's issues like female ordination and reproductive rights. These liberal Catholics often point to the documents of Vatican II, especially *The Pastoral Constitution on the Church in the Modern World*, which they believe called for a paradigm shift in our understanding of a theological vision of the world. Instead of conceiving the world as tainted and a place to withdraw from, members of the Catholic community were called to redirect their energies in a quest for holiness and the encounter with God to the world.[40] Some interpreted this engagement with the world as an acceptance of the changing culture of the modern world—an embrace of egalitarianism and a rejection of what they viewed as the archaic hierarchical system of teaching. Some went even further—maintaining that even our relationship with God needed to be altered from one that was hierarchical to one that is more "horizontal."

For many pro-choice progressive Catholics, the abortion debate suggests there is a need to address attention to the "common life" of the individual—moving beyond the authoritarian or "vertical" relationships of the past. As former Jesuit priest Bernard Cooke pointed out in a series of lectures at the College of the Holy Cross, "the Vatican Council reintroduced an understanding of the divine-human relationship that was more horizontal than vertical. God is less above the people, sending down messages through delegates, than abiding with them."[41] For these progressives, even God is not "above" the people. As historian David O'Brien, of the University of Dayton, writes: "the older, now resurgent position leads to a moral teaching that, however skilled its intellectual rationalization, remains in essence an articulation of truths handed down from above."[42] Instead, O'Brien suggests that what is needed is a theological method that is anchored in the experience of Christians who "necessarily must be consulted in moral formulations. . . . The more horizontal understanding fastens the vision of the church beyond itself, in the historic liberation of the human family."[43]

In contrast, as Reverend Richard Neuhaus, the editor of *First Things*, wrote a few years before his death in 2009, the denial of authority and refusal to submit to official Church teachings implicit in O'Brien and Cooke's horizontal formulation and Dillon's argument in favor of prochange Catholics "is at the heart of the problem within our Church. . . . When a university decides not to say that Jesus is the way, the truth, and the life, it is not saying nothing. Rather, it is saying that adherence to this way, this truth and this life is not necessary to, or is a hindrance to being the kind of university it wants to be."[44]

This denial of the authority of the Church was predicted more than fifty years ago in the works of T. S. Eliot. Writing about the sense of alienation that occurs when social regulators begin to splinter and the controlling moral authority of a society is no longer effective, Eliot used his play *The Cocktail Party* to present the dilemma of what happens to a society when no one recognizes the presence of sin. In his play, a troubled young protagonist visits a psychiatrist and confides that she feels a "sense of sin" because of her relationship with a married man. She is distressed not so much by the illicit relationship but by the strange feeling of sinfulness. Eliot writes, "Having a sense of sin seems abnormal to her—she had never noticed before that such behavior might be seen in those terms. She believed that she had become ill."[45]

When Eliot writes of his protagonist's feeling unease or uncertainty about her behavior, he is really speaking of the sense of normlessness that has traditionally been a focus of sociologists. In many ways, Eliot's play is about anomie—the state that sociologists identify as resulting when one is caught between the loosening moral norms regulating behavior and one's own moral misgivings. Eliot's play echoes the scholarship of Durkheim. Both men saw that the identification and stigmatization of deviant behavior is functional for society because it can produce certainty for individuals and solidarity for the group. And, both recognized that dramatic social change through rapid redefinitions of deviance can be dysfunctional for society. Strong cultural values and clear concepts of good and evil integrate members into the group and provide meaning. When traditional cultural attachments are disrupted, or when behavior is no longer regulated by these common norms and values, individuals are left without a moral compass.[46]

Durkheim knew that social facts like crime statistics, abortion rates, and poll data on support for gay marriage can be explained only by analyzing the unique social conditions that evolve when norms break down. The resulting anomic state leads to deviant behavior as the individual's attachment to social bonds is weakened. According to this view, people internalize social norms because of their attachments to others. People care what others think of them and attempt to conform to expectations because they accept what others expect.[47] However, when these same people are unsure about the norms, or when the norms are changing rapidly, as they have for the past few decades, there is a growing unwillingness to make moral judgments about behavior. This reluctance to judge has even permeated the culture of those who have been entrusted to make these moral judgments—the bishops themselves.

Bishop Armando X. Ochoa, formerly of the Diocese of El Paso, Texas, received national attention in 2011 when he reassigned a parish administrator, Reverend Michael Rodriguez, for publicly condemning homosexuality and writing guest columns in the *El Paso Times* in response to the city's decision to extend health insurance benefits to domestic partners, regardless of marital status or sexual orientation, which he called "gravely harmful to the common good of our city." Father Rodriguez wrote four controversial columns that ran in the *El Paso Times*, speaking out against the gay lifestyle. He also challenged El Paso mayor John Cook and city representatives Susie Byrd and Steve Ortega to a public forum.[48] In a column titled "Every Catholic Must Oppose Certain Things," Father Rodriguez wrote that "any Catholic who supports homosexual acts is, by definition, committing a mortal sin, and placing himself/herself outside of communion with the Roman Catholic Church." Father Rodriguez ended his column by calling homosexuality "an intrinsic moral evil."[49]

In news releases from the Diocese of El Paso, Bishop Ochoa said that Father Rodriguez's comments "raised serious issues regarding whether his participation could be attributed to the Diocese of El Paso." In an interview for a local television news affiliate, Bishop Ochoa said that "Father Rodriguez has recently challenged city officials to participate with him in a partisan debate on issues related to an upcoming election. This type of intervention in the political process by religious organizations such as the Diocese of El Paso and San Juan Bautista Church is not permitted under Section 501 of the Internal Revenue Code."[50]

Value-Free Ideology

Again, we return to the work of Philip Rieff, who warned over forty years ago in his now classic book *The Triumph of the Therapeutic*, that "psychological man" was beginning to replace "Christian man" as the dominant character type in our society.[51] Unlike traditional Christianity, which made moral demands on believers, the secular world of "psychological man" rejected both the idea of sin and the need for salvation. Replacing the concept of sin with the concept of sickness was predicted by Eliot's *Cocktail Party* but was documented by Rieff, who wrote in 1966 that the authority that had been vested in Christian culture had been all but shattered. Nothing had succeeded it. What worried him was that the institutions of morality—especially the Church—lacked authority and could no longer persuade others to follow them. Further, Rieff believed that this failure of authority was no accident but the program of "the modern cultural revolution," which was conducted "not in the name of any new order of communal purpose, but rather, for the permanent disestablishment of any deeply internalized moral demands."[52]

Rieff believed that once the religious authority is removed from the culture, a kind of anticulture emerges. It is a culture in which religion is privatized—completely removed from the public square and used only as a type of therapy for individuals. For Rieff, "psychological man becomes a hedger against his own bets, a user of any faith that lends itself to therapeutic use."[53] In *Fellow Teachers*, Rieff's subsequent book, he goes even further to say that "at the end of this tremendous cultural development, we moderns shall arrive at barbarism. Barbarians are people without historical memory. Barbarism is the real meaning of radical contemporaneity. Released from all authoritative pasts, we progress towards barbarism, not away from it."[54]

Rieff further relates society's attempt to "level all of the verticals in authority" in his later books, *Sacred Order/Social Order: My Life among the Deathworks* and *Charisma: The Gift of Grace and How It Has Been Taken from Us*, the latter published shortly after his death in 2006.[55] Rieff asserted that one of the reasons we have such problems with social order is that "moral constraints are now read as social constructions that have no status in being beyond what is given by those who have constructed these constraints."[56] While defining down the deviance of abortion or homosexual relations that has occurred within the culture—including Catholic culture—the reality remains that it is simply a symptom of a much bigger problem. The real problem is the failure to recognize that there are indeed rules, and a natural law basis for such rules, that for centuries have led to sacred orders, or what Philip Rieff calls "interdicts."

The faithful know that teachings on life issues and marriage and the family cannot be changed. For faithful Catholics, these teachings are Rieff's "interdicts." And, although there are some issues—including some liturgical changes and devotional practices—that are constantly being redefined and strengthened within the Church, there remain the enduring truths, those that Philip Rieff calls "commanding truths," that cannot be changed: "commanding truths will not be mocked, except to the destruction of everything sacred."[57] Of the family as a commanding truth, Rieff wrote: "the destruction of the family is the key regimen of technological innovation and moral deviance."[58] And, of life itself, Rieff wrote: "we must stand against the re-creation of life in the laboratory and the taking of life in the abortion clinic."[59] Rieff knew, as the earliest bishops of the Church knew, that culture survives by faith in the highest absolute authority and its interdicts. For Catholics, there can be no Catholic culture and no true Catholic Church without such commanding truths.

Rieff points out that the challenge to social order is the growing inability of the culture to translate sacred order into social order. In the past, the faithful knew that their identity as Catholics came from what Rieff calls the "vertical axis in authority." Believers looked to authority figures like priests and bishops for guidance as these clergymen were willing to do the hard work of translating sacred order—helping others to understand the scriptural and natural law basis for the interdicts. Rieff warned us that there must be a conscious and intense established order of interdicts or rules that are unchanging. In a review of *Charisma*, R. R. Reno, editor of *First Things*, writes that "for Rieff, the central and defining purpose of culture is to regulate the relationship between the no-imposing voice of commandment and the yes-seeking desires of the individual. According to Rieff, the traditional approach to the felt difficulties of bringing personality into coordination with authority involves internalizing and intensifying cultural norms. Religious at their core, traditional cultures stamp our inner lives with their creeds and in so doing, deliver the human animal from its slavery to instinct."[60]

Charisma describes the gift of what Rieff calls a "high and holy terror," which instills the power of divine command so deeply in the soul that we can bear the thought of "evil in oneself and in the world." For Rieff, holy terror is actually fear of oneself, fear of the evil in oneself and in the world. It is also fear of punishment. Without this necessary fear, charisma is not possible. To live without this fear is to be a terror oneself, a monster—a barbarian. And, yet, for those who want to change Church teachings on faith and morals, the goal is to live without fear—to remove all holy terror by removing all of the rules. One of his intentions in writing *Charisma* is "to make us again more responsive to the possibility of holy terror."[61] It is this concept of "holy terror" that is being slowly recovered by charismatic leaders of the Church—steeped in the truths of her Creed—who are responsible for the first fruits of today's renewal.

6 | Blurring the Boundaries

While we have been critical of progressives who have distorted the documents of Vatican II to suit their own goals for women's ordination, a noncelibate priesthood, and a general promotion of one's own individual experience over the Church's Creed, we acknowledge that there is much to celebrate in the Church as the decades following the end of the Vatican Council in 1965 brought new opportunities for lay Catholic participation in ministerial activities. Both of the authors of this book are grateful beneficiaries of these opportunities as we have each participated in several Catholic ministries. The first author has served on a diocesan review team, a liturgy committee, and a vocations committee. She has also provided assistance to migrant workers through a Catholic ministry on the San Diego border with Mexico and spent nearly a decade serving as a prison minister within a San Diego Juvenile Detention Facility. The second author of this book has worked in a youth ministry, has volunteered in urban ministries to assist the homeless, and has led educational programs at the parish level. Both authors have served on parish councils and worked in Catholic programs to support pregnant women and single mothers. And both have dedicated much of their professional writing careers to bringing the "Good News" of the Gospel to others.

We are thankful for the opportunity to serve the Church in these many ways and acknowledge that Vatican II helped to make all of these opportunities possible. The

Council reminded all Catholics—including lay Catholics like us—of the principle of shared responsibility. Shared responsibility means that every Catholic, by reason of Baptism, is charged with the task to make Christ present here on earth. We are all required to participate in the salvific mission of Christ in the world. Many of us, from both the progressive and more conservative Catholic perspectives, have taken that responsibility seriously—including those with whom we may disagree on how best this mission can be fulfilled. And, although we have devoted pages of this book to critically evaluating the methods used by progressive Catholics to blur the boundaries between the ordained and the laity, we must acknowledge that most of the self-described "Vatican II" Catholics share our love for the Church and believe that they are doing what is best for the Church.

The problem is that the ways in which some Catholics have interpreted Vatican II's call to the laity continues to cause confusion about the boundaries between the laity and the ordained. This has created problems for the Church as the ambiguity surrounding the position of the priest may have deterred young men from accepting such an uncertain role. While few would want to return to the days before the Council when the laity played a passive role in helping to support the Church, we all must acknowledge that it was a simpler time because the roles were clear and well defined as bishops headed the dioceses, priests led their parishes, and the laity prayerfully complied with their direction. This is no longer true. And, in some dioceses, female lay ministers have assumed the role of the pastor of a given parish—relegating the priest to the role of what dioceses like Rochester, New York, calls "sacramental ministers," or "priest assistants," who are called on to celebrate the Mass, consecrate the Eucharist, and administer the sacraments. All other pastoral duties, including the day-to-day parish administration and financial decision-making, is done by the lay pastoral administrator—even when there are priests available within the very same parish the lay administrator is leading. Last year, San Jose bishop Patrick McGrath named a female lay "minister for parish life" to lead a large Santa Clara parish instead of appointing a new pastor. He did this despite the fact that there are three priests listed in the parish's online staff directory. *California Catholic Daily* reported that Dorothy Carlson is now leading St. Justin Parish in Santa Clara, even though Father Mancha is listed as the parochial vicar, Father Edsil Ortiz is listed as parochial vicar and minister to the sick, the dying and the grieving, and Father Joseph Penderast is listed as "in residence." According to the diocesan website, the reasons for the appointment of Carlson to lead the parish were: "the number of priests is dwindling; some priests may choose not to become pastors; there are increasing numbers of highly educated, experienced, and motivated lay Catholics who view ministry as a profession; and closing or merging some parishes was a negative option."[1]

There does not appear to be a shortage of priests at St. Justin Parish. And there is no real shortage of priests in the San Jose diocese. Currently the San Jose Diocese has ninety-nine active diocesan priests and twenty-two religious priests serving fifty-three churches. It likely that a shortage of priests is not what is driving the movement toward appointing female lay administrators to lead parishes throughout the country. Rather, it is a way to meet the growing demand from women to gain leadership roles in the Church. In the Diocese of Rochester, there is an extensive liturgical function for the lay pastoral administrator that includes leading prayer or worship services, leading penance services, and according to a recent article in the *Wanderer*, often means delivering the homily at Mass. In Rochester the homilies delivered by the lay parish administrators are called "Dialogue Homilies" to differentiate them from those administered by priests or deacons.[2] Lay parish administrators in Rochester also provide pastoral counseling to parishioners, officiate at graveside services, and supervise the activities of the "priest assistants" involved in parish sacramental ministry.

There are costs to this structure as few men have been attracted to a priesthood that has been so severely restricted that the priest himself is viewed purely in instrumental terms as sacramental minister or priest assistant rather than pastoral leader. In the dioceses of Rochester and Albany, the empowerment of large numbers of female lay parish leaders—at the expense of priestly leadership—may have contributed to the dramatic declines in vocations in those dioceses. Our research on ordination rates reveals that when large numbers of lay leaders assume control over parishes, there are few vocations to the priesthood in those dioceses. And, while we cannot claim causality because we cannot say that the lay leadership itself caused the lack of ordinations in a specific diocese, we can say that the presence of large numbers of parish life coordinators or lay ecclesial ministers in a diocese is correlated to a lack of ordinations to the priesthood in that diocese. In fact a review of the ordination data for the past decade reveals that the greater the number of lay pastoral leaders in parishes without resident priest-pastors, the lower the number of ordinations.

The Feminization of Parish Leadership in Rochester, New York

After more than thirty years as bishop of the Rochester Catholic Diocese, Most Reverend Matthew Clark retired at the end of 2012. He leaves behind a legacy of shuttered churches, closed schools, large numbers of priestly resignations, few ordinations to the priesthood, and a steadily declining rate of Mass attendance for Catholics in the diocese. According to an analysis published recently in the *Wanderer*, from 1995 to 2005, the Diocese of Rochester lost more than 45 percent of its priests, and Mass attendance has dropped more than 25 percent in the past decade.[3] The rates of priestly ordination in the Rochester diocese are among the lowest in the country. According to the *Official Catholic Directory*, the Diocese of Rochester ordained twenty-four (or seven per 100,000 Catholics) to the priesthood from 1992 through 2009. During that same time period, Bishop Fabien Bruskewitz's Diocese of Lincoln ordained sixty-three men (or sixty-six per 100,000 Catholics) to the priesthood.

Still, ordination rates do not appear to concern Bishop Clark as his 2009 book, *Forward in Hope: Saying Amen to Lay Ecclesial Ministry*, ignores the lack of priestly ordinations and instead, celebrates the fact that the Rochester diocese has led the nation in empowering women to lead parishes. From the earliest days of his Episcopal appointment as Rochester's bishop in 1979, Bishop Clark has made it a priority to enhance women's roles in parish and diocesan leadership. In his earliest pastoral letter, titled *Fire in the Thornbush: A Pastoral Letter on Women in the Church*, Bishop Clark presented his vision for a more inclusive Church in which women were given opportunities for leadership in every aspect of parish life—including newly created roles in the liturgical life of the parish. In that first pastoral letter, Bishop Clark promised "the inclusion of women in liturgical functions, in those roles now open to them or in new roles that may be legitimately created." Writing that "it will be a priority of the Diocese of Rochester, all of its agencies, divisions and departments, to encourage and to invite women to participate in full measure in volunteer and paid positions within the diocese and its organizations," thirty years later, it is clear that Bishop Clark has succeeded in creating roles for women that few could ever have imagined. But the empowerment of women has come at a high price in terms of the loss of priestly ordinations in the Diocese of Rochester.

Currently there are twenty-three churches that are led by women in Rochester—all of them without a resident priest-pastor. Of these twenty-three churches, twelve are led by six lay women: Deb Housel is in charge of four churches, including St. Michael's, Corpus Christi, St. Andrew's, and the Church of the Annunciation. Housel is assisted in her ministry by "sacramental minister" Father Paul Gitau. The Church of Our Lady of Perpetual Help was the fifth church led by Housel, but that church recently closed. Charlotte Bruney leads St. Vincent de Paul Church; Irene Goodwin leads St. Mary of the Assumption; Anne Marie Brogan leads St. Mary's Church in downtown Rochester; Margaret Ostromecki runs two churches, St. Thomas More and Our Lady Queen of Peace. Barbara Swiecki has leadership over three churches: Good Shepherd, Guardian Angels, and St. Joseph.

In addition to the six lay female parish administrators leading 12 churches in the Rochester Diocese, there are 5 women religious leading eleven Rochester Diocese churches, including Sister Joan Sobala, S.S.J., who leads two churches, St. Anne and Our Lady of Lourdes; Sister Karen Dietz, S.S.J., who leads three churches, St. Agnes, St. Rose, and St. Paul of the Cross; Sister Chris Treichel, O.S.F., who leads two churches, Sacred Heart and St. Ann; Sister Joan Cawley, S.S.J., who leads the Church of the Resurrection; and Sister Diane Dennie, S.S.J., who leads three churches, St. Michael. St. John the Evangelist, and St. Patrick's. Out of a total of thirteen lay parish administrators in the Rochester diocese, there are only two lay men leading Rochester's parishes—William Rabjohn and Michael Sauter.[4]

In *Forward in Hope: Saying Amen to Lay Ecclesial Ministry*, Bishop Clark uses the word "amen" in the subtitle to express his "hearty approval" of the practice of using female parish administrators and devotes the entire book to making the argument that the future of the Church depends on empowering the laity to assume pastoral leadership roles. Looking back at the heady days that surrounded Vatican II, Bishop Clark recalled that he was "thrilled hearing the Church referred to as the People of God. . . . I recognized the profound shift in the documents talking about the Church, not as the hierarchy but as the People of God . . . and the laity share in the one mission of God's people, and in the triple office of Jesus Christ as priest, prophet, and king."[5]

Interpreting the Vatican II documents to mean that all God's people are "ordained" through Baptism has helped to encourage a whole generation of progressive theologians and historians to maintain that there is no difference between the laity and the ordained. Bishop Clark recalls that the Rochester diocese was "among the first in the nation" to employ a female pastoral assistant, proudly claiming that this "soon led to other pastors hiring lay people to help them."[6] Only a few years later, the Rochester women moved from their "pastoral assistant" role to assume the leadership of the parishes—employing priests as "priest assistants." This was replicated first in Albany and later in dioceses throughout the country led by progressive bishops who shared Bishop Clark's commitment to elevating the laity sometimes at the expense of the priests. In *Fire in the Thornbush*, Bishop Clark acknowledged his gratitude to a number of bishops—including Archbishop Raymond Hunthausen of Seattle, Bishop John Cummins of Oakland, Bishop Raymond Lucker of New Ulm, Minnesota, and Archbishop Peter Gerety of Newark—who were beginning to make the kinds of changes that Bishop Clark would also implement.

Bishop Clark's enthusiasm for the empowerment of women as pastoral leaders in his diocese's churches has not lessened since 1979. In fact, in his recently published book, he writes—replete with an exclamation point—"How wonderful, really, for us to be a part of the birth of this new era of Church life!"[7] Bishop Clark also offers tips to other bishops who may want to implement the kind of ministries he has presided over. In an effort to "preserve communion among the various vocations and ministries . . . both ordained and lay," Bishop Clark advises that in the Diocese of Rochester he implemented the use of the term "ministerium" to describe "all those who exercise in the local Church an official ecclesial ministry whether they are ordained or not." Bishop Clark believes that this term can help such ministers "avoid the temptations of individualism and parochialism, the antidote to which is precisely this sense of a diocesan ministerium to which they belong together with the clergy and to which they hold some greater degree of accountability." Each year, Bishop Clark convenes a "Gathering of the Ministerium" for hundreds of priests, deacons, and lay ecclesial ministers to "create a sense of togetherness, mutual purpose and communion among all those present."[8]

The Origins of the Role of the Pastoral Administrator or Parish Life Coordinator

The role of the pastoral administrator or parish life coordinator as this position is defined in dioceses like Rochester and Albany emerged from *Lumen Gentium*, Vatican II's *Dogmatic Constitution on the Church*, which many progressive Catholics interpreted as including a call for lay parish leadership for the laity. On the surface, the *Constitution* is a welcome invitation for all to share in the responsibility for accomplishing the salvific mission of the Church: "the Pastors know well how much the laity contributes to the welfare of the whole Church. For they know that they themselves were not established by Christ to undertake alone the whole salvific mission of the Church to the world, but it is their exalted offices to be shepherds of the faithful and also recognize the latter's contributions and charisms that everyone in his own way will, with one mind, incorporate the common task."[9] The message was a call to all Catholics to share with their priests a commitment to the mission of saving souls. But the *Constitution* has become so distorted by progressive theologians that many members of the laity now believe that the documents of Vatican II erased the distinction between the laity and the ordained.[10]

In 1978, Bishop Hubbard released "We Are His People," his first pastoral letter as bishop of Albany. In it, Bishop Hubbard, like Bishop Clark, cited the Second Vatican Council's *Dogmatic Constitution on the Church* to call the faithful to "shared responsibility" that needs to be "relearned and experienced." Focusing first on the priests of his diocese in his pastoral letter, Bishop Hubbard's 1978 pastoral letter first assured the priests that they have been a "special blessing to the Church of Albany." But then Bishop Hubbard offered the following caveat to his priests:

> While your role is unique and indispensable, it is not and cannot be self-contained. . . . As we look to the future, you must be willing to share with the deacons, religious and laity of our Diocese many of the roles and ministries you have tradition-

ally been required to exercise. With other persons entering the sanctuary as lectors, acolytes and ministers of the Eucharist, or assuming responsibility for religious education, health care, social services and financial matters related to the life of the parish or diocese, there can well emerge questions about the proper role of the priest. As a result, there can develop the natural human reaction to cling to one's own identity or vested interest. But, in point of fact, what is emerging, I believe, is not a challenge to your role or identity but an opportunity for greater service, an opportunity to explore the interrelatedness of all ministries of the Church and to facilitate their development. . . . I envision your role to be initiators, coordinators and facilitators of ministries.[11]

Bishop Hubbard's 1978 admonishment to priests that they should not "cling to one's own identity" as priests was prescient. It is difficult today to avoid thinking that this has been the major problem in the Albany diocese over the past three decades as many priests have indeed given up their identity as priests there—and few are entering the priesthood. There have only been six ordinations to the priesthood for the five-year period 2006–2010. During three of those years there were no ordinations at all. Resignations from the active priesthood in the Albany diocese mirror those in Rochester. And, like Rochester Bishop Clark's earliest pastoral letter, Bishop Hubbard's 1978 pastoral letter welcomed the laity to "be Church" because "being a member of God's people gives to each of you, no matter what your call or state in life, a great dignity and empowerment." Now, more than thirty years later, the Diocese of Albany joins the Diocese of Rochester in the largest numbers in the country of lay pastoral associates leading parishes throughout the diocese. In fact, Bishop Hubbard went even further than Bishop Clark in calling on the Albany diocese to share personnel and resources on an "ecumenical basis" with those of other faiths: "administration is a crucial ministry which must be shared, especially with competent lay people. . . . Also to be considered is a willingness to share resources, personnel and other advantages on an inter-parochial, regional and ecumenical basis."[12]

The Demographics of Church Leadership

To understand how the role of parish life coordinators or lay pastoral administrators has developed over the years, it is helpful to look at the demographics of those currently in the role of leading parishes without resident priest-pastors. About 90 percent of all lay parish life coordinators throughout the country are female.[13] The most comprehensive national study of the role of the parish life coordinator was released in 2004 by the Center for Applied Research in the Apostolate at Georgetown University. They conducted a national random sample telephone poll that included interviews with 795 lay ecclesial ministers in Catholic parishes in the United States. The CARA researchers focused on interviews from a random oversampling of lay persons and religious sisters and brothers entrusted with the care of a parish without a resident priest-pastor (often called parish life coordinators, or in Rochester, lay pastoral administrators). Interviews with ninety-six parish life coordinators were conducted, and attempts were made to compare the demographic characteristics of current parish life coordinators with lay ecclesial ministers in general. Comparisons were also made to a previous study of parish life coordinators and a previous study of lay ecclesial ministers, both conducted more than a decade prior to their current poll.

The 2004 CARA study revealed that nearly nine in ten lay parish life coordinators were female. Seventy-one percent were women religious, and 18 percent were other lay women. Only 6 percent of parish life coordinators were lay men, and 5 percent were religious brothers. Although the majority of parish life coordinators were women religious, the researchers point out that this is a declining trend (in 1990, 81 percent of parish life coordinators were religious sisters). Although the portion of parish life coordinators who were male (religious or lay) nearly doubled from 1990 until 2003, when the CARA researchers collected their data for their 2004 report (from 6 percent to 11 percent) the percentage of lay females (as opposed to women religious) serving as parish life coordinators increased from 13 percent to 18 percent during the same period.

According to the 2004 CARA study, the use of parish life coordinators was much more prevalent in Midwest parishes than anywhere else as nearly half of all parish life coordinators served in parishes in the Midwest. Thirty percent of all parish life coordinators resided in the South, 16 percent in the West, and only 6 percent in the Northeast during the period of data collection for the 2004 CARA study. It also revealed that the average age of a parish life coordinator was sixty-one, with two-thirds of all parish life coordinators being fifty-five or older. Nearly six in ten parish life coordinators came of age before Vatican II. But, a significant number of parish life coordinators (four in ten) were part of what CARA calls the Vatican II Generation—the baby boomers who were born between 1943 and 1960, a time of great demographic and economic growth. They came of age during the time of the Second Vatican Council, and their formative years are most likely to have spanned the time of profound changes in the Church. This generation "is sometimes considered a "questioner generation," CARA points out, because "in Church life they tend to share common memories of a Catholic childhood but now exhibit a wide variety of forms of religious practice and understanding. . . . They are more likely than the generations before them to emphasize concerns of individual self actualization over institutional commitment." When the 2004 CARA data were collected, about 40 percent of all parish life coordinators were part of this "questioning" generation.[14] With the aging of the cohort, it is likely higher today.

Nearly a decade has passed since the CARA data were collected in 2003, and although some parishes have continued to draw on parish life coordinators, the 2011 Kennedy Directory demonstrates some decreases in the total number of parishes without a resident priest-pastor employing these lay leaders. After decades of steady increases in the number of lay persons heading parishes without resident pastors, the number of pastoral administrators or parish life coordinators has actually declined from a high of 553 in 2005 to 469 in 2011. This has occurred despite the fact that the number of parishes without resident pastors has stayed constant (3,251 parishes without resident pastors in 2005 compared with 3,249 in 2011).

Despite the optimism represented in Bishop Clark's book *Forward in Hope: Saying Amen to Lay Ecclesial Ministry* it is possible that the ambiguity surrounding the role of the lay parish administrator has created problems not just for priests but for the female pastoral administrators themselves. In his own book, Bishop Clark includes short chapters by a few of the women who are leading parishes in his diocese. Their narratives reveal some of that ambiguity. One of the pastoral leaders appears angry that she has not been accepted by parishioners and priests alike as equal in status to that of the priest. In a chapter titled "Voices from the Vineyard," pastoral administrator Anne-Marie Brogan introduces herself by saying that she "collaborates with a talented pastoral staff, including a priest who serves as sacramental minister."[15] Although she has found several rewards to being an ecclesial minister, including being able to "rejoice with a family over the birth and baptism of a new child," Brogan also writes that being a lay ecclesial minister has been hard when

> I have not felt accepted by some priests, deacons or other companions at the table.
> I have been told that I can't possibly be called to pastoral ministry as a woman.
> I have prepared someone for marriage and then the service is presided over by someone who does not have a relationship with the couple.

Most revealing, Brogan writes that being a lay ecclesial minister is hard when "my ability to do my job is questioned; or when people assume that the sacramental minister is the decision maker for the community."[16] It is clear that Brogan wants parishioners and priests alike to know that she is making the decisions for her parish community—and that the priest (sacramental minister) in her parish is under her supervision.

In a second chapter in *Forward in Hope*, written by one of Rochester's female lay pastoral administrators, Deb Housel writes that as a child she was often excluded from the street baseball games by her brothers and the neighborhood boys—even though she "could run faster than some, catch and pitch as well." It left an impression on her and she resolved: "just as that young girl baseball player in me who prepared my bat, ball and mitt nightly to be ready in case I could be a member of the team the next day, I have prepared to answer the call that God offers me. God willing, acceptance will grow in the hierarchy of the Church and among the people in the pews."[17] Even though she has achieved this parish leadership position—heading four parishes—Housel laments that her ministry "became for some people a gender issue . . . it hurt that in all of my desire and call to help keep communities open, vital and raised up, my anatomy became more important than my gifts or my spirit. . . . Once again I felt like that young girl waiting to see if she would be allowed to be on the baseball team."[18]

Housel is not the only lay member of Rochester's ministry teams to bemoan the exclusivity of the male-only priesthood. The *Wanderer's* Paul Likoudis has documented several cases in which female lay ministers from the Rochester diocese have been leaders in the women's ordination movement through their membership in the Women's Ordination Conference. Some have actually left lay ministry to become "ordained" in alternative "Catholic communities." "Catholic women in Rochester have been ordained such as Denise Donato, a graduate of St. Bernard's School of Theology and Ministry, who recently formed the St. Mary Magdalen community in suburban Fairport." The latest woman to announce her departure from the Catholic Church is the music director at the Church of the Assumption. In May 2011, parishioners learned that Mary Van Houten was "leaving to enter more deeply into ministry." In a letter to parishioners, Van Houten wrote: "For the past several years I have sensed a deeper call from God in my life. . . . I have discerned that I am being called by God to the vocation of ordained ministry. . . . I am convinced that without the support, love and stability of Assumption Parish, I would never have had the spiritual space in which to do this kind of discernment."[19]

The support Van Houten may have been referring to was likely from Deni Mack, then, the "pastoral associate" at the Church of the Assumption. Paul Likoudis writes that Mack is "one of the most prominent women in the diocese, who, along with Sr. Joan Sobala and Nancy DeRyck, is affiliated with the Women's Ordination Conference." According to Likoudis, Mack delivered the homily at Church of the Assumption on various occasions and has also been one of the presiders at liturgies for Rochester's chapter of Dignity/Integrity—the support ministry for gay and lesbian Catholics.[20]

Special liturgy services for gays, lesbians, and their friends and families have been held in the Rochester diocese as Bishop Clark has been very supportive of the gay community and has participated in national conferences sponsored by New Ways Ministry, a gay support organization that is not recognized by the Catholic Church. Despite the fact that New Ways Ministry describes itself as a "gay-positive" ministry of advocacy for lesbian and gay Catholics and dismisses

Church teachings on homosexual behavior, Bishop Clark has been supportive of their initiatives.

In contrast, Bishop Clark has not allowed faithful Catholic groups and organizations to issue public statements supporting Catholic teachings on homosexuality. In fact, he has reprimanded any Catholic group that has issued statements that may be construed as critical of homosexual behavior. According to Women for Faith and Family, when the Catholic Physicians Guild and the St. Thomas More Catholic Lawyers Guild issued statements reiterating Church teachings on the immorality of homosexual behavior, Bishop Clark told the two professional groups that henceforth they would not be allowed to hold meetings or disseminate literature in the diocese without his permission. He accused the groups of undermining his authority.[21]

In an interview in 2011 in the *Rochester City (New York) Newspaper*, Bishop Clark dismissed a statement from the Vatican banning individuals with "deep-seated homosexual tendencies" from entering the priesthood, saying that he "has always been open to such candidates." Bishop Clark told the interviewer: "I know some magnificent gay priests. . . . If they are openly gay in terms of living a lifestyle that is incompatible with their basic commitment, we have to intervene. But, I have always tried to be open to such candidates."[22]

When asked by the interviewer about how the Rochester diocese might be able to grow again, Bishop Clark responded that the reason that the diocese has lost Catholics is "because population growth is flat in the region and the city itself is really losing population. . . . It is not much better in the suburbs because a lot of our young people are moving away. It's always been ironic to me that we have all these fine colleges and universities, but there aren't sufficient jobs here to keep as many young people as we would like. . . . We're all rooting for our new governor [Cuomo] and other elected officials to help us get out of this difficult time. A better economic situation in Upstate New York would help everyone including those of us in the faith community."[23]

And, when asked about the shortage of priests in Rochester, he acknowledged: "we're older and fewer in numbers than I think is good for us. . . . but there is no parish church that we can't provide sufficient priests for Mass on Sunday."[24] Bishop Clark neglected to mention that many of those parishes he referred to are being led by female lay administrators—with visiting "sacramental ministers."

Can We Go Back—Or Would We Want To?

Recently, Tricia Wittman-Todd, the parish life coordinator at Seattle's St. Mary's Church, wrote a letter titled "Dear People of St. Mary's" in which she advised the parishioners that she had decided to reject Archbishop Peter Sartain's request that Churches become signature-gathering points for Referendum 74, the ballot measure to roll back Washington's recently passed same sex marriage law. In making what was essentially a unilateral decision, Wittman-Todd wrote: "after much prayer and reflection, I have decided we will not collect signatures at the parish. I am certain you will find ample opportunity elsewhere to sign whatever petitions you choose."

Wittman-Todd claimed that her decision was based on two considerations: "St. Mary's mission is *House of God, Home for Everyone.* One of our highest values is inclusion and welcome. I fear that the collection of signatures would be hurtful and divisive to our parish. I am particularly concerned about our youth who may be questioning their own sexual identity and need our support at this time in their lives." Her second consideration was that "as Catholics, each of us is asked to form our conscience and decide how to vote on this and other issues, i.e. tax policies, services to the poor, environmental laws, capital punishment, etc."[25]

Lumen Gentium, the Vatican II *Dogmatic Constitution on the Church,* ushered in the current changes in roles of leadership. Vatican II took a decidedly positive and inclusive approach to the laity, establishing the relative autonomy of the laity from the hierarchy and affirming the role of the laity in the Church as well as in the world.[26] Marti Jewell, a professor of theology at the School of Ministry at the University of Dallas, was the director of the Emerging Models Project of the Church from 2003 to 2009 has said on many occasions that there is no going back, and she is likely right about that. But the model of implementation can be changed. There are some dioceses that have implemented the lay pastoral leader model in ways that protect the integrity and dignity of the priest as well as the pastoral leader.

In fact, it is possible that the divisive Rochester model may be a model that is dying. In their most recent book, *The Next Generation of Pastoral Leaders: What the Church Needs to Know,* Dean Hoge and Marti R. Jewell provide survey data from young adults from across the country who are involved in either college campus ministry programs or diocesan young adult groups—in an effort to understand their thoughts about faith and their attitudes toward the Church.[27] Hoge and Jewell also interviewed program administrators of lay training programs, who unanimously agreed that there is an adequate supply of candidates for available positions but acknowledged that lay ministry does need more young people. The administrators also noted a "more conservative ecclesiology" among the newer generation of Catholic lay leaders than the Vatican II generation.[28] Because of their appreciation for ecclesiology, this new generation may have a greater appreciation for the unique role of the priest.

Likewise, the trend toward a more faithful servant leadership model for lay ministry was noted in a new book by Michael Novak and William E. Simon. In *Living the Call: An Introduction to the Lay Vocation*, Novak and Simon introduce readers to nine faithful lay persons now serving in various ministry capacities within the Church. We meet Cambria Smith, a convert to Catholicism who is now serving as the recently installed parish life director at Holy Family Church in South Pasadena. We learn that she was intellectually attracted to the faith after reading *Mere Christianity* by C. S. Lewis, but it was not until she began attending Mass regularly for more than three years that she began to realize that the Catholic Church "offered a more profound sense of mystery, a deeper sense of the presence of God," than she had experienced in Anglicanism. Smith converted and said that she was surprised to find that even though the Church only has male priests and a male hierarchy, "it is a profoundly feminine religion . . . there is a beautiful sense of the feminine in the rituals and practices of Catholicism that really resonates with me."[29]

Unlike many of the Rochester lay leaders, Smith speaks appreciatively of the ordained clergy. Novak and Simon describe her as working "closely with Monsignor Connolly" and point out that she is grateful for the opportunity to be given a "window into the life of a priest and a great admiration for what they do." She recalled how in the course of one day, "Monsignor Connolly had to perform a funeral for a young child who had died of brain cancer, and then he did a wedding . . . they have to have an enormous amount of spiritual strength and reserve."[30] Smith also said that she found the congregation has been very welcoming. But her parishioners have a choice of meeting with her or the priests: "parishioners who want counseling have the choice of speaking with one of the three priests or with Smith. . . .

Although she does not do any of the official premarital counseling, she has met with people struggling in their marriages. . . . A lot of her counseling sessions are simply praying with people on issues causing them pain and grief."[31]

Novak and Simon demonstrate the ways in which a parish can indeed benefit from the presence of the pastoral life administrator—as long as the priest is not viewed as a visitor who is there only to say Mass and consecrate the Eucharist. Parishioners want to know that a priest—even a visiting priest who cannot devote full time to a parish—is present to the people and interested in the life of the parish. Catholics know that the lay parish coordinator cannot do the things that a priest can do. Priests are ordained for a reason. And parishioners feel cheated when parish administrators and their bishops pretend that a lay person can fulfill the role just as well. Some of them leave the Church.

In 2011, Bishop Hubbard of Albany published a column titled "The Failings of the Church" in the *Evangelist*, his diocesan newspaper. The column listed all of the areas that Bishop Hubbard believes have contributed to the exodus of large numbers of Catholics from the Church. He named seven, which included clergy sexual abuse; parish closures; anemic parish life; pastoral insensitivity; poor preaching and liturgies; deficiency in technology; feeling unaccepted or exploited. Refusing to even acknowledge that there may be some of Albany's Catholics who continue to be unhappy with the lay parish administrator model, the lack of priestly leadership, and the dearth of vocations, Bishop Hubbard did not even mention the massive structural changes he implemented over the previous thirty years as possibly contributing to the "failings" of the Church.[32]

Following the publication of Bishop Hubbard's column on the failings of the Church, the usual progressive commentators praised it as "prophetic." Reverend Richard McBrien used Bishop Hubbard's column to publish his own criticisms of the Church in the *National Catholic Reporter*. Lauding the column as one that "other bishops should read," McBrien cited the Hubbard column to complain that the Church has failed to appreciate the unique gifts of women, the contributions of gay men and lesbian women, as well as divorced and separated Catholics, and noncelibate men for ministry. Concluding that the real reason Catholics leave the Church is because of the hierarchy's "fixation" on issues "related to human sexuality and reproduction,"

McBrien cautioned that the Church has "abandoned the path marked out by the Second Vatican Council."[33]

Indeed, it almost always comes back to the Second Vatican Council for progressive Catholics of the McBrien generation. They came of age in the turbulent 1960s when everything seemed possible. Shelby Steele once wrote that the 1960s were a time when seemingly every long simmering conflict, every long-standing moral contradiction in American history, presented itself to be made right even as an ill-conceived war raged on. And the resulting loss of moral authority was the great vacuum that literally called the counterculture consciousness into being.[34] The 1960s culture redefined gender, sexual behavior, and sexual relationships, giving little thought to the old norms. The situation of every young girl like Deb Housel, Rochester's lay parish administrator, who was excluded from playing baseball with the boys, became a national calamity that could only be fully addressed by the courts—and a law to address the grievance. Structures of institutional authority toppled as college students and seminarians occupied the offices of the college president—or the seminary director—until their demands were met. Columnist William Murtchison writes that in the 1960s, "verticality and top-down-ness in culture gave way slowly but inexorably to horizontality—a side-by-side-ness of ideas, outlooks, postures and assumptions, and beliefs, especially moral and social beliefs. . . . As for religion, wasn't the nice God a decided improvement on the old God of Judgment, high in the heavens, thundering His displeasure with His creations, demanding from them reverence and obedience?"[35]

When a parish becomes accustomed to the nonjudgmental "nice God" it is difficult for a bishop, priest, or deacon to remind the parishioners that sin still exists—and that the temptation to sin is real. Many churches rightly use the pulpit to warn their parishioners about the sin of corporate greed or unbridled capitalism, but sins against moral teachings on abortion and same-sex marriage are not often mentioned in most parishes. Yet, if all Catholics are to play a role in salvation, that is exactly what has to happen.

The Role of the Deacon

Deacons may have the most difficult role to play in this mission because they are ordained and therefore, no longer members of the laity.

While they are unable to celebrate the Mass, they can preach the homily and therefore influence parishioners in the pews. Because of this, the role of the deacon has drawn a special kind of venom from many within the McBrien generation.

Most faithful Catholics agree that the restoration of the diaconate has been a source of tremendous grace and blessings for the Church. Because the men who enter the permanent diaconate are ordained, they are surely the more appropriate leaders of parish life than the female lay parish leader. But even the role of the deacon can become problematic, and recently Most Reverend Alexander K. Sample, now archbishop of Portland and previous bishop of Marquette, wrote a long pastoral letter to address some of the confusion that has surrounded this role.

In his pastoral letter, *The Deacon: Icon of Jesus Christ the Servant*, Bishop Sample begins with gratitude for the ways in which "this local Church has been richly blessed by the witness and sacrifices of the fine men who have received ordination as permanent deacons." But Bishop Sample also cautions that "alongside such blessings, however, there have been some misunderstandings and misinterpretations of the essential identity of the permanent deacon that have led to some confusion regarding his ministerial role in the life and mission of the Church."[36]

In an effort to address these misunderstandings and misinterpretations of the role of the deacon, Bishop Sample formed a study group in 2008 that included many deacons, priests, women religious, and lay persons. The principal task of this committee was to address the essential identity of the permanent deacon in the life of the universal Church; the essential role of the permanent deacon in diocesan and parish ministry within the local church of the Diocese of Marquette; where and how many permanent deacons do we need; the qualifications and qualities needed in those men recruited; the formation process; and particular issues and concerns that have been encountered in light of the experience of the permanent diaconate in the Diocese of Marquette. Bishop Sample wanted to be clear that the reflections and conclusions of the committee should in no way be seen as a criticism of the history of the permanent diaconate in the Diocese of Marquette. Rather, Bishop Sample wanted the report to be seen as a maturing of our understanding of the diaconate in light of that history and experience.

The report first gives the history of the permanent diaconate by describing the way in which the role was created. According to the study committee, the institution of the Order of Deacons by the apostles arose from an early necessity of service in the church that was too demanding for the apostles to manage alone. The solution was to appoint seven men of good repute to assist them in the daily ministry. "Through prayer and the laying on of hands they entrusted to those chosen men the ministry of serving at table." With the spread of the Faith in the early Church, deacons began to have a liturgical function. Emphasized throughout the Gospels, the Greek word that became the designation for the office of deacon, *diakonia*, was grounded in Jesus Christ himself when Jesus offered himself in total service to the Father: "I am among you as one who serves [*diakonia*]."

Far from Lakeland's definition of a "monster creation" of the bishops, the role of the deacon is nearly as old as the Church. But the diaconate declined in 400 A.D. when abuses of power and conflict over the status of priests, often over monetary compensation, led to the demise of the diaconate as a permanent order. The role returned in Europe in the 1950s when the need began to emerge for ministry assistance. And, in the 1960s, the Second Vatican Council proposed that the ministry of the deacon came from the apostles and as such should be restored as a permanent order of the Church. *Lumen Gentium* states clearly: "it will be possible in the future to restore the diaconate as a proper and permanent rank of the hierarchy." Assigned to the deacon were his traditional ministries of administering baptism, ordinary minister of Holy Communion, witnessing of marriages, bringing viaticum to the dying, proclaiming the sacred scriptures, instructing the people, officiating at funeral rites, and being dedicated to charitable works.

Bishop Sample's committee makes it clear that "of his threefold ministries of the Word, the liturgy and charity, the deacon's distinctive call is to charity."[37] This means that the deacon must always have some particular focus of his diaconal ministry on specific needs in the community. They are not ordained for any particular parish, even their own. They are ordained for service to the Church, a service exercised in the Diocese of Marquette under the authority of the bishop.

Bishop Sample reminded the deacons of his diocese that as permanent deacons they enjoy all the rights afforded them in the Code of Canon Law and are also subject of all of the obligations required of him under the same law. But issues of competition with the ordained priest were also addressed by Bishop Sample's committee. The report cautioned: "the deacon must remember that the pastor is the one whom he helps and serves under the authority of the bishop. Mutual respect and charity must govern this relationship. . . . To be avoided at all costs is any sense of rivalry or competition between priests and deacons. All must remember that they are there to serve Christ and the Church. A sense of selfless service to Christ and the People of God should animate the ministry of bishops, priests and deacons. The permanent deacon must remember that the pastor possesses the ultimate authority in the parish or mission, always under the authority of the diocesan bishop."

One area that became controversial when Bishop Sample's committee report was released was the practice of having the deacon give the homily at Mass. The committee advised: "the liturgical norms presume that the one who presides at a liturgical service, or who is the principal celebrant at Mass is also to give the homily. This should be the ordinary practice. . . . He may entrust it to a concelebrating priest or occasionally according to circumstances, to the deacon."

This statement rules out the notion of the deacon preaching the homily at Mass on a routine or scheduled basis. It has become the practice in many parishes for priests to relegate the role of preaching to the deacon on a regularly scheduled basis. Bishop Sample wants to end that practice—and there are many faithful Catholics who have applauded that decision. Faithful Catholics attend Church to learn from their priests. Bishop Sample's report makes it clear that the primary ministry of the deacon is "not in the sanctuary but in the service of charity—in care for the poor, the sick, the elderly, or the imprisoned."

An Unresolved Tension

The tension between differing understandings of what a lay person is and what a priest is remains. Ordination in the Church begins with the recognition of the ability to lead the people in Word and Spirit given through charism. The person ordained is given a formal authority within the community. In "The Basis for Official Ministry in the Church," David Power writes that the conferral of the charism of leadership is transferred through "orders": the spirit, through the bishop to the one ordained gives the charism. This charism equips the ordained to fulfill the leadership function.[38] The lay person does not receive this charism from the bishop.

Yet we must acknowledge that Vatican II endorsed the term "priesthood of all believers" to denote the baptismal priesthood of all Catholics. Progressive theologians have interpreted that to mean that all believers are "priests" and therefore see no need for the ordained priesthood. The bishops have attempted to clarify the boundaries in documents like *One Who Serves: Reflections of the Pastoral Ministry on Priests in the United States* and a second report on priestly life and ministry titled *A Shepherd's Care: Reflections on the Changing Role of Pastor.*[39]

In 2005, the USCCB released *Co-workers in the Vineyard of the Lord*, which attempted to clarify roles. But the document met a mixed response from most bishops because it minimized the tensions that remained—and the effects that such a ministry has on priestly ordinations. Those like Bishops Clark and Hubbard welcomed the document because they believe it validated their work. In his book *Forward in Hope*, Rochester's Bishop Matthew Clark writes that *"Co-Workers in the Vineyard* says 'amen' to the development thus far and is an expression of confidence that what is well begun will continue to grow, realistic in acknowledging that we are not all in the same place around the country. . . . My experience has vividly revealed to me the beauty of this development and how deeply it is enriching our daily lives as Catholics."[40]

Pope John Paul II worried about fidelity to the priestly tradition. An article in the *National Catholic Reporter* stated that Pope John Paul II refused to talk about "lay ministries" and preferred to use the language of "lay apostolate."[41] And, in a speech to the Congregation for the Clergy, the pope himself noted that this language about the "ministry" might be "booby trapped."[42] In this speech, Pope John Paul II reaffirmed his belief that the need for lay ministers will recede as soon as the Church is successful in recruiting more priestly vocations. . . . He reminded all that "only the priest can act as shepherd to the flock, and thus, even when lay people are serving in ways similar to priests they are never properly speaking, pastoral."[43] He further clarified: "only in virtue of sacred ordination does the word ministry obtain the full meaning that tradition confers." And he called for "attention to the urgent pastoral need to clarify and purify terminology, because behind it there can lurk dangers far more treacherous than one may think."[44]

Pope John Paul II accurately predicted our current dilemma decades ago. He called for a renewed commitment to the ordained priesthood —and the hierarchical ordering of charism to serve the Church. And he warned that empowering the laity in this way is not the right order of the Church but a temporary arrangement to meet a crisis.[45]

7 | The Campus Culture Wars

If we are to have a strong and well-trained laity to participate in the New Evangelization, then there is no better
place for this formation to take place than on the campuses
of Catholic colleges and universities. Unfortunately, over
the past fifty years these institutions have proven hostile
to the Church rather than contributors to the necessary
renewal of the faith as encouraged by popes John Paul II,
Benedict XVI, and now Pope Francis. Looking back over
the history of Catholic higher education, it is difficult to be
able to say exactly when the culture wars began on Catholic campuses. Some historians point to the 1960s as the
beginning of the end of a commitment to a strong Catholic identity for most Catholic colleges and universities—
mostly because of the residual effects of major cultural
changes that affected all institutions. Other historians believe that the campus culture wars began even earlier as
the pursuit of progressivism and modernism of the 1950s
led status-seeking Catholic college professors and administrators to begin to distance themselves from any per-
ceptions of control by the Church. And, although there is
little agreement on exactly when the battles began, almost
everyone agrees that the Catholic campus culture wars
reached their peak in 2009, when the University of Notre
Dame announced its decision to invite President Barack
Obama—the most committed supporter of abortion
rights we have ever experienced in the White House—to
give the commencement address and receive an honorary

degree. Creating divisions on campus and off, more than 350,000 faithful Catholics signed an online petition to protest the decision—and eighty-three bishops joined Notre Dame's presiding bishop, the late John D'Arcy, to publicly protest Notre Dame's actions in honoring the president in this way.

This was not the first time Catholic college leaders publicly battled their own bishops. The 1960s ushered in a new religious pluralism, the sexual revolution, the civil rights movement, the protests over the war in Vietnam, and most important, the questioning of the authority of social institutions like the Church. It was a time when Catholics, formerly part of an inner-city "immigrant Church," began to move out of Catholic ghettos and achieve upward mobility and higher status in the suburbs. And, as Catholic historian David O'Brien points out, it was when a popular pope, John XXIII, assembled Church leaders in 1962 for the Second Vatican Council. As this council, with its call to renewal and reform, intersected with the social transformation of what had been the American immigrant Church, the pace of change was astonishing—and unsettling—as Catholics began to question their own relationships with the Church, and the Church's relationship with its colleges.[1]

All of these events surely had an impact on Catholic colleges. Still, it is far too easy to blame the liberalizing trends within society and the Church that began in the 1960s for all of the problems within Catholic higher education today. The truth is that concerns about secularization and status surrounded the earliest Catholic colleges. Patterned on the sixteenth-century Jesuit plan of study, *Ratio Studiorum,* the curriculum at Georgetown, founded in 1789, the first Catholic College in the country, consisted of three successive stages: humanistic, philosophical, and theological. Students were required to develop the ability to speak Latin fluently and "with persuasive power" as it was a practical necessity for advancement in lay, as well as clerical, careers.[2] But even in these early days, the focus on philosophy and the classical languages, including Greek and Latin, was viewed dismissively by secular academic leaders. In his book on the history of Catholic colleges, Philip Gleason recalls that in 1896, the president of Harvard, Charles W. Eliot, publicly humiliated Catholic colleges by publishing an article in *Atlantic Monthly* that compared the Catholic college curriculum to the most backward educational system of the Moslem countries: "where the Koran prescribes the perfect education, to be administered to all children alike." Having instituted a system of electives at Harvard more than a decade before, Eliot was especially critical of the uniform education found in the curriculum of the Jesuit colleges, which had remained almost unchanged for four hundred years, disregarding some concessions made to natural science. And, in a mocking attack on Catholicism, Eliot concludes: "that these examples are ecclesiastic is not without significance. . . . Direct revelation from on high would be the only satisfactory basis for a uniform, prescribed school curriculum."[3]

While the Harvard president's article contained the most publicly devastating attack of Catholic colleges at the time, the sentiments it contained were part of a common response from secular academic leaders. What was somewhat more surprising was the attack on Catholic colleges from Catholic college leaders themselves. Even today, assessing the progress of Catholic colleges, Reverend Theodore Hesburgh, president emeritus of the University of Notre Dame, acknowledges that while some Catholic colleges come close, "there has not been in recent centuries a truly great Catholic university, recognized universally as such." While Father Hesburgh, who stepped down in 1987 after thirty-five years as head of Notre Dame, acknowledges that although some Catholic colleges have made progress, "one would have hoped that history would have been different when one considers the Church's early role in the founding of the first great universities in the Middle Ages: Paris, Oxford, Cambridge, Bologna, and others."[4]

Unlike Harvard's Charles Eliot, who was critical of the Catholic college plan of study, Father Hesburgh is most critical of the Catholic college's historic relationship to the Church itself. In Father Hesburgh's opinion, the early European universities in the Middle Ages were great because they encouraged a culture of freedom and independence from the state as well as from the authority of the Catholic Church. Claiming that unlike American Catholic universities, these early colleges provided "an atmosphere of free and often turbulent clashing of conflicting ideas, where a scholar with a new idea theological, philosophical, legal, or scientific, had to defend it in the company of peers, without interference from the pressures and powers that neither create nor validate intellectual activities."[5] In Hesburgh's book *Challenge and Promise of the Catholic University,* the theme of independence from the "external authority" of the Church is clear. For Hesburgh, "the best and only traditional authority in the university is intellectual competence. . . . It was great wisdom in the medieval church to have university theologians judged solely by their theological peers in the university. . . . A great Catholic university must begin by being a great university that is also Catholic."[6]

Few questioned this statement of distancing from the Church because until recently, Father Hesburgh's musings were simply accepted as "fact" because of his own high status in the academy and beyond. The recipient of more than 150 honorary degrees, the most ever awarded to one person, Father Hesburgh became the first person in higher education to be awarded the U.S. Congressional Gold Medal in 2000. Father Hesburgh has held sixteen presidential appointments over the years involving him in civil rights, peaceful uses of atomic energy, campus unrest, and immigration reform—including the U.S. policy of amnesty for immigrants in the mid-1980s. Father Hesburgh was the first priest ever elected to the Board of Directors of Harvard University and served two years as president of it. He also served as a director of the Chase Manhattan Bank. A longtime champion of nuclear disarmament, Father Hesburgh has served on the board of the United States Institute of Peace and helped organize a meeting of scientists and representative leaders of six faith traditions who called for the elimination of nuclear weapons.

On many occasions, Father Hesburgh found himself the first Catholic priest to serve in a given leadership position on boards of secular organizations. Much of his success can be viewed as stemming from his ability to distance himself from the authority of the Church and sometimes from its teachings. Such was the case during the years he served as a trustee, and later, chairman of the board of the Rockefeller Foundation, a frequent funder of causes counter to Church teachings.[7] His appointment as ambassador to the 1979 UN Conference on Science and Technology for Development was the first time a priest had served in a formal diplomatic role for the U.S. government.[8]

One of the ways in which Catholic college faculty and administrators have achieved higher status has been to take the route chosen by Father Hesburgh—by publicly embracing the social gospel on civil rights and social justice and by distancing themselves from those teachings less acceptable to the liberal establishment on sexual morality and reproductive rights.

In many ways, the foundation for the distancing from the authority of the Church emerged in the 1950s as a backlash against what was regarded as undue Catholic influence in politics, public morality, and general social policy.[9] In 1955, an obscure Catholic college professor published an essay in a long-forgotten journal accusing faculty on Catholic campuses of "perpetuating mediocrity" by giving too great a priority to the moral development of students instead of scholarship and intellectual excellence.[10] Within six months, as historian Philip Gleason points out, more than 3,500 reprints had been distributed: it had been commented on in the Catholic press, noted by *Newsweek*, read aloud in the refectories of many religious communities, and discussed at meetings of Catholic educators, including two sessions at the National Catholic Education Association's 1956 convention.[11] The author, Monsignor John Tracy Ellis, became a Catholic celebrity—and Catholic higher education has yet to recover.

Looking back on these early days of what can only be viewed as the "revolution" in Catholic higher education, it is difficult to understand how such a bitter little essay could have generated such emotional debate among faculty and administrators on Catholic campuses. By 1955, with the publication of Monsignor Ellis's essay on the inferiority of Catholic colleges, there was a renewed focus on the failure of Catholics to contribute to American intellectual life. And, in 1958, the decision was finally made to remove the course of studies in Latin at Boston College, and permission was given by Jesuit Provincials to eliminate the classical language requirement in any of the twenty-seven Jesuit colleges and universities that thought it best.[12] This ended the last vestige of the classical tradition that defined Catholic colleges.

By the end of the decade of the 1950s, Scholasticism—the study of Thomas Aquinas and natural law—had been so thoroughly discredited on Catholic campuses that any academic who dared "speak its name" risked ridicule. In fact, the chairman of DePaul University's philosophy department made *Time* by deriding "the closed system Thomists who still shadowbox the ghosts of the 13th century."[13] It is possible that Scholasticism itself became a casualty of the pursuit of upward mobility as even Gleason suggests that "a too exclusive emphasis on Thomism could still count heavily against a Catholic institution seeking approval for a chapter of Phi Beta Kappa."[14] Notoriously biased against Catholic applications, Phi Beta Kappa gave the "disproportionate place of philosophy," which effectively reduced the number of electives students might take, as the grounds for turning down Boston College for membership as late as 1962.[15] It is also possible that Scholasticism became an inconvenient reminder of moral absolutes in an emerging 1960s culture of tolerance for diversity in lifestyle and a growing cultural relativism. As the new decade dawned, Scholasticism became more inconvenient than ever because it provided an embarrassing reminder of what increasingly came to be viewed as provincial Catholic teachings on sexual morality. The emerging liberation movement for women's rights—including reproductive rights, along with the demands from an increasingly politically powerful gay rights movement—could not easily coexist with a philosophy that stressed moral absolutes.

Upward mobility and status concerns began to affect individual Catholics. By the early 1960s, the Catholic Church was no longer predominantly an immigrant Church—and Catholicism began to contain diverse social classes. While Catholics still remained underrepresented in top business and professional jobs, they occupied many of the same occupations as Protestants.[16] For these newly middle-class Catholics, the religion itself had promoted much of the self-denial and disciplined attitudes required for success in a highly organized society as the Church in general and Catholic education in particular had been vehicles of Americanization and upward mobility. Sociologists Christopher Jencks and David Riesman pointed out that "a Catholic elite began to emerge that was American first and Catholic second."[17] Anticommunism in the 1950s had given Catholics an evil to defeat— and an opportunity to show they were real Americans. While Hungarian, Polish, and German Catholics may have been anticommunist because of what they had experienced in their homelands, Jencks and Riesman wrote in 1968 in *The Academic Revolution*, "the Irish Catholics seemed more often to be anti-communist because it was a useful club with which to beat the Anglo-American Establishment, made up of men like Acheson, Marshall, and Hiss."[18] The late senator Daniel Patrick Moynihan, a Catholic Democrat from New York, suggested: "anti-communism gave the Fordham men in the FBI a chance to get even with the Harvard men in the State Department and the White House."[19]

Once they had established their American credentials, the next generation was ready to move on. Gleason points to a "perfect storm" in the 1960s of academic, social, and Church currents that rocked Catholic colleges. "The priority of individual conscience over the law diffused itself. . . . Catholics may have been particularly susceptible to the message because of the modernizing trends of the Second Vatican Council. It legitimated change, it reinforced assimilative tendencies, with its emphasis on religious freedom, collegiality, ecumenism, pastoral approaches and openness to the modern world."[20] These changes intersected with faculty demands for academic freedom, fewer clergy and women religious on campus, coeducation, more faculty and student participation in university governance, the growing liberation movements on campus and off, and the complete abandonment of the Scholastic approach. While Catholic colleges had been accused of being "too Catholic" in the 1950s, the charge in the 1960s and beyond was that the institutions were not Catholic enough.

In 1967, that "perfect storm" in Catholic higher education reached maximum strength at the meeting of Catholic academic leaders in Land O' Lakes, Wisconsin, where a crucial statement on the nature of the Catholic University emerged. The opening paragraph of the fifteen-hundred-word statement began: "to perform its teaching and research function effectively the Catholic university must have a true autonomy and academic freedom in the face of authority of whatever kind, lay or clerical, external to the academic community itself."[21] While liberal academics nostalgically look back on the Land O' Lakes gathering with great fondness as a kind of "Catholic Woodstock" for professors and administrators anticipating independence from the authority of the Church, Gleason described the Land O' Lakes statement as a "symbolic manifesto" that marked a new era in Catholic higher education.[22]

Within the next few years most Catholic colleges moved to laicize their boards of trustees. Some colleges went even further. Manhattanville College of the Sacred Heart and Webster College publicly and officially declared themselves "no longer Catholic." Manhattanville promptly dropped part of their name, deleting the now too-Catholic-sounding "College of the Sacred Heart." Webster, under the direction of the Sisters of Loretto, was not only the earliest Catholic college to announce that it was choosing to relinquish its Catholic identity; its president, Sister Jacqueline Grennan, S.L., renounced her religious vows and withdrew from her own religious order to became a lay leader so that she too could function as president of the now secular institution "without the embarrassment of being subject to religious obedience."[23] Pronouncing that "the very nature of higher education is opposed to juridical control by the Church," Grennan was just the first of many other women religious who renounced their vows and assumed leadership positions in the now more secularized Catholic higher education.[24]

Concerns about upward mobility were so high during the 1960s and 1970s that any hint of obedience to the authority of the Church became an embarrassment. And although many of the Jesuit colleges and, of course, Notre Dame, maintained that members of their founding religious orders would continue to hold the office of the president of what became increasingly secular institutions, many of those colleges that had been founded by women from religious congregations were more than eager to turn the leadership over to lay leaders as women's colleges increasingly merged with men's and coeducation became the norm. Having abandoned their earlier preoccupation with integrating the curriculum around a core of philosophy and theology, Catholic colleges entered the final decades of the twentieth century devoting themselves to the pursuit of upward mobility.[25] Unfortunately, as Gleason points out, this pursuit became increasingly defined as the way things were done at Harvard. This was a fateful decision for Catholic higher education. It was a decision that still reverberates on many Catholic campuses—and one that directly led to Notre Dame's decision to honor President Obama in this way.

"Open Hearts, Open Minds, Fair-Minded Words?"

Acknowledging the controversy that surrounded his invitation to Notre Dame, President Obama began his commencement address by praising the diversity of thought and culture that characterizes Notre Dame—and singling out Father Hesburgh for creating an institution that is "both a lighthouse and a crossroads. . . . A lighthouse that stands apart, shining with the wisdom of the Catholic tradition, while the crossroads is where differences of culture and religion and conviction can coexist with friendship, civility, hospitality, and especially love." He also praised Father Jenkins for his "courageous and contagious commitment to honest, thoughtful dialogue."[26] And then President Obama turned his attention to praising the graduating seniors for the "maturity and responsibility" with which they had approached the debate surrounding the graduation ceremony. Lauding the Notre Dame tradition of "open hearts, open minds and fair-minded words," the president assured the graduates that he and they would "work together to reduce the number of women seeking abortion" and would "honor the conscience of those who disagree with abortion by drafting a sensible conscience clause."

Unfortunately, President Obama kept neither of those promises. Passing the Affordable Care Act in 2010, replete with public funding for abortion, President Obama directly defied the Catholic bishops in signing the health-care legislation. And, in 2012, President Obama denied the conscience protections of all Catholic institutions, including Catholic colleges and universities, by forcing them to provide employees with free access to contraceptives—including abortifacients—through the Health and Human Services mandate contained within the Affordable Care Act. This decision was considered so offensive that even Notre Dame filed its own lawsuit against the federal government, though the suit's fate remains to be seen. Even before his appearance at Notre Dame in 2009, President Obama had already ended restrictions that prevented taxpayer dollars from funding abortions overseas; opened a path for using taxpayer dollars to encourage the destruction of embryos for research; and began to dismantle the "conscience clause" designed to protect doctors, nurses, and others from being forced to participate in procedures, including abortion, that violate their consciences.

Although President Obama praised the "maturity" of the members of the senior class in attendance at the graduation ceremony, he neglected to mention the nine Holy Cross priests and the hundreds of alumni who protested the decision to invite him. He ignored the fact that many members of Notre Dame's senior class formed an ad hoc committee to lead the student response in condemning the university's invitation to President Obama. The coalition, including Notre Dame Right to Life, Notre Dame College Republicans, the student newspaper *Irish Rover*, and six other campus groups, created a website and released a formal statement denouncing Father Jenkins's choice of speaker. Unable to even meet with Father Jenkins, these students boycotted the Obama-led graduation ceremonies and instead enlisted faithful faculty leaders to help organize an alternative graduation celebration. There, the graduates prayed the rosary in reparation for Notre Dame's decision to invite President Obama, and some of Notre Dame's priests offered a Mass for the graduating seniors. Although the furor that surrounded the honoring of the president in this way demonstrated the divisions in the Church, and offered yet another sign of the Catholic campus culture wars, the incident appears to have moved many of the bishops to begin to deal with the duplicity that has been occurring on Catholic campuses for decades now.

While courageous, the eighty-three bishops who publicly spoke out against the Notre Dame honors to the president were simply implementing an important decision made by their own USCCB. After several decades of scandal over speakers and activities on Catholic campuses, a nearly unanimous vote by the USCCB approved the statement "Catholics in Political Life" in June 2004: *"The Catholic community and Catholic institutions should not honor those who act in defiance of our fundamental and moral principles. They should not be given awards, honors or platforms, which would suggest support for their actions."*[27] It is likely that this document was influenced by ongoing concerns about inappropriate commencement speakers and honorees at Catholic colleges and universities. Since 1998, the Cardinal Newman Society—a higher education advocacy group dedicated to helping Catholic colleges and universities recover their commitment to a strong Catholic identity—has been documenting the scandalous behavior of honoring pro-choice politicians and celebrities on Catholic campuses. In fact, just weeks prior to the USCCB's 2004 meeting, the Society released a report titled "The Culture of Death on Catholic Campuses: A Five Year Review," documenting nearly two hundred incidents of speakers and honorees who have vocally opposed Catholic teachings on abortion, euthanasia, and contraception. The previous year, the Society sent a letter to each of the U.S. bishops urging them to consider diocesan policies banning inappropriate speakers and honorees at Catholic institutions.

Although the USCCB issued the strong statement blocking inappropriate speakers, the Cardinal Newman Society has documented that many bishops have chosen to ignore it. For example, Bishop Edward Kmiec of the Diocese of Buffalo refused to block an honored appearance at Canisius College by pro-choice Hilary Rodham Clinton, then the senator from New York. Claiming to have voiced his displeasure to college officials, Bishop Kmiec said he would reluctantly allow the event to proceed in order to maintain channels of communication with Senator Clinton and others who hold her views.

St. Mary's College of Moraga, California, hosted Jack O'Connell as its graduation speaker in 2009—despite the fact that during his twenty years as a Democratic state legislator he compiled a nearly perfect proabortion, pro–Planned Parenthood voting record. O'Connell was a high-profile opponent of Proposition 8, the initiative constitutional amendment promoted by Bishop Salvatore Cordileone and most California voters in 2008 that defined marriage in California as between one man and one woman. That same year, the University of San Francisco gave an honorary degree to Lloyd Dean, president of Catholic Healthcare West. While Dean is not a politician, he joined Sister Carol Keehan in defying the bishops in helping to pass President Obama's Affordable Care Act—even though the Act removed conscience protections for employers and health-care workers, and contained provisions for the public funding for abortion.

Georgetown University honored Supreme Court justice Sandra Day O'Connor, and she proceeded to attack the pro-life lawmakers who had sided with Terri Schiavo's parents in their efforts to prevent their daughter's euthanasia death. O'Connor, who has sided with the abortion rights justices in the partial-birth abortion case before the Supreme Court, claimed a congressional effort to have federal courts review the Schiavo case was "a first step toward a dictatorship."

President Obama was also an honored guest speaker earlier that same year at Georgetown University, where his appearance created yet another scandal when Georgetown agreed to cover up all of the sacred symbols of Christianity in Gaston Hall before the president would agree to speak there. Covering crucifixes, statues, and the symbol IHS, the millennia-old monogram for the name of Jesus Christ, Georgetown willingly removed any trace of Christianity from the hall where President Obama was to speak. A White House statement claimed that the motivation to remove the appearance of Christian symbols was not based in bias against such symbols but was simply so that the president would have a "consistent background of American flags, which is standard for many presidential events."

Continuing to ignore the USCCB's directive on honoring supporters of abortion, Georgetown University also presented a legal award to the pro-choice Catholic vice president Joseph Biden in 2009. When Vice President Biden was a candidate for the Democratic primary race for president in 2008, he promised that he would have a pro-abortion litmus test for his own possible judicial choices—and would only appoint judges who would respect a woman's right to choose abortion. In one of the primary debates Biden said: "I would not appoint anyone who did not understand that Section 5 of the 14th Amendment and the

Liberty Clause of the 14th Amendment provided a right to privacy. . . which means they would support *Roe v. Wade*."[28]

Until the Notre Dame scandal over honoring President Obama, it appeared that the bishops would continue trying to persuade administrators on Catholic campuses to embrace a Catholic identity by respecting Church teachings on moral issues, and these same leaders would continue ignoring them. During the first year following the release of the 2004 Catholics in Public Life directive, twenty Catholic colleges chose commencement speakers for their 2005 graduation ceremonies who were public advocates of abortion rights, stem cell research, physician-assisted suicide, or same-sex marriage. Yet only three bishops publicly protested their decision.

In 2006, the second year following the release of the USCCB's statement "Catholics in Political Life," the Cardinal Newman Society documented an additional twenty-four Catholic colleges and universities that hosted advocates of abortion rights, stem cell research, and gay marriage. And, although few bishops publicly protested these honors, Notre Dame's presiding bishop, the late John M. D'Arcy of Indiana's Fort Wayne–South Bend diocese, made some courageous public statements on Notre Dame's recalcitrance. In 2007, Bishop D'Arcy issued a statement denouncing the annual Notre Dame Queer Film Festival as "an abuse of academic freedom." In response, Matthew Storin, a Notre Dame spokesman, responded that although the university has "great affection and respect for Bishop D'Arcy," the faculty and administrators "disagree with his interpretation of academic freedom." Storin issued a press release asserting that "we would prefer that our students encounter the secular American culture, with all its faults, in the context of their Catholic education rather than attempting to cloister them till the time they graduate, only then to confront reality."[29]

This dismissive response to Bishop D'Arcy reduced the role of the bishop to that of a single voice among many voices responding to a controversial Notre Dame decision. Ignoring the authority of the office of the bishop, the theological underpinnings of his critique, and his fiduciary responsibility under *Ex Corde Ecclesiae* as bishop of the diocese in which Notre Dame resides, the university rejected the bishop's concerns—while still claiming to have "great affection and respect" for the bishop. Most important, the Notre Dame spokesman failed to recognize that it is unlikely that most students are offered the opportunity to debate about Catholic teachings on homosexuality in the context of their Notre Dame education. Notre Dame's Queer Film Festival has included a presentation of films by gay and lesbian filmmakers, with panel discussions, including those supporting gay marriage. None of these panels addressed Catholic teachings and the natural law underpinnings for these teachings. Rather than inviting speakers who might support Catholic teachings, Notre Dame invited speakers and presenters who have historically criticized Catholic teachings on homosexuality. Sister Jeannine Grammick, a nun who was suspended from her gay ministry by the Vatican because of her dissident views on the nature of homosexual acts, was an honored guest at Notre Dame's Queer Film Festival in 2005. Defying a Vatican directive to discontinue speaking out on the goodness of homosexual acts, Sister Grammick remains a member in good standing of the School Sisters of Notre Dame and was quoted in an online interview saying that she believes that "the greatest sin for lesbians and gay people is to want to be straight."[30]

Beyond honored guests like Grammick, Notre Dame has provided a home for several tenured faculty members who have creatively deconstructed Catholic moral teachings to conform to what the late Notre Dame professor Ralph McInerney calls the "secular zeitgeist." Theologians like the (former) chairman of Notre Dame's Theology and Religious Studies Department, Richard McBrien, have received a great deal of attention in the secular media and the liberal Catholic press by attempting to redefine Catholic teachings on abortion, birth control, homosexuality, and same-sex marriage, and embryonic stem cell research, to make them more acceptable to a secular audience.

McBrien has been especially recalcitrant in his response to *Ex Corde*. In a published statement in the *Chronicle of Higher Education*, McBrien's contempt for the bishops was clear: "The idea of even suggesting any kind of oversight by non-academic operations of a university—Catholic or not—is odious to anybody in an academic institution. I'm not saying we're above criticism, but I want the criticism to come from people with the credentials to criticize. Bishops should be welcome on a Catholic-university campus. Give them tickets to ball games. Let them say Mass, bring them to graduation. Let them sit on the stage. But there should be nothing beyond that. They should have nothing to say about the internal academic affairs of the university or any faculty member thereof."[31] McBrien has had a long history of defying Church teachings. In 1985, the USCCB, in consultation with the Vatican, declared that the views presented by McBrien in his published encyclopedic work *Catholicism* are contrary to "authoritative" Church doctrine. In an unusual statement, the USCCB's Committee on Doctrine issued a warning about the contents of McBrien's *Catholicism,* claiming that the insights contained in the book are "difficult to reconcile with authoritative Church doctrine." In particular, the committee cited sections of the book questioning the "virginal conception" of Jesus, the "perpetual virginity" of Mary, and the binding nature of Catholic dogma. The bishops also objected that the book is "not supportive" of Church teaching on such controversial issues as the ordination of women, homosexuality, and artificial contraception.[32] Still, none of this kept Notre Dame from granting Professor McBrien tenure and promoting him to chairman of the Theology and Religious Studies Department.

It is in this context that the strong response from the bishops on the Notre Dame invitation to President Obama arrived—and thus was so surprising to those who had become so accustomed to supporters of abortion rights being honored at Catholic colleges and universities— including Notre Dame. No one seemed more surprised by the strong response from the bishops than Reverend John Jenkins, the president of Notre Dame, who claimed that he did not even realize that it might not be appropriate to honor the president of the United States. Stating that he was confused about whether the "Catholics in Political Life Statement" would even apply to President Obama, since the president is not Catholic and thus not bound to following the teachings of the Church, Father Jenkins remained resolute in his decision to honor the president. Other Catholic college administrators lent their support in maintaining that it was the bishops' document itself that was the problem. The Reverend James L. Heft, formerly the provost at the University of Dayton and currently president of the Institute for Advanced Catholic Studies at the secular University of Southern California, told an interviewer for the *Baltimore Sun* that "it is not entirely clear who should be barred from honors."[33] In a column in the *New York Times,* Peter Steinfels went even further, dismissing the document as a "hastily composed statement." Steinfels complained that the USCCB's statement is now being treated as highly authoritative and is "being waved at Notre Dame to criticize the Obama invitation. . . . It includes the injunction that Catholic institutions should not honor those who act in defiance of our fundamental moral principles. . . . Exactly what the bishops meant by 'in defiance' is unclear, especially as it might apply to non-Catholics whose adherence to Catholic teaching can hardly be presumed."[34]

In his defense, Father Jenkins said that "presidents from both parties have come to Notre Dame for decades to speak to our graduates. . . . We are delighted that President Obama will follow in this long tradition of speaking from Notre Dame on issues of substance and significance."[35] Escalating his defensiveness in response to the growing protests a few weeks later, Father Jenkins told a Town Hall meeting at Notre Dame that "we are very proud and honored to welcome the first African-American President of the United States in a few weeks as our commencement speaker. . . . This is a tremendous event for us. . . . President Obama clearly could have chosen any university in the country to give a commencement address, and they would have been just delighted to have him, but he is coming to Notre Dame and we are exceptionally proud."[36] And, expanding his support for the President, Father Jenkins wrote a letter to the graduating class just days before commencement saying that "there is much to admire and celebrate in the life and work of President Obama . . . his views and policies on immigration, expanding health care, alleviating poverty, and building peace through diplomacy have a deep resonance with Catholic social teachings." Finally, in an attempt to minimize the controversy, Father Jenkins said "I think it is unfortunate that the great event of President Obama coming to this campus has been a little clouded by that controversy, but we believe what we believe and we're clear on that, but at the same time, we recognize this remarkable leader and this remarkable person who has accomplished so much. . . . He is one of the great orators of our time and we're just so proud to have him."[37]

Supporting President Jenkins were twenty-four self-described "Catholic leaders" who allied with the group Catholics in Alliance for the Common Good to purchase a full-page ad in the *South Bend Tribune* titled "Catholic Leaders and Theologians Welcome President Obama to Notre Dame." Catholics in Alliance is a progressive advocacy group that has received more than $1 million from MoveOn.org founder George Soros to support progressive causes and candidates. The ad lauded Notre Dame's decision to invite Obama as part of a "long tradition of honoring presidents" and warned against "those who seek to disrupt these joyous proceedings or to divide the Church for narrow political advantage."[38] Presumably, this was intended as a warning to the bishops.

Far from ending the Catholic campus culture wars, the Notre Dame controversy helped to harden the battle lines among all Catholics as research released by the Pew Forum on Religion and Public Life revealed that almost half of Catholics agreed that inviting Obama was the right choice. Twenty-eight percent said it was the wrong decision, and 22 percent had no opinion. However, of those who attend Mass at least weekly, 45 percent said it was wrong for Notre Dame to invite Obama, while 37 percent believed it was the correct choice. Of those who do not attend Mass regularly, only 23 percent said it was wrong, and 56 percent agreed with Notre Dame president Father John Jenkins. The numbers should not be surprising, for 54 percent of all Catholics voted for President Obama in the 2008 election and 50 percent in the 2012 election.[39] Even regular-church-attending Catholics only opposed presidential candidate Obama on a narrow 50-to-49 percent margin. The Pew poll also surveyed Catholics on abortion and found that 47 percent of Catholics say abortion should be legal in all or most circumstances while 42 percent say abortion should be illegal in all or most cases.[40]

It is clear that many Catholics—including many of the faculty and administrators at Notre Dame—view abortion as just one of many social issues. This has continued despite the best efforts of Pope Emeritus Benedict XVI to instruct the faithful that not all moral issues are the same. In a letter to the U.S. bishops during the 2004 presidential campaign, then-cardinal Ratzinger wrote: "Not all moral issues have the same weight as abortion and euthanasia. For example, if a Catholic were to be at odds with the Holy Father on the application of capital punishment or on the decision to wage war he would not for that reason be considered unworthy to present himself to receive Holy Communion. . . . There may be a legitimate diversity of opinion even among Catholics about waging war and applying the death penalty, but not however with regard to abortion and euthanasia."[41] In his letter to the bishops, Cardinal Ratzinger was clear on whether a Catholic can support a political candidate who promises to continue to support access to abortion when he said that "a Catholic would be guilty of formal cooperation in evil, and so unworthy to present himself for Holy Communion if he were to deliberately vote for a candidate precisely because of the candidate's permissive stand on abortion and or euthanasia."[42]

In 2012, Pope Benedict reiterated his concerns about the poor catechesis that many Catholics have experienced—especially on issues of abortion and sexual morality. In a recent *ad limina* visit by the bishops to report on the status of their dioceses, the pope said ignorance of, or challenges to church teaching on marriage and sexuality were part of the intellectual and ethical challenges to evangelization in the United States today. Pope Benedict told the bishops that the Church itself "must acknowledge deficiencies in the catechesis of recent decades, which failed to communicate the rich heritage of Catholic teaching."[43]

Pope Benedict's sentiments on the failure of catechesis were echoed by many of the eighty-three bishops who publicly criticized the Notre Dame decision to honor President Obama. Now deceased Notre Dame professor Ralph McInerney wrote that "the teaching of the faith since the close of Vatican II has been scandalously inadequate.... With time, the difference between the moral teaching of dissenters and what was dismissively called official teaching blurred.... No wonder that Catholic politicians undertook to support policies in flat contradiction to what they purportedly believed privately." McInerney concluded that at Notre Dame on that graduation Sunday, "surrounded by priests and all the panoply of Notre Dame, the smiling Caesar, thumb turned down on life, was engulfed in allegedly Catholic applause."[44] At Notre Dame, faithful Catholics were regarded as dissenters.

But, this time, these faithful Catholics had allies in those eighty-three bishops who found a very public way to defend the faith that was being so distorted at Notre Dame. In a published statement to the faithful, Bishop John D'Arcy decried the invitation to President Obama and asked Father Jenkins to correct the statements he had made to the media to try to justify his invitation because these statements were "simply wrong and give a flawed justification for his actions."[45] Likewise, Phoenix bishop Thomas Olmsted sent an email to Notre Dame's president in late March when he became the second of dozens more bishops to criticize President Obama's appearance. In a note to the pro-life community accompanying his email, Bishop Olmsted called Father Jenkins's invitation a "public act causing widespread public scandal due to the President's clear support for policies which fail to protect and even attack innocent human life."[46] The parish bulletin on Easter Sunday in 2009 at Phoenix's St. Thomas the Apostle Church carried the headline "Anti-life Politician Honored by Top U.S. Catholic University." Introducing a copy of Bishop Olmsted's email to Father Jenkins, the bulletin noted President Obama's ardent support for abortion, including even late-term, partial birth abortion, and forcing Catholic medical personnel to perform abortions. Bishop Olmsted's email to Father Jenkins concluded: "I am saddened and heavy of heart about your decision. . . . I pray that you come to see the grave mistake of your decision."[47]

By the end of March 2009, Archbishop Edwin O'Brien had joined the protest, writing that he was "disappointed and bewildered" by the decision to invite President Obama and "fully supports Bishop John D'Arcy's plans to boycott the ceremony." By April 3, 2009, the Birmingham, Alabama, diocesan newspaper had published a letter from Birmingham's bishop, Robert Baker, to "express my deep disappointment over the Obama invitation." Bishop Baker called it a "travesty" and concluded that the situation constituted a "public act of disobedience to the bishops of the United States."[48]

A week later, an additional thirty bishops joined the protest—all issuing public statements decrying the invitation to the President. Archbishop Daniel Buechlein of Indianapolis posted his letter to Father Jenkins on the archdiocesan website on April 8, 2009: "I join my voice to the chorus of thousands of faithful Catholics around the United States and those of the Archdiocese of Indianapolis in particular who are appalled and embarrassed by your invitation to President Obama to address the 2009 graduates of Notre Dame. . . . You dishonor the reputation of the University of Notre Dame and abdicate your prestigious reputation among Catholic universities everywhere." Bishop Alexander Sample of Marquette, Michigan, the nation's youngest bishop, called the decision "unconscionable" in a statement published April 8. Writing that "it saddens me beyond words that the great university named after Our Lady would bestow distinction and honor on a politician who would seek to expand threats to such innocent human life, Bishop Sample said that he had written to Father Jenkins urging him to withdraw the invitation because it "weakens our united Catholic efforts in defense of life."[49]

By the end of April, there were sixty-five bishops (one-fifth of the total number of U.S. bishops) involved in the very public protest. Bishop Edward Cullen of Allentown, Pennsylvania, called the decision "disappointing" and "not in harmony" with the USCCB's directive on honoring proabortion politicians. Bishop Robert Hermann of St. Louis, Missouri, wrote that Father Jenkins had no excuse for not standing up for a strong Catholic identity at Notre Dame, and he encouraged Notre Dame alumni to organize in such a way that funding and students would be withheld until there is a change in the direction on the Board of Directors. And Bishop Raymundo Pena of Brownsville, Texas, published an April 24 letter addressed to Father Jenkins condemning the scandal, and cautioning: "the prestige that the president will lend to your commencement is not sufficient reason to disregard these principles."[50]

On May 3, 2009, Bishop Thomas Wenski of Orlando, Florida, led a Mass of Reparation for Notre Dame's invitation to President Obama and "the sins and transgressions committed against the dignity and sacredness of human life." Criticizing Catholic "complacency," he urged the faithful to be "for the world" by living the Gospel. Warning about becoming "too complacent about the legal killing of unborn children," Bishop Wenski said that "this complacency contributed to the climate that led Notre Dame's president to think that it would be no big deal to defy the bishops in granting this honorary degree to President Obama.... We have become complacent, because we have become comfortable—too accommodating and too uncritical of the larger culture in which we live. Perhaps, as Catholics, we have become victims of our own success."[51]

Following the Notre Dame commencement Archbishop Charles Chaput, then the leader of the Denver archdiocese, published a strong statement on May 18, 2009, that described Father Jenkins's introductory remarks at the commencement ceremony as "embarrassing." Archbishop Chaput wrote of President Obama that "we have the duty to oppose him when he is wrong on foundational issues like abortion, embryonic stem cell research and similar matters. And we also have the duty to avoid prostituting our Catholic identity by appeals to phony dialogue that mask an abdication of our moral witness.... There was no excuse—none, except intellectual vanity—for the university to persist in its course. Father Jenkins compounded a bad original decision with evasive and disingenuous explanations to subsequently justify it."[52]

Echoing his brother bishops, Chicago's Cardinal Francis George suggested that Notre Dame did not understand what it means to be

Catholic well before these events began. While hardly a revelation to faithful Catholics who have taught on these campuses, Cardinal George's statement was important, though, because it was the first time a bishop said anything like that in public. The fact that eighty-three bishops waged such a strong battle against the honoring of President Obama is significant. After decades of silence on what most faithful Catholics view as the scandalous honors and awards given to proabortion politicians, the bishops seem to have found their collective voice—and have begun again to assert their authority. Professor McInerny saw the Notre Dame graduation scandal as the "unequivocal abandonment of any pretense of being a Catholic university."[53] But he also saw a silver lining in the cloud of scandal cast over the Church at Notre Dame: "it may prove to have been providential, an opportunity for Catholics to recognize that their house is indeed divided."[54]

For many Catholics, there is hope that the Notre Dame controversy has proven to be a turning point for a reclaiming of Catholic identity on these campuses. The courage exhibited by the bishops evidence a new and zealous commitment to this cause and perhaps a new embrace of *Ex Corde Ecclesiae*. Catholic University of America president John Garvey knows firsthand how difficult it is to try to create a Catholic campus that is faithful to the tenets of *Ex Corde Ecclesiae*—but he has risen to the challenge. In 2011, in an attempt to address problems within campus student life—including binge drinking and concerns about sexual activity by students—Garvey and the Board of Trustees made the decision to reimplement single-sex residence halls. Garvey told a reporter for the *National Catholic Reporter* that "at a school like Catholic University of America, we're concerned not only about forming their minds, but their character, and this was the kind of message we wanted to send about appropriate and respectful behavior toward the opposite sex."[55] Research in the *Journal of Studies on Alcohol* and the *Journal of American College Health* has revealed that students in coed housing report weekly binge drinking more than twice as often as students in single-gender housing. Students in coed housing were also more likely than those in single-sex dorms to have had a sexual partner in the last year, and more than twice as likely to have had three or more.

While Garvey's decision received praise from orthodox Catholics like Patrick Reilly, the founder and president of the Cardinal Newman Society, an organization committed to strengthening Catholic iden-

tity at Catholic colleges and universities, there was much criticism—
including a major legal challenge to the same-sex dorm decision. John
Banzhaf, a law professor at George Washington University, sued CUA
over its decision. In a statement published in the *Washington Post*,
Banzhaf said that the District of Columbia's antidiscrimination law
"prohibits any discrimination based directly or indirectly upon sex
unless it is strictly necessary for the entity to remain in business." The
lawsuit garnered so much attention that even Supreme Court justice
Antonin Scalia criticized Banzhaf's suit during a speech at Duquesne
Law School. Citing the Catholic University lawsuit over the same-sex
dorm policy, Justice Scalia said that "our educational establishment
these days, while so tolerant of and even insistent upon diversity in
all other aspects of life seems bent on eliminating diversity of moral
judgment—particularly moral judgment based on religious views."[56]

Justice Scalia was correct about the difficulties facing any Catholic
college administrator who attempts to implement a policy that appears to make a moral judgment. This is exactly what *Ex Corde Ecclesiae* was intended to address. In 1999, faced with the recalcitrance of
Catholic college administrators and their lobbyists at the ACCU, Cardinal George spoke sharply in response when Monica Hellwig, the
now-deceased executive director of the ACCU, refused to implement
the mandatum prescribed in canon 812 of the 1993 Code of Canon Law,
which required that theology professors teach in communion with the
Church. Hellwig told an interviewer at the *National Catholic Register*
that the mandate "would move Catholic institutions in the direction
of fundamentalist Bible schools." She concluded that "the pope doesn't
want colleges and universities to become Catholic ghettos in which
students and faculty shut themselves off from the outside world."[57]
Cardinal George dismissed these concerns, saying "that is not serious
criticism. She really can't be serious. Is she implying all bishops are
fundamentalists?" Cardinal George reiterated his strong support for
the implementation of *Ex Corde,* claiming that this would simply "set
up a mechanism for bishops to certify theologians." Cardinal George
continued: "all colleges want autonomy and independence, and that is
certainly something we should respect. But colleges and universities
must conform to state laws, standards of accrediting agencies and all
sorts of things force them to conform in some manner. The idea that
they exist in complete autonomy simply isn't true."[58]

Cardinal George's statement was verified in 2012, when the federal government's Department of Health and Human Services mandated that all religious institutions—including Catholic colleges and universities—dispense contraceptives, including abortion-producing drugs, and pay for sterilizations or pay a steep fine. The list of required services includes the "morning after" and "week after" pills that cause the death of an unborn child within days of its conception. The Health and Human Services mandate was issued to all religious institutions in August 2011, and the Beckett Fund for Religious Liberty protested the mandate and responded with a lawsuit on behalf of both Belmont Abby College, a Catholic liberal arts college, and Colorado Christian University, an evangelical college located outside Denver. In February 2012, the Becket Fund filed a suit on behalf of Ave Maria University, and in July 2012, Wheaton College, the leading evangelical liberal arts college, filed a lawsuit in partnership with CUA, making it the first ever partnership between Catholic and evangelical institutions to oppose the same regulation in the same court.[59] In the fall of 2012, East Texas Baptist University and Houston Baptist University also filed lawsuits challenging the Obama administration's Health and Human Services mandate.

The Franciscan University of Steubenville also responded to the Health and Human Services mandate by announcing that it will no longer furnish students with health care coverage. Citing the Health and Human Services mandate as the reason, a spokesman for Franciscan said: "the Obama Administration has mandated that all health insurance plans must cover women's health services including contraception, sterilization, and abortion causing medications . . . we will not participate in a plan that requires us to violate the consistent teachings of the Catholic Church on the sacredness of human life."[60]

In July 2012, Catholic University's president, John Garvey, coauthored an op-ed in the *Wall Street Journal* with Wheaton College's president, Philip Ryken, that protested the Health and Human Services mandate, saying that "we must cherish life, not destroy it. This belief is shared by both campus communities. The Catholic Church's unqualified defense of the unborn is too well known to need restatement. Wheaton's commitment is equally firm. . . . A government that fails to heed the cries of its religious institutions undermines the supports of civil virtue and puts in jeopardy our constitutional order."[61]

In light of this affront to religious liberty, it seems that even Father Jenkins may be trying to make right his decision to invite President Obama with his decision to invite New York's Cardinal Timothy Dolan to deliver the 2013 commencement address and receive an honorary doctorate. In accepting the award, Dolan cautioned Notre Dame and the rest of Catholic higher education not to be tempted by the status or rankings of other institutions but instead to remain centered in Christ. "Here at Notre Dame we do not strive to be like Harvard or Oxford, but like Bethlehem, Nazareth, Cana, Calvary, and the Upper Room at Pentecost . . . with Mary, as the 'Word becomes flesh' in the one who called Himself "the Way, the Truth and the Life." [62]

We can hope that the strong negative response that President Obama and Health and Human Services director Kathleen Sebelius met from Catholics and their Episcopal leaders over the Health and Human Services mandate may be viewed as a continuation of the conversation started by the Notre Dame controversy, which was perhaps a trial run for future challenges against the Church. It is likely that this show of strength will continue, and as the following chapter will demonstrate, the Manhattan Declaration is yet another courageous manifestation by an increasing number of bishops and faithful Catholic leaders and new allies in the battle to defend traditional marriage, protect all human life, and defend religious liberty.

8 | Forging Alliances

In his newest book, *A Heart on Fire: Catholic Witness and the Next America*, Archbishop Chaput warns of the need for Catholic and Christian witness to public life. He notes that "next to America's broad collection of evangelical churches, baptized Catholics now make up the biggest religious community in the United States." For Chaput, "the issue is faith—always and everywhere, whether we're scholars or doctors or priests or lawyers or mechanics. Do we really believe in Jesus Christ, or don't we? And if we do, what are we going to do about it?"[1] Despite this plurality in numbers, the evidence suggests that Catholics continue to need better formation in what authentic Christian living means.

For more than three decades, pro–gay marriage foundations and individuals have been funding a coordinated attempt to subvert the Catholic Church's teaching on homosexuality and same-sex marriage. Yet in response is a growing and heartening defense by the bishops. In 2010, Cardinal Donald Wuerl, archbishop of Washington, D.C., and chairman of the U.S. Bishops' Committee on Doctrine, issued a statement, "Marriage Equality: A Positive Catholic Approach." This statement publicly criticized New Ways Ministry—a progressive Catholic organization that openly defies Catholic teaching on marriage. In his statement, Cardinal Wuerl warned Catholics about New Ways Ministry's attempt to redefine marriage by saying that "no one should be misled by the claim that New Ways

Ministry provides an authentic interpretation of Catholic teaching and an authentic Catholic pastoral practice. Their claim to be Catholic only confuses the faithful regarding the authentic teaching and ministry of the Church with respect to persons with a homosexual inclination. . . . New Ways Ministry cannot speak on behalf of the Catholic faithful in the United States."[2]

New Ways Ministry has been attempting to undermine Catholic teachings on homosexuality for more than twenty years. They have been able to do this because of generous funding from pro-gay foundations and individuals. Thomas Peters of the blog "American Papist" pointed out that New Ways Ministry received more than $100,000 from the Arcus Foundation in 2009. Arcus was founded by Jon Stryker, a close friend of Tim Gill, an openly gay billionaire from Colorado who has promised to spend the entirety of his fortune on redefining marriage in the United States. Targeting Catholic organizations and institutions has been the primary way that Arcus has attempted to undermine Catholic teachings. Peters lists the financial grants Arcus has made to progressive Catholic organizations and colleges and universities to help change Catholic opinion on homosexuality and same-sex marriage. In addition to the New Ways Ministry, the following are Catholic beneficiaries of Arcus's largesse on behalf of same-sex marriage:

> 2010 *Dignity USA:* $200,000 to increase the impact of Catholic pro-LGBT advocacy in the United States through the work of Equally Blessed, a coalition of pro-LGBT Catholic advocacy organizations.
>
> 2010 *Women's Alliance for Theology, Ethics and Ritual:* $70,000 to create a cadre of Catholic lesbian, bisexual, and transgender women and their allies that would play a leadership role within the Catholic community on issues related to gender, sexuality, reproductive health, and other justice issues.
>
> 2010 *Fairfield University:* $100,000 to hold a series of forums at four Catholic colleges in order to expand the current discussion on homosexuality within Roman Catholicism to include diverse opinions of progressive Catholic thought leaders and theologians.
>
> 2009 *Dignity USA:* $36,000 to define strategies to expand Dignity's national membership base of pro-LGBT Catholics.

2009 *National Gay and Lesbian Task Force:* $152,625 for a collaborative strategic planning process focused on building a pro-LGBT movement within the Roman Catholic Church in the United States.

2009 *New Ways Ministry:* $93,345 to educate Maryland's Catholic laity and lawmakers about marriage equality.

2008 *Dignity USA:* $20,000 to support media and advocacy activities in connection with the first visit of Pope Benedict XVI to the United States in April 2008.

2008 *Mainstream Media Project:* $23,000 for the Mainstream Media Project to work with four leading Catholic LGBT organizations to conduct a messaging campaign and schedule interviews in the broadcast media that promote pro-LGBT messages in connection with Pope Benedict XVI's visit to Washington, D.C., and New York City in April 2008.

Since 2008, Arcus has given more than $700,000 to progressive Catholic organizations and institutions to change the attitudes and beliefs of Catholics about homosexuality and same-sex marriage. Regrettably, it appears to have been money well spent. National polls indicate that Catholics are more likely than other Americans to support access to marriage by same-sex couples.[3] The most recent Pew poll found that not only are Catholics more likely than Protestants and other Americans to support same-sex marriage, this support has increased dramatically in the past decade. In 2004, 55 percent of Catholics were opposed to same-sex marriage, and 28 percent said they were strongly opposed. By 2012, these figures had dropped to 42 percent opposed and only 17 percent strongly opposed. Protestants are much more likely than Catholics to oppose same-sex marriage. In 2012, 56 percent of Protestants were opposed, and 32 percent were strongly opposed. And white evangelical Protestants are the most opposed to same-sex marriage, with 78 percent opposed and 56 percent strongly opposed.[4]

Shamefully, this "Catholic" support for same-sex marriage has had an impact on public policy. In fact, the strongest predictor that a state will pass legislation permitting same-sex couples to marry is whether that state has a large population of Catholics. On May 17, 2004, Massachusetts—a state where 46 percent of the population is Catholic—became the first state in the country to strike down a law banning same-sex marriage. Connecticut, a state where 42.7 percent of the population is Catholic, soon followed, as did New York, with a 38.4 percent Catholic population, and New Hampshire, with a population that is 34.3 percent Catholic. The Massachusetts decision marked a defining moment for the debates surrounding marriage in the United States because it was not only a denial by Catholic voters of Catholic teachings on the sanctity of marriage as the union of one man and one woman, it was also a rejection of the Defense of Marriage Act (DOMA) restricting marriage to heterosexual couples. In February 2011, the U.S. Justice Department announced that it would no longer defend DOMA—tacitly eliminating the federal role in supporting traditional marriage in the United States. In June 2013, the Supreme Court ruled Section III of DOMA unconstitutional which now presents new challenges for defenders of traditional marriage.

Similarly, California—the state with the greatest number of Catholics in the country (10,463,330)—has been the site of the biggest battles to redefine marriage. After years of heavy lobbying by the pro–gay marriage coalition, the conflict intensified on May 15, 2008, when the California Supreme Court opened the door to same-sex marriage in the state. Ruling that sexual orientation "does not constitute a legitimate basis upon which to deny or withhold legal rights," the Supreme Court appeared to end the debate.[5] As California is a politically liberal state, with a large population of liberal Catholic voters, it appeared to most observers that it was just a matter of time before same-sex marriage would be a reality in that state.

Yet these observers never anticipated the tremendous grassroots movement nurtured by religious leaders from across the state. Beginning with San Diego's then auxiliary bishop Salvatore Cordileone, and strengthened by leaders from the Mormon and evangelical communities, more than one hundred thousand volunteers gathered sufficient signatures from voters throughout the state to hold a statewide voter referendum known as Proposition 8—an initiative on the ballot that would overturn the state's Supreme Court decision.[6] The initiative was successful as 52 percent of California's voters cast ballots in favor of protecting marriage as the union of one man and one woman—halting same-sex marriage in the state. However, in 2010, this decision by the voters was overturned by the historically liberal Ninth Circuit Court of Appeals—and in June 2013, the U.S. Supreme Court dismissed an appeal of California's Proposition 8 on grounds of standing. This means that the lower court's ruling stands and same-sex marriage must be recognized in California.

While the protection of traditional marriage through Proposition 8 was overturned, the movement to protect marriage in the state showed the country that even in a liberal state like California, religious leaders can indeed have a significant influence. Early in the fight, California's bishops rallied the troops with a strong statement issued by the California Catholic Conference. Reminding the faithful of the importance of the underlying issue at stake in Proposition 8, California's bishops also warned the faithful of their duty to be involved: "the issue before us with Proposition 8 is 'marriage'—an ancient, yet modern, human institution which pre-exists both Church and government. . . . The ideal relationship between a man and a woman for the purpose of procreation and the continuation of the human race." Calling on all Catholics, "as citizens of California," the bishops advised the faithful of their obligation to overturn this ruling by the California Supreme Court.[7]

The Knights of Columbus, the world's largest Catholic family fraternal service organization, donated $1 million to the cause—noting that the donation was "an indication of how important we believe this referendum to be, and an encouragement to other groups and individuals of all faiths to lend their support as well . . . we are proud to join the Catholic bishops and priests of California."[8] Although Catholics were highly visible because of the leadership of Bishop Cordileone, they were not the only warriors on this battlefield. In fact, the truth is that exit poll data following the November voter referendum revealed that evangelical or born-again Christians (85 percent) were far more likely than others (42 percent) to vote yes to protect traditional marriage.[9] While 64 percent of all Catholics voted in favor of the proposition to protect marriage as the union between one woman and one man, the vote was largely decided by evangelical voters.[10]

A United Front

In many ways, the battles over the attempted redefinition of marriage in California were a harbinger of things to come. The continued success by the pro–gay marriage forces in redefining marriage in states throughout the country, coupled with the support for these initiatives by the Obama administration, predicted a long and difficult war for faithful Catholics—and all people of faith. Religious leaders recognized these latest threats and attempted to join forces to present a united front to create a document that would help identify issues and coordinate a unified response.

Assembling in New York City in September 2009, religious leaders representing the Eastern Orthodox Church, the Roman Catholic Church, the Anglican Church, and various evangelical leaders gathered to discuss what they defined as "threats" to their faith communities. Identifying these threats, and developing strategies to meet them, characterized the early days of the formulation of what would soon become known as the Manhattan Declaration. Princeton University professor Robert P. George, a Catholic, teamed with evangelical leaders Timothy George, a professor at the Beeson Divinity School, and the late Chuck Colson, founder of the Prison Fellowship, to write the first draft of the document. After several revisions, on November 20, 2009, almost 150 Christian leaders joined together for the official release of *The Manhattan Declaration: A Call of Christian Conscience*.[11]

The focus of the Declaration was on three major areas. First, the Declaration provided a robust defense of marriage as a union exclusively between a man and a woman—identifying the threats to such a defense—and identifying strategies designed to meet these threats. The second focus of the Declaration was on protecting all human life from conception to natural death. Issues of abortion, embryonic cell destruction, and euthanasia were all identified as areas of concern—and, as with the defense of marriage, strategies to defend life were developed. Finally, the Manhattan Declaration identified the threats to religious liberty—and the need to provide a strong defense of such liberty as a natural right. Identifying their commitment to fight, the signers of the Manhattan Declaration pledged to "speak and act in defense of biblical truths with respect to the three issues it addresses. Each [of the signers] agrees that these truths are not open to compromise. And each has become part of a growing movement of people standing shoulder to shoulder in defense of these three vital moral issues."

Among the first signers were fourteen Roman Catholic bishops and archbishops, including Archbishop Charles Chaput, Archbishop Salvatore Joseph Cordileone, Timothy Cardinal Dolan, Archbishop Joseph Kurtz, Adam Cardinal Maida, Bishop Richard Malone, Archbishop John Meyers, Archbishop Naumann, Archbishop Nienstedt, Bishop

Thomas Olmsted, Justin Cardinal Rigali, Bishop Michael Sheridan, Donald Cardinal Wuerl, and Bishop David Zubik.

This collaboration between Catholic and non-Catholic Christian leaders in signing the declaration marks a significant escalation in Christian opposition to the growing secularization of the public square. Realizing their strength in unity, Christian leaders throughout the country have understood that their previous inability to collaborate in confronting these threats has had serious costs in corroding traditional beliefs and values once held in common by a large majority of Americans. The continued support that the Declaration continues to receive—now almost four years after its drafting—indicates that many faithful Catholics and a large number of evangelicals see the declaration as not just a strategic means of winning the cultural and political battles over marriage, abortion and religious liberty, but as the means to true Christian renewal. Shortly after signing the declaration, Archbishop Kurtz of Louisville publicly lauded the declaration, stating: "We have a commitment to working hard in these three important areas. This declaration speaks from the convictions held by its authors and signers—and it is something worth fighting for, and it's a recognition that our resolve needs to be stronger."[12]

Archbishop Chaput, then of Denver, also expressed his enthusiastic support for the document. In an interview with the Catholic News Agency, he said: "I was glad to be invited to sign the declaration, and glad to sign because I believe in its content. . . . In a sensible world, none of these things would be in question. But we no longer live in a sensible world." Ultimately, Archbishop Chaput hoped the declaration would serve as a means to "galvanize good people."[13] Similarly, Father Fessio, founder of Ignatius Press, offered his praise for the declaration: "It's a magnificent document. It's a beautiful expression of fundamental principles and a wonderful weaving of clear, evangelical, biblical and the Catholic contribution of respecting natural law."[14]

And "galvanize good people" it did. In addition to the original 150 signers, the petition has now received over five hundred thousand signatures from Christians throughout the world.[15] Evangelical pastors and Catholic parish priests alike have used the declaration as both a pedagogical tool to educate their flocks and as a way to stir them to action. Since November 2009, more than fifty Catholic bishops have joined the ranks of those who have added their name to the petition. Perhaps no other document has done as much good in forging a united front in the culture wars surrounding life, marriage, and religious liberty.

Forming Consciences for Faithful Citizenship

It is likely that the alliance between evangelical Protestants and orthodox Catholics will continue as these Catholics find that they share similar values and goals. In fact, the truth is that orthodox Catholics have much more in common with evangelical Protestants on marriage and life issues than with their own progressive coreligionists. While the Church is nonpartisan, and will never embrace a specific political party, all Catholics are called to take positions that reflect Church teaching. As *Faithful Citizenship* states, "these themes from Catholic social teaching provide a moral framework that does not easily fit ideologies of 'right' or 'left,' 'liberal' or 'conservative,' or the platform of any political party. They are not partisan or sectarian, but reflect fundamental ethical principles that are common to all people."[16] Likewise, the signers of the Manhattan Declaration state clearly that they do not represent any political party. "We make this commitment not as partisans of any political group but as followers of Jesus Christ, the crucified and risen Lord, who is the Way, the Truth and the Life."

In an attempt to assist voters in assessing the suitability of candidates for public office and combat groups like New Ways Ministry and Dignity who falsely label themselves as "Catholic," the USCCB released *Forming Consciences for Faithful Citizenship: A Call to Responsibility*. First issued in 2007, and then updated in 2011, the USCCB has created a document intended to serve as a tool for faithful Catholics to better understand the moral implications of political life. The introductory note of the document advises that "it does not offer a voters guide, scorecard of issues, or direction on how to vote." Rather, the USCCB document "applies Catholic moral principles to a range of important issues and warns against misguided appeals to conscience to ignore fundamental moral claims, to reduce Catholic moral concerns to one or two matters, or to justify choices simply to advance partisan, ideological, or personal interests."[17] The *Catechism of the Catholic Church* defines conscience as "a judgment of reason whereby the human person recognizes the moral quality of a concrete act that he is going to perform, is in the process of performing, or has already completed. In all he says and does, man is obliged to follow faithfully what he knows to be just and right."[18]

Faithful Catholics who follow Church teaching on abortion or marriage are often labeled as single-issue voters. While such labeling is an unfair exaggeration, all Catholics are called to first and foremost prioritize policies that protect the dignity of life. As the USCCB's document *Faithful Citizenship* states, "Catholics are not single-issue voters. A candidate's position on a single issue is not sufficient to guarantee a voter's support. Yet a candidate's position on a single issue that involves an intrinsic evil, such as support for legal abortion or the promotion of racism, may legitimately lead a voter to disqualify that candidate from receiving support."[19] Taking such advice to heart—and implementing it in practice—will be an essential step for continued Catholic renewal in public life.

The Newest Front: Religious Liberty

As the Obama administration refuses to offer any serious relief for Catholics or Evangelical institutions over the Health and Human Services mandate, this will prove to be yet another opportunity for both sides to work together toward a shared end. While an exemption was granted to churches, there was no exemption for church-related institutions. Since Catholic Church teachings hold contraception, sterilization, and abortion to be gravely immoral acts, the ruling amounted to an ultimatum. Cardinal Dolan, as the head of the USCCB, responded quickly and forcefully by issuing a statement identifying what the bishops labeled as "the false claims" issued by the Obama administration and clarifying exactly what the mandate would require. Cardinal Dolan made it clear that the bishops would not comply. Although White House officials responded "no one will be forced to buy or use contraception" under their mandate, the bishops countered that the mandate "forces Catholic institutions to pay for things they consider immoral, since they must sponsor and subsidize coverage of contraception, sterilization, and abortifacients." When the White House claimed that "drugs that cause abortion are not covered by this policy," the bishops countered that claim also—calling it "false"—and pointing out that "by including all drugs approved by the FDA for use as contraceptives, the HHS [Health and Human Services] mandate includes drugs that can induce abortion, such as 'Ella,' a close cousin of the abortion pill RU-486."[20]

In the months that followed the release of the January 2012 mandate, more than 160 individual bishops issued public statements decrying it. Archbishop Charles Chaput of Philadelphia issued an action alert stating that "Bishops and lay Catholic leaders across the United States have made it clear that we cannot comply with this unjust law without compromising our convictions and undermining the Catholic identity of our service ministries. . . . This is not just another important issue among the many we need to be concerned about. This ruling is different. This ruling interferes with the basic right of Catholic citizens to organize and work for the common good as Catholics in the public square."[21] "We cannot and we will not comply with this unjust federal order. We cannot and we will not accept this egregious affront to our religious liberty,"

Now retired bishop Fabian Bruskewitz of Lincoln warned Catholics that they must be prepared to "suffer" for the integrity of their Church: "Like the martyrs of old we must be prepared to accept suffering, which could include heavy fines and imprisonment. . . . This means that all of our Catholic schools, hospitals, social service agencies will be forced to participate in evil." According to the *National Catholic Register*, Bishop Bruskewitz described Secretary Kathleen Sebelius as a "bitter fallen-away Catholic" and urged Catholics to call their representatives to protest the outrage of the contraception mandate.[22]

Bishop Olmsted, of the Diocese of Phoenix, declared that people of faith would not be "stripped of their God-given rights." Archbishop Alexander Sample said: "we Catholics will be compelled to either violate our consciences or drop health coverage for our employees and suffer the penalties for doing so." Bishop Kevin Rhoades of Ft. Wayne-South Bend, Indiana, wrote in a statement to be read at all parishes in his diocese. He advised Catholics to "pray hard" and to ask political candidates about their position on religious liberty in general and conscience protection specifically. And Baltimore's bishop, William Lori, who chairs the U.S. Bishops' Ad Hoc Committee for Religious Liberty, denounced the mandate in the *Washington Post*, warning of the "horrific and alarming consequences" that would come from forcing Catholic organizations and institutions to limit their services to members of their own faith in order to protect their religious liberty.

Bishop Lori put it starkly by saying that forcing Catholic organizations to choose between following President Obama's mandate and Jesus's mandate "strikes at the very heart of the right to religious liberty on which our country was founded."

Cardinal Dolan directly addressed the reality of these threats when he published a statement decrying the Obama administration's attempt to divide Catholics by reminding the bishops that there was great diversity of opinion from Catholics on the health-care mandate. The implication was clear to Cardinal Dolan that the Obama administration wanted the bishops to listen instead to the progressive Catholic voices—those the cardinal called the "enlightened voices of accommodation" from the progressive Catholic side. And, while the Obama administration can be forgiven for their ignorance of the fact that it is the bishops who speak for the Church, what was more difficult to forgive was when some Catholics inserted themselves into the controversy in an attempt to marginalize the voices of the bishops.

The editors of *America* chastised the bishops for "stretching the religious liberty strategy" and claiming that "official Catholic rights theory proposed that people should be willing to adjust their rights claims to one another." Maintaining that the government—and not the Church—has the "responsibility to coordinate contending rights and interests for the sake of the common good," the editors of *America* lectured the bishops on the limits of their authority by citing Pope Benedict's admonition that "the church does not seek to impose on those who do not share the faith."[23] The editors concluded their piece by warning the bishops that their campaign against the mandate "devalues the coinage of religious liberty."[24]

Cardinal Dolan must have anticipated that the editorial in *America* would embolden the other side in the debate surrounding the contraceptive mandate—and it did. When members of the USCCB met with the White House staff, they were told that the bishops should follow the "enlightened" voices at *America*. In yet another statement published on his website, Cardinal Dolan called the *America* editorial "hardly surprising, yet terribly unfortunate."[25] Archbishop Lori responded even more strongly by saying that "if the editorial is to be believed, bishops should regard it (the mandate) not as a matter of religious liberty but merely policy that, as providers they teach one thing but as employers they are made to teach something else. In other words, we are forced to be a countersign to Church teaching and to give people plenty of reason not to follow it . . . the detail in question here is called 'scandal.'"[26] The editorial was just one more sign to faithful Catholics and their bishops that the progressives had enlisted to fight for the Obama side in helping to implement a mandate that the bishops had already identified as evil.

Of course, this was not the first time that President Obama had attempted the divisive strategy of enlisting progressive Catholic culture warriors to help him fight his battles. From the earliest conflict over his health-care mandate in 2009, President Obama recruited progressive Catholic leaders like Sister Carol Keehan, president of the Catholic Health Association, to lead from the front—attacking any faithful Catholic who criticized her tactics. For faithful Catholics, it was discouraging to see that the Catholic Health Association embraced a plan that many of their bishops had decried. Still, there was division even among the bishops. While Cardinal Justin Rigali, then, chairman of the USCCB's Committee for Pro-life Activities, urged lawmakers to block the health-care legislation unless it was amended to prohibit public financing for abortion, his was a lonely voice. In a commentary posted on the website of the San Bernardino diocese in California, Bishop Gerald Barnes denigrated those who participated in what he called the "anger-fueled conduct" at Town Hall meetings and directed followers to the bishops' website to learn about Catholics' moral obligation to help others gain access to quality health care.

The bishops' website advised Catholics to "join the efforts of local groups funded by the Catholic Campaign for Human Development." As it happens, the Catholic Campaign has been involved in funding progressive organizations and activities from its earliest years, subsidizing not only the Industrial Areas Foundation but also Acorn, both of which have promoted pro-choice candidates for office. And though funding irregularities at Acorn ended financial support from the Catholic Campaign, an organization called the Pacific Institute for Community Organizations has stepped in to fill the void. Founded in 1972 under the leadership of Father John Baumann, a Jesuit who learned community organizing in Chicago, the Institute has become heavily invested in promoting the president's health-care reform. It organized "Faith and Health Care Sundays" throughout the country. When the San Diego Organizing Project (an Institute affiliate) held an "action on health care at Our Lady of Guadalupe Church," Pastor

Bob Fambrini accused opponents of misleading the faithful on health care in the same way that they had supposedly "lied about weapons of mass destruction in Iraq."

To allay fears about President Obama's health-care plan, PICO teamed up with the progressive Christian group Sojourners and the Catholics in Alliance for the Public Good to provide congregations with a "Health Care Tool Kit." While the kit's brochure does not deny that the proposed health care reform will fund elective abortion, it states rather neutrally: "how Congress applies current policy on federal funding for abortion to new systems created through health reform will be an important issue for the faith community." It also reassures readers that conscience protections will remain in place— even though it was clear then (and now) that no conscience protections remained for faithful Catholics.

Drawing support from progressive Catholics and agencies is a strategy that worked well for Obama during both of his presidential campaigns. In the 2008 campaign, Catholics in Alliance for the Common Good and Catholics United tried to neutralize the abortion issue during the presidential campaign by suggesting that Obama's proposal on "social justice" issues like poverty were the way to reduce abortion rates without restricting abortion rights. Once he was elected, personnel from the same progressive Catholic organizations who helped him played a central role in enlisting Catholic support for the Health and Human Services mandate. Alexia Kelley was appointed to head the President's Center for Faith Based and Community initiatives; she coupled a decade of experience of working on the USCCB's own Catholic Campaign for Human Development with her most recent work as cofounder and director of Catholics in Alliance for the Common Good. In November 2012, Kelley left her position at the White House to return to working for progressive Catholic causes as the president and CEO of the board of Foundations and Donors Interested in Catholic Activities (FADICA).

In addition to Kelley, Chris Korzen, a former organizer for the Service Employees International Union and a cofounder of Catholics United and the Catholic Voting Project, helped to organize support for Kathleen Sebelius's appointment as secretary of Health and Human Services by gathering signatures for an online petition titled "Catholics for Sebelius." Since joining the administration, Sebelius has played a key role in helping to pass the president's health-care reform, and attempting to implement the president's mandate on contraception.

Sister Carol Keehan has been an even more valuable ally to President Obama than Sebelius because she is ostensibly "outside" the administration, and a woman religious, this providing much more Catholic credibility than Sebelius. Appearing to speak for the Church, Sister Keehan defended what faithful Catholics find reprehensible—a health-care reform package that will provide federal funding for abortion. Despite the fact that the leadership of the bishops continued to point out that unless a correction was applied to the proposed health care bill, the bill Sister Keehan was defending, the bill would greatly expand public funding for abortion—and likely expand access to abortion.

It was difficult not to conclude that Sister Keehan and her organization supported the health-care reform plan of the president—replete with funding for abortion, and despite the bishops' reluctance to support such a plan. One only had to view the video posted on the Catholic Health Association website titled "I Can't Wait for Health Reform" to see this support. The video opens with a film clip of President Obama giving a speech in which he declares that "health-care reform cannot wait, it must not wait, and it will not wait another year." This is followed with priests, nuns, and health care workers—and even a few bishops—holding up signs claiming that they too "Can't Wait" for health-care reform—implying that the Catholic Church cannot wait for health-care reform either.

Follow-up videos by the Catholic Health Association claimed that President Obama's health-care reform "draws on Catholic social teaching" and "is an ethical necessity, a building block for the common good of the nation and the strength of its community." This time, Sister Keehan enlisted Catholic Democratic senator Robert Casey to star in the video to contradict the bishops by claiming that the health-care reform was "pro-life legislation." Of course, Casey is the same "pro-life" Catholic progressive Democrat who had no problem voting in favor of funding abortions overseas when he voted the previous year to allow President Obama to end the Mexico City Policy, a Reagan-era policy that prohibited taxpayer funds from going to organizations that promote or perform abortions overseas.

The goal of propaganda videos in any war is simply to win people over to an idea so deeply and emotionally that it no longer matters whether the idea is true. Calling the Obama health-care reform "pro-life" was always a lie. But, it is possible that the lie had been repeated so often and portrayed on Catholic Health Association films so compellingly that even the filmmakers began to believe it. The star of the final Catholic Health Association health-care reform video was once again President Obama as the crowd of more than eight hundred participants at the Catholic Health Association annual meeting applauded when President Obama appeared on the Catholic Health Association video and thanked everyone at the Association for their "help and courage in passing health care reform." Referring to what he obviously saw as the effective Catholic Health Association video, President Obama reassured all of those gathered in Denver that those in the Catholic Health Association video "won't be waiting much longer." And, once again, in the video, the president singled out Sister Keehan for "the extraordinary leadership she has shown in advancing our national discussion." Showing how grateful he was to Sister Keehan for convincing so many Catholics to disregard their bishops and support his health care reform, the president awarded her one of the twenty silver-tipped signing pens after the signing ceremony.

Noticeably absent from all of the Catholic Health Association propaganda videos—or any speeches by Sister Keehan or other officials of the Catholic Health Association—were the growing list of bishops who were critical of Sister Keehan and her activities. Labeling this dissent as a "wound to Catholic unity," the leadership of the USCCB seems to have learned an important lesson in the passage of the health-care reform that prepared them to face the Health and Human Services contraceptive mandate. The bishops learned to lead from the front—to get out early to define their stand on Catholic teachings so that they were not defined by the opposition. In the lead-up to passing health-care reform, Sister Keehan appeared to speak for the Church and all Catholics. However, faithful Catholics remain optimistic that the proactive response of their bishops in the battles over the Health and Human Services mandate will prevent this from happening again. In contrast, President Obama thought he could be successful, as he had been in passing his health-care reform, by using similar tactics to divide Catholics. Just as generals are always fighting the last war, President Obama attempted to enlist Sister Keehan yet again in the contraception battles. Who could blame him? It worked so well the last time. But this time the bishops had already mounted a strong fight against the mandate—making their presence much more difficult to ignore. Of course, this did not stop Jack Lew, the White House chief of staff, from attempting to portray the Catholic Church as supportive of the Health and Human Services mandate. Lew appeared on all of the major Sunday morning television news shows to defend the administration's contraception mandate. Claiming Catholic support, he said: "we had a broad range of groups endorse where the president's policy is. . . . We had the Catholic Health Association, which understands health care extremely well and is true to Catholic beliefs." Lew must have known that Sister Keehan's position in support of the president's mandate conflicted (again) with the official teaching of the bishops—the authentic teaching body of the Church. But it seems that the Obama administration does not really care where the bishops stand on this. Once again, Sister Keehan has given them the "Catholic cover" they need. While the bishops had posted their disapproval of both the mandate and the accommodation offered by the president on February 10, 2012, Sister Keehan ignored the bishops *yet again* and supported President Obama's proposed accommodation.

On March 14, 2012, the Administrative Committee of the USCCB released a statement calling the Health and Human Services mandate "unjust and illegal." In their statement, the bishops maintained that their protest was not about contraception, and not just about Catholic religious rights. Rather, it was about the Obama administration attempting to impose its agenda on all: "the introduction of this unprecedented defining of faith communities and their ministries has precipitated this struggle for religious freedom. . . . Government has no place in defining religion and religious ministry."[27]

The bishops' statement concluded by "calling upon the Catholic faithful and all people of faith, throughout our country to join us in prayer and penance for our leaders and for the complete protection of our First Freedom—religious liberty—which is not only protected in the laws and customs of our great nation, but rooted in the teachings of our great Tradition." While the progressive side continues to denigrate what they view as the bishops' refusal to compromise, faithful Catholics have been encouraged by the strength shown by their shepherds throughout this latest battle to define Catholic teaching.

In 2010, at the occasion of his retirement from leading the USCCB, Cardinal Francis George predicted many of these threats to religious liberty. He reminded the bishops of their ecclesiological charge in speaking for the Church: "we speak for the apostolic faith, and those who hold it, gather round. We must listen to the *sensus fidei*, the sense of the faith itself in the lives of our people, but this is different from intellectual trends and public opinion. . . . The bishops in apostolic communion and in union with the successor of Peter, the bishop of Rome, speak for the Church in matters of faith and in moral issues and the laws surrounding them. All the rest is opinion."[28]

9 | Priests Matter

How great is the priest! God obeys him: he utters a
few words and the Lord descends from Heaven at his
voice—to be contained within a small host. Without the
sacrament of Holy Orders, we would not have the Lord.
Who put him there in that tabernacle? The priest. Who
welcomed your soul at the beginning of life? The priest.
Who feeds your soul and gives it strength for the journey?
The priest. Who will prepare it to appear before God,
bathing it one last time in the blood of Jesus Christ? The
priest—always the priest. And if the soul should happen
to die as a result of sin, who will raise it up—who will
restore its calm and peace? Again, the priest. After God,
the priest is everything. Only in heaven will he fully
realize what he is.

—ST. JOHN VIANNEY, PATRON SAINT OF PRIESTS

On the occasion of the 150th anniversary of the death of
St. John Vianney, the patron saint of priests, Pope Benedict
proclaimed a year for priests in 2009.[1] Vianney was an inspired choice for the pontiff. Born at the start of the French
Revolution in 1786, in the French town of Dardilly—when
priests risked execution for celebrating the Mass—Vianney
learned as a child to view priests as heroes. Forbidden to
perform the sacraments following the Revolution, Dardilly's priests secretly instructed Vianney so he could receive
his First Communion and Confirmation. The Churches
were closed, but the sacraments continued because of the

heroism of the priests. After the Church was again restored in 1802, Vianney was ordained to the priesthood and assigned to lead the parish of Ars, a town of just 230 people. While Vianney soon became known internationally as a priest with the gifts to spiritually transform the parish and the surrounding community, he always thought of himself as a simple parish priest.

For faithful Catholics, priests are still heroes. Even in the aftermath of the clergy abuse scandal, national surveys consistently indicate that most Catholics deeply respect their priests. They are grateful for the sacrifices these men have made on their behalf, and faithful Catholics are optimistic about the future of the priesthood and the Church itself.[2] Progressives maintain that no priest deserves such an honor—and define such respect as leading to "clericalism." Many progressives do not even see the need for priests. In 1972, theologian Hans Kung published his provocative book *Why Priests?* in which he proposed that the term "priest" be abolished as a reference to the ministers of the Church. In 1975, the Congregation for the Doctrine of the Faith condemned Kung's work, though this did not diminish his influence on theologians and lay Catholics like Gary Wills, who in early 2013 published a similar work: *Why Priests: A Failed Tradition.*[3]

Despite the efforts by the Church to publicly correct Catholic theologians like Kung whose teachings run contrary to official Church teachings, their influence continues on the progressive side. For progressive theologians, especially those teaching on Catholic campuses, the emphasis on the "priesthood of all believers" involves a diminishment of the role of the priest—from one who brings the real presence of Christ to his people to one who is simply a minor player in the greater community. For these progressives, it is the community that celebrates the Eucharist—not the priest. As University of San Diego theology professor Bernard Cooke claims, it is the celebrating congregation—not the priest—that "does the Eucharistic action."[4]

It is not surprising, then, to find that progressive Catholics are much less likely than orthodox Catholics to be optimistic about the future of the priesthood or the Church itself. Many progressives do not believe that priests matter. When asked whether they were optimistic or pessimistic about the future of the Church, 40 percent of self-described progressive Catholics said they were either somewhat pessimistic or very pessimistic. In contrast, only 7 percent of orthodox Catholics claim to be somewhat or very pessimistic about the future of the Church.[5] There are also dramatic differences between orthodox or progressive Catholics regarding the priesthood. While 69 percent of orthodox Catholics believe it is somewhat or very important that the priesthood remain all male, only 6 percent of the progressives believe a male priesthood is important to their faith. Similarly, 61 percent of those identified as orthodox say a celibate priesthood is important to their faith, while only 6 percent of progressives agree with the need for celibacy for priests.[6]

Priests are Qualitatively Different from Others

In 2010, as he was concluding the Year of the Priest, Pope Benedict's homily reminded the faithful that "the priest is not a mere office-holder, like those which every society needs in order to carry out certain functions. Instead, he does something which no human being can do of his own power in Christ's name." Echoing Vianney, Benedict reminded the faithful that the priest "speaks the words which absolve us of our sins and in this way, he changes, starting with God, our entire life. . . . The priesthood is not simply office, but sacrament."[7]

Catholic novelist Walker Percy, who converted to the faith in the 1940s and lived as a faithful Catholic for nearly fifty years until his death in 1990, describes the important role priests play when he says: "more than one pilgrim finds himself standing at a strange rectory door, wondering how he got there, never having said two words to a priest . . . and, here I have to smile, remembering how it felt, and also hoping that I would not run into some exhausted, unhappy or otherwise messed up human being."

Percy knew that priests matter—even exhausted and unhappy ones. Priests play a central role in several of Percy's novels. None of them are perfect. In fact, most of them are rather flawed. But Percy's priests are often heroes nonetheless because they do what only priests can do—administer the sacraments. Sometimes, as in his *Last Gentleman*, the priest is there at the hospital deathbed—arriving just in time, looking disheveled and quite annoyed—using the water in the water glass on the bedside table to baptize a dying convert to the faith. Percy does not romanticize his priests. There is no attempt to give the reader a sense of awe or mystery; rather, Percy describes a simple priest doing what he is supposed to be doing—reminding a young dying man of the hope of heaven. In other novels, like his story *Lancelot,*

Percy's priest says almost nothing throughout the entire book. Much of the novel is devoted to the murderous Lancelot and his constant musings on why he was justified in murdering his adulterous wife and her lover. The silence of the priest is attractive to Lancelot as he tells him "your silence is the only conversation I can listen to." It is not until the final pages of the three-hundred-page novel that the priest finally begins to speak—and his speaking finally helps Lancelot begin to see what he has become.

Percy's priests do not have to be perfect to matter—nor do our priests. Catholic theology teaches that God acts through his ordained ministers, however unworthy they may be. This is the doctrine that the sacraments work *ex opera operato* with God or Christ as their agent, irrespective of the worthiness of the priest administering them.[8] In *Thanatos Syndrome*, when one of Percy's most memorable priests, a reformed alcoholic, is asked why he became a priest or even stayed a Catholic, he simply answered: "in the end one has to choose between life and death." And, whatever else Catholicism is, it is certainly life-affirming. For Percy the convert, the great attraction of the Catholic Church was "Christ's commission to Peter in Matthew 16:18, both in the founding of the Church and the power to loose and to bind. This, and the no less mysterious historical fidelity of the Catholic Church to this commission, through thick and thin, decay and renewal, for some 2,000 years."[9] In a 1987 interview with the author, he quipped, "The Church even has St. Peter buried in the basement of a cathedral in Rome. Other churches can't produce evidence like that."[10] Percy knows, like all faithful Catholics must know, it is the very timelessness of the teachings of the Church that continues to attract Catholics to the faith. Faith is a gift. It's a grace, an extraordinary gift. But faith is also a gift that can be lost. Sometimes it can only be recovered through extraordinary means through the sacraments. Priests matter because only priests have been entrusted with the authority to administer the sacraments. This is why so many progressives have been trying to diminish the centrality of their role.

Holy Orders is the general term used to refer to the sacrament in which men are ordained to the priesthood—it is "the sacrament through which the mission entrusted by Christ to his apostles continues to be exercised in the Church until the end of time: thus, it is the a sacrament of apostolic ministry."[11] To understand this fully, it is helpful to look at the scriptures in which the ministry of the Church finds its origins. Through the Old Covenant, or the Old Testament, God selected the Jewish people—the nation of Israel—as his chosen people. Within this nation, he selected the tribe of Levi, led by the brother of Moses, Aaron, to serve as priests, "appointed to act on behalf of men in relation to God, to offer gifts and sacrifices for sins" (Hebrews 5:1). The priesthood of the Catholic Church finds its roots here yet is fulfilled in the New Covenant, with the coming of Christ as the one true priest. The gospel writings of the New Testament provide accounts of how Christ chose to share his priesthood with others—the apostles— and how he established the sacraments of the Church. The apostles, often referred to in the scriptures as "the twelve," were selected by Christ to take on an elevated role in his ministry. As theologian Scott Hahn observes in his book *Many Are Called*, priests in the Old Testament received their priestly duties through inheritance. In the New Testament, however, priests are called by vocation through favorably responding to Christ's call to his disciples when he says, "Come, follow me."[12]

The Church teaches that the defining role of a priest is his sacramental ministry. This is, of course, modeled after Christ and his earthly ministry: the celebration of the Eucharist was instituted by Christ during the Last Supper (Luke 22:19), the sacrament of reconciliation was established by Christ when he conferred to his apostles the ability to forgive sins (John 20:23), and Baptism and the Anointing of the Sick were defining aspects of Christ's earthly ministry that he transferred to his apostles (Matthew 28:19; Mark 6:7–13). *Presbyterorum Ordinis*, the Decree of the Ministry and Life of Priests, produced during the Second Vatican Council, states that "the priest shares in the authority by which Christ himself builds up, sanctifies, and rules his Body." This is why the Church teaches that the priest acts in *persona Christi* when he is offering the Mass, hearing and forgiving sins through the sacrament of reconciliation, and teaching and leading his flock. Regardless of the priest's personal sins and human weaknesses, the sacraments and his priestly duties remain effective because faithful Catholics know that it is actually Christ serving as the minister.

Christ established an authority and a hierarchy to lead his Church and serve the people and the priesthood. Appointing Peter to serve as the vicar of Christ on earth as the first bishop and pope of the Catholic Church, we find the scriptural account of this in Matthew's Gospel: "and I tell you, you are Peter, and on this rock I will build my Church, and the powers of death shall not prevail against it. I will give you the keys of the kingdom of heaven, and whatever you bind on earth shall be bound in heaven, and whatever you loose on earth shall be loosed in heaven" (Matthew 16:18–19).

As the Church continued to grow in influence and membership throughout the early centuries of the Christian faith, the other apostles looked to Peter and his successors and respected this authority. The title "bishop" designates the authority of the apostolic successor over both the priests he oversees and the parishioners of his flock. The Nicene Creed, which was adopted during the Church Council at Nicea in 325 A.D., affirms Catholic belief in the "one, holy, catholic and apostolic Church." While Catholics recite this every time they attend Mass, they often do so without even thinking about the profound theological implications of the words. "Apostolic" means that the Catholic Church is one that is rooted in the apostles and it acts by and through the authority that was given to them by Christ. As Christ was leaving this earth before his return to heaven, he told his apostles: "all authority in heaven and on earth has been given to me. Go therefore, and make disciples of all nations; baptize them in the name of the Father and of the Son and of the Holy Spirit. Teach them to observe all the commands I gave you. And, look, I am with you always, yes, to the end of time" (Matthew 28:18–20).

Referred to as "The Great Commission," this authority—this mission—that the apostles were instructed to carry out anchors the Church. The apostles, led by Peter, knew that their earthly ministry would be confined to their lifetime and that they now shared in the same responsibility to continue to spread the gospel of Christ. This is why the first apostles then handed down their knowledge and authority to other apostles. This line of unbroken authority continues today. Within each diocese, there is a bishop who serves as the local authority over all of the priests in the diocese. The bishop is the sole authority. This is why when a priest is ordained, it is the bishop of the diocese who presides over the Rite of Ordination. As the Catechism decrees: "Though each bishop is the lawful pastor only of the portion of the flock entrusted to his care, as a legitimate successor of the apostles, he is, by divine institution and precept, responsible with the other bishops for the apostolic mission of the Church" (Catholic Catechism, 1560).

Celibacy and the All-Male Priesthood

Two of the defining features of the priesthood that contribute to the most contentious battles of the Catholic culture wars are the Church's requirement for the all-male priesthood and the celibacy requirement. In order to understand the Church's reasoning for this, it is helpful to look again at the scriptural basis for the priesthood. In the book of Genesis, we learn that at creation, God made both man and woman for specific purposes—both different and complementary. Adam, the first man, was created to "be fruitful and multiply" and to "inhabit the earth." God also made him ruler over Eden and placed him in charge of nurturing and caring for his wife, Eve, and the rest of creation. In this role he not only served as a husband and provider, he was also a Father.

As we know from the book of Genesis, Adam failed in this important role. This is why when Christ comes in the New Testament, he is considered the new Adam—now made perfect. When Jesus chose his apostles, he chose twelve men to act in his name and continue his ministry. As Jesuit theologian Father Jean Galot observed, "Jesus did not call any woman to be one of the twelve . . . this fact should not be traced to conformity with the prevailing ethos, since Jesus dissented from the prejudices prevalent in his surroundings and firmly refused to abide by the discriminations practiced in relation to women. The apostles grasped the permanent validity of this stance, for they continued to assign the ministerial priesthood exclusively to men."[13] At the Last Supper, when Christ instituted the Eucharist, he chose only twelve men to be present at this event, for it was here that he would provide the instructions to carry this on after his death. Father Galot also points to the importance of understanding the historical context in which the Last Supper occurred, for it was a Passover meal. In the Jewish tradition, the Passover was a family event that always included women and children. By specifically inviting only men to this event, Christ made a deliberate decision to limit the ministry of the priesthood to men.

This does not mean, however, that Jesus did not see men as equal with women. Jesus recognized that women were then, and will continue to be, vital to the spiritual life of the Church. In fact, it was Jesus who rebelled against the societal norms of the time by entering into deep friendships with women, such as Mary and Martha, and by defending their worth and dignity. The Gospel of Mark reveals that Jesus provided hope to the Samaritan woman at the well and praised the poor widow who brought all of her worldly possessions to sacrifice at the Temple. Through Baptism in Christ, all believers have equality before God—though we are different in our identities in his Kingdom. Before his death, Jesus instructed the apostles to revere and respect his mother, Mary. Mary is the mother of the Church, and Christ chose men to be of service to the Church as spiritual fathers and husbands. Throughout the scriptures, the theme of marriage is used to describe God's relationship with his people. In the New Testament, Christ chooses the Church to be his bride, and in the New Covenant, it is the priest who functions in the role of Christ. The priest must be male to fulfill this covenant.

Despite the assertions contained in Santa Clara University theology professor Gary Macy's book *The Hidden History of Women's Ordination: Female Clergy in the Medieval West*, there is absolutely no credible evidence to indicate that women have ever been ordained to priesthood throughout the Church's long history.[14] Citing "hidden gospels" and a preposterous reading of letters between Abelard and Heloise, Macy—and his comrades—stretch the truth to support their heresy. Counter to the beliefs of the radical feminists and the other dissidents in the Church, the inability to ordain women to the priesthood is not an arbitrary decision on the part of sexist Church leaders who could easily do things differently if they chose. Rather, the inability to ordain women is the result of the Church's conscientious attempt to be faithful to the teachings and the will of Christ.

In contrast, priestly celibacy is a law or a regulation, not revealed truth or a rule derived from basic moral principles. Vows of celibacy—a promise to live a chaste, unmarried life—is a component of the priesthood that is modeled after Christ's example of giving himself solely for the ministry of his disciples and his Church. Still, priestly celibacy reflects the teaching of Jesus about the urgency of the Kingdom of God. Jesus taught that nothing is more important than God's love and God's action in our midst. Even the deepest human associations are secondary to the demands of God's love. The celibacy of the priest is witness to this teaching. It is not a matter of marriage being a less desirable vocation—or that women have the potential to "corrupt" the priest. Rather, priestly celibacy is a reminder to the faithful of the primacy of the role of the priest in helping to save souls. The presence of priests whose central purpose in life is to care for the Christian community as ordained leaders is a reflection of the love and attention that God provides to those who believe in him. The practice of celibacy has been a part of the priesthood for most of its history, and became a part of the Church's canon law in the Fourth Century. On February 10 in the year 385, Pope St. Siricius wrote that "the Lord Jesus wished the figure of the Church, whose Bridegroom he is, to radiate with the splendor of chastity, . . . so that from the day of our ordination we may devote our hearts and our bodies to moderation and modesty, to please the Lord our God in the daily sacrifices we offer him."

Despite this historical commitment to celibacy, the practice has been challenged from within and outside the Church. Even Pope Paul VI reconsidered the teaching in 1967, during the Second Vatican Council, releasing his encyclical *Sacerdotalis Caelibatus,* in which he affirmed the Church's teachings on celibacy and provided three primary reasons for its defense: Christological, ecclesiological, and eschatological. Priestly celibacy is Christological in the sense that it mirrors Christ's life on earth and his complete sacrifice and service to God and his people. Second, the vow of a priest to live a celibate life is ecclesiological, meaning that it allows him to give of himself in complete service to his pastoral duties within the Church and her people. *Sacerdotalis Caelibatus* teaches that celibacy allows the priest to come to the altar and offer his whole life as a sacrifice. Finally, it is eschatological in the sense that it is a foreshadowing of the end of time, because as the scriptures state, "in the resurrection they neither marry nor are given in marriage, but are like the angels in heaven."

When a priest completes his formal seminary training, he is officially ordained a priest within the Church, and is radically altered forever during the Rite of Ordination. During the Ordination Mass, the local bishop calls each new priest by name and calls on the power of God to conform these men for priestly ministry within the Church. The actual ordination takes place at the laying on of hands and prayer by the bishop, and in that moment, the priest is sealed for Christ and his Church—not just during his earthly life, but forever. The Catechism describes this as an indelible seal that can never be altered— even in the unfortunate cases when a priest is defrocked and removed from his priestly ministry, he is still a priest: it is in his spiritual DNA: "as in the case of Baptism and Confirmation this share in Christ's office is granted once for all. The Sacrament of Holy Orders, like the other two, confers an indelible spiritual character and cannot be repeated or conferred temporarily. While it is true that someone validly ordained can, for grave reasons, be discharged from the obligations and functions linked to ordination, or can be forbidden to exercise them, he cannot become a lay man again because the character imprinted by ordination is forever. The vocation and mission received on the day of his ordination mark him permanently.[15]

Despite the Attacks, the Joy of Priesthood Remains

The clergy abuse scandal of the last decade and the recent attacks on the religious liberty of the Church herself have made the job of the priest a difficult one indeed. In the midst of the clergy abuse scandals, priests were verbally abused and sometimes physically attacked. In an October 2011 opinion piece in the *Huffington Post,* writer Michele Somerville disparagingly described the Catholic Church as a

> corrupt organization led by a there-but-for-the grace-of-extradition-agreements-go-I pontiff. . . . Were Ratzinger not head of a sovereign state, the world might well have witnessed his perp walk by now. . . . The Vatican is on Amnesty International's list of torturers for its human rights violations/crimes against children. . . . Survivors Network of Persons Abused by Priests have filed a lawsuit against the Vatican in the Criminal Courts. Yet, even as it faces the possibility of a trial at the Hague, the Vatican continues to show poor faith in addressing the hundreds of thousands of brutal crimes against its own children.[16]

Such criticisms have become commonplace in the media. One needs to look no further than the reader comments section of any online news article or editorial that mentions the Church to conclude that Catholicism—and the priesthood in particular—is one of the most corrupt institutions in society. Much of the criticisms are directed at the hierarchy—and the priests—and reflect a spirit of anti-Catholicism in which the charism of the priesthood is denigrated. Opinion editors like Maureen Dowd and Nicholas Kristof of the *New York Times* are constant critics of the Catholic Church. In a recent Dowd piece she calls Catholic priests and bishops the "crepuscular, medieval men who run the Catholic Church." Dowd complains that "Church leaders behave like adolescent boys, blinded by sex.... That's the problem with Inquisitors and censors: they become fascinated by what they deplore."[17] Dowd has been especially vitriolic in her attack on the celibacy requirement for priests and bishops—claiming that it is celibacy itself that has caused the clergy abuse scandal in the Church.

Like Dowd, some within the media present priests and bishops as psychologically inferior or defective compared with the laity, who are portrayed as leading normal and balanced lives. Father Stephen Rossetti, the president of the Saint Luke Institute in Silver Spring, Maryland, a place that is dedicated to the healing of troubled priests, recalls that he often hears from those outside the priesthood that "a celibate, male Roman Catholic priesthood is defective and abnormal." In such a climate it is not hard to understand how such disparagement might cause a weakening of priestly identity and morale.[18] But, it has not. Rossetti concludes that it is not celibacy that is the cause for "troubled priests."

Despite the continued attacks on the priesthood, survey data demonstrate that most priests are happier than ever with their vocation—even happier than most lay persons are in their careers. Two surveys completed by Father Rossetti—the first in 2004, and a follow-up in 2009—provide compelling evidence that not only demonstrates that priests are happy with their vocation, but that they are engaging in greater spiritual discipline, and have strongly embraced the celibate life as one of the essential elements of the priesthood. In 2004, only two years after the *Boston Globe*'s Pulitzer Prize–winning coverage of the clergy sexual abuse scandal, 90 percent of priests agreed with the statement "Overall, I am happy as a priest." In 2009, the number of priests who agreed with that same statement had increased to 92.4 percent.[19] In addition, when asked if they would choose the priesthood if they could go back and do it all over again, over 80 percent said yes. While many Americans suffer from depression and serious work-related stress, on the whole, priests are one of the happiest and most fulfilled working classes in the country. These positive data on priestly satisfaction compare favorably with job satisfaction for other Americans. In 1987, the Conference Board completed a survey of five thousand households in America and found that 61.1 percent of Americans were satisfied with their jobs. The same survey, in 2009, found that the number of Americans who were satisfied with their jobs had decreased to 45 percent of households.

The high levels of job satisfaction for priests is something that emerges when priests fully embrace the teaching of the Church and her devotional practices. When priests were surveyed about their spiritual habits, devotion to Mary was consistently found to be an important characteristic in the life of priests—and a strong predictor for priestly success and satisfaction. In addition, devotion to Mary is consistently found as increasing one's devotion and closeness to God. Cardinal Edwin O'Brien, former archbishop of Baltimore and now grand master of the Equestrian Order of the Holy Sepulchre of Jerusalem, has observed: "in those parishes and dioceses where there is an abundance of Eucharistic adoration, there is an abundance of priestly vocations."[20]

At their ordination, all priests make a vow to pray the Liturgy of the Hours. While some priests may consider this too time consuming, the priests who are faithful to this promise reveal that they find themselves to be closer to God. Moreover, the priest prays the Liturgy of the Hours for the Church and the world. This means that when priests are consistent in their prayer, they are not the sole benefactors—we all benefit from the grace that is given by God. When Pope Benedict instituted the Year for Priests in 2009, he made a specific call for priests to receive the Sacrament of Reconciliation (Confession) more frequently. The same 2009 survey by Father Rossetti confirms that the priests who participate in the Sacrament of Reconciliation more often are not only closer to God but also have higher morale. All Catholics are required to go to Confession once a year, and if the priest who offers the sacrament is not regularly receiving it as well, he does a disservice to his flock.

While public opinion polls indicate that non-Catholics and progressive Catholics see celibacy as a deterrent for future vocations to the priesthood, the reality is that among newly ordained priests, support for celibacy is actually on the rise. Over 75 percent of priests agreed with the statement "despite its challenges, celibacy has been a grace for me," with only 11.8 percent disagreeing with the statement. As Father Rossetti concludes in his study, if these trends continue, support for mandatory celibacy will continue to increase among priests, and the challenges to celibacy will cease to be a "hot button issue" for critics of the priesthood.[21]

Beyond a strong spiritual life, Father Rossetti found that one of the strongest contributors to priestly happiness and morale is the ability to build healthy relationships with other priests and people in the community. A happy priest is one who has close friendships with other priests and with lay people—able to share his life, emotions, and challenges with others: "building communion and community is constitutive part of priestly life." The relationship with his bishop is also important. Father Rossetti's survey data reveals that if a priest has a good relationship with his bishop and continues to value his promise of obedience, he is much more likely to be a happy priest. In *Presbyterorum Ordinis* of the Second Vatican Council, the bishop is counseled to regard the priest as his "indispensable adviser." On the priests' part, the same document states: "the very unity of priests' consecration and mission requires their hierarchical union with the order of bishops."[22]

Father Rossetti writes that promising obedience to one's bishop is an integral part of the Rite of Ordination and we priests ought not to dismiss it: "I believe it is fair to say that the priest who is not obedient to his bishop, barring major and obvious malfeasance on the part of the bishop, is not being faithful to his priesthood. . . . This is not the obedience of slaves, but of free men. . . . Exercising our priestly promise of obedience is inherently an affirmation that, as individuals, we do not know everything. It is also an affirmation of our belief that the Holy Spirit works through our Church, especially its leaders."[23]

Similarly, *Same Call, Different Men*, a new book by Mary Gautier, Paul Perl, and Stephen Fichter, research associates at the Center for Applied Research in the Apostolate at Georgetown University, reveals that not only are priests relatively satisfied with their lives and ministries but priestly satisfaction with their chosen vocation has been increasing over time even in the midst of the decline in the total number of priests, and the sexual abuse scandal. For example, the 91 percent of priests who described themselves as either "somewhat" or "very" satisfied in response to the 2002 *Los Angeles Times* survey of priests, conducted at the height of the sexual abuse scandal, was actually up slightly from 89 percent in 1993. In 2009, 97 percent of all priests indicated that they would "probably" or "definitely" not leave the priesthood. This proportion has risen steadily from 88 percent when the question was first asked in 1970. Similarly, the percentage who would probably or definitely choose the priesthood again, currently at 95 percent, is up from 79 percent in 1970.[24]

Gautier and her colleagues noted that that today's younger priests are more satisfied than younger priests were in years past. In 1985, 44 percent of full-time associate pastors said they would "definitely not" leave the priesthood. By 2009, this proportion had risen to 93 percent.[25] It is likely that the underlying reason that satisfaction has increased so much among the younger priests is, as Gautier and her colleagues acknowledge, "the greater orthodoxy among priests of the millennial ordination cohort—a cohort that includes some older members, but two thirds of which consists of priests currently in their 30 and 40s. By greater orthodoxy, we mean the more 'traditionalist' positions they take on theology, ecclesiology, liturgy, sexual morality, faithfulness to the magisterium and related topics."[26] Today's millennial priests find affirmation for their beliefs from the Church's hierarchy—and this may translate into a feeling of greater support from Church leadership. In the Gautier study, 73 percent of priests under forty report receiving "strong" support from the Vatican. In 1993, this was the case for just 33 percent of priests under thirty. These young priests are also more likely to report strong support from their own bishops (79 percent of those under forty in 2009 compared to 52 percent of those under forty in 1993).

Satisfaction with their choice of vocation to the priesthood is also enhanced when priests believe more strongly in maintaining a clear distinction between priests and laity. Gautier, Perl, and Fichter found that younger priests are more satisfied with the priesthood if they have embraced what these researchers call the "cultic" model of priesthood—one that tends to place more emphasis on maintaining a distinctive priestly identity, concerned with maintaining the view of the priest as a "man set apart." While we would not call this a "cultic" model as these researchers have done, we would suggest that an orthodox view of the priesthood would indeed view the priest as a "man set apart" because he has been set apart through the laying on of hands at ordination in his distinctive ministry as a representative of Jesus Christ here on earth.

The New Evangelization

Many of the newly ordained priests during the last decade have been referred to as evangelical priests. While the meaning of the term "evangelical" may differ for some, the labeling of newer priests as evangelical priests indicates that those entering the priesthood share the same religious fervor in their priestly ministry that many of their evangelical (Protestant) counterparts are known for and what George Weigel refers to as a "deep friendship with Jesus Christ." The same intensity and excitement that fueled the Protestant camp meetings during the Second Great Awakening and the Billy Graham crusades of the later 20th century is now being matched by Catholic priests and bishops who are participating in what Pope John Paul II, coining the term, called "the new evangelization." While the roots of the new evangelization begin with the papacy of Pope Paul VI, it was John Paul II's 1990 encyclical *Redemptoris Missio* (Mission of the Redeemer), that clearly defined the term. In the encyclical, John Paul II identifies three aspects of the Church's evangelical work: reaching those who have never heard the gospel, a special focus on those already living a faithful Christian life, and finally, a new target area "in countries with ancient Christian roots, and occasionally in the younger Church as well, where entire groups of baptized have lost a sense of the faith, or even no longer consider themselves members of the Church, and live a life far removed from Christ and his gospel." In this case what is needed is a "new evangelization" or a "reevangelization."[27] During his papacy, John Paul II witnessed firsthand the growing nominalism of Catholic faith and practice in Europe and much of the Western world.

In John Paul II's 1990 apostolic exhortation *Ecclesia in America*, he advised: "the commemoration of the 500 yeas of evangelization will achieve its full meaning if it becomes a commitment by the bishops, together with the priests and people, a commitment not to a reevangelization, but to a new evangelization—new in ardor, methods, and expression." To meet the needs of a growing Catholic population, the USCCB has made a commitment to increasing priestly vocations. John Paul II famously remarked: "the Church does not impose, she only proposes."[28] Part of this proposal requires a renewed appreciation for the leadership role of priests and bishops—especially as they confront greater challenges to religious liberty and authority from outside and within the Church.

CATHOLIC RENEWAL: THE GOOD NEWS

For the Church to continue on her path to renewal, she must present a bold witness to Catholicism—one that is unapologetic in its defense of the timelessness of its teaching, yet one that is inviting and attractive. During the papacies of John Paul II and Benedict XVI—and now Pope Francis—we have seen several movements that reflect this and offer a necessary roadmap for the future.

The New Evangelization and New Media

The Reverend Robert Barron probably knows better than any other contemporary Catholic how the media can help the Church come to be viewed again as what he has called "the integrating heart of the culture."[1] Dedicated to proclaiming the gospel through the use of modern media, Father Barron founded the organization Word on Fire Catholic Ministries, at the request of Cardinal George of Chicago. In 2011, Word on Fire created *Catholicism*, a ten-part DVD series that was broadcast on EWTN and ninety public broadcast television stations throughout the country. The series covers the major themes of the Catholic faith in what can only be called a breathtakingly beautiful worldwide tour of Catholicism's most beautiful art, architecture, music, doctrine, liturgy, and extraordinary people.[2] In an interview published in *Catholic World Report*, Father Barron said that he was motivated to create the series because he "wanted to show the life-affirming message of the Gospel—that God became human that we might become like God." Most viewers of the series have indicated that this message has indeed come through. One priest who viewed the program told the interviewer for the *Catholic World Report* article that he had never seen such a confident public presentation of the Catholic faith. Father Barron replied: "I wanted the program to be a bold and confident, but not a cocky or off-putting, presentation. But bold and confident has been the way of the Church before me. There was St. Paul, who obviously represented a bold Catholicism. Think of G. K. Chesterton, think of Archbishop Fulton Sheen, and their boldness in proclaiming the gospel and the Church. We have this well-established instinct for self-critique nowadays, but I wanted to present the fuller and affirmative picture of the Church."[3]

Father Barron said that he wanted to reach three different audiences: inactive Catholics, active Catholics, and finally, the wider secular culture. His hope was that regular Catholics will feel proud and uplifted and newly informed about their faith. He also hopes that what he calls the

> "drifted-away Catholic" will find that it intrigues him enough
> to take another look . . . I hope he will be given a new sense
> of Catholicism . . . I am a von Balthasar guy so I believe that it
> is beauty that will bring people to God. You look at La Sainte-
> Chapelle in Paris, at the Sistine Chapel, and you cannot help
> but be drawn into something outside yourself. The visuals
> throughout the series are meant to draw people into the mes-
> sage of Catholicism . . . a way to address the good, the true, and
> the beautiful . . . Jesus Christ is the proper lure of all three of
> these dimensions of culture. . . Jesus addresses them all. And
> so you propose Jesus under those rubrics in terms of the series
> . . . we are using the arts and using the intellectual tradition.
> We wanted to show that there is something for those people in
> those cultural realms in the series.[4]

Father Barron has said that Pope John Paul II had a large influence on his decision to undertake what most would view as an overwhelming project. He recalls that "the new evangelization was what he [Pope John Paul] was proposing. . . . The idea of trying to evangelize a culture that knows Christ but that has lapsed into a certain forgetfulness was something he highlighted."[5] The project was guided by a love for the faith that all faithful Catholics can understand and celebrate.

Catholics Come Home

Beyond Father Barron's extraordinary series, the Catholics Come Home initiative has been a successful evangelizing effort designed to "inspire, educate and evangelize inactive Catholics and others, and invite them to live a deeper faith in Jesus Christ, in accord with the Magisterium of the Roman Catholic Church."[6] Catholics Come Home is an independent, nonprofit Catholic apostolate that creates effective and compassionate media messages and broadcasts them nationally and internationally, in an effort to lead to a genuine "enculturation of the Gospel."

Like the *Catholicism* series, Catholics Come Home was inspired by Pope John Paul's call to a new evangelization by reaching out to inactive Catholics using the media in creating inspiring TV commercials and an interactive website. Without obligation or pressure, Catholics Come Home offers an opportunity to learn the truth about the Catholic faith in a nonjudgmental atmosphere. As many as one hundred thousand baptized Catholics in the United States drift away from church each year. This initiative attempts to address this population by offering resources that will help nonpracticing Catholics learn more about returning to the Church. Their slogan is "We are Family . . . Coming Home Has Never Been Easier."

Their work has already made a difference. Most Reverend Michael Sheridan, bishop of the Diocese of Colorado Springs, wrote that the television campaign has had a significant impact on hundreds of viewers in his diocese. Many of his priests received positive feedback from parishioners and non-church-attending Catholics who accepted our invitation to "come home" to the Church. While the campaign is not yet a nationwide presence, there has been a 6–10 percent increase in Mass attendance in those dioceses where the campaign has been implemented—including the dioceses of Colorado Springs, Venice (Florida), Atlanta, Savannah, Chicago, Rockford, Joliet (Illinois), Baton Rouge, New Orleans, Lafayette, Boston, Manchester (New Hampshire), Winona, Charlotte, Bismarck, Fargo, Omaha, Lincoln, Erie, Providence, Corpus Christi, Seattle, and Green Bay.

In an endorsement on the Catholics Come Home website, Boston College professor and author Peter Kreeft, a convert to the faith, wrote that "Catholics Come Home is a powerful sacramental, a means of grace. . . a willing, waiting taxi to take us home, to our home away from Home, the Catholic Church, the Mystical Body of Christ."[7]

As important as is the message to those Catholics who have drifted away, an equally valuable effect of the Come Home campaign has been the nurturing of the importance of a welcoming parish. Evangelical Churches in the Protestant tradition are places where families are celebrated. Many Catholic parishes have lost that spirit of evangelization—but the Come Home campaign is helping them reclaim it. In addition to the Catholics Come Home initiative, the EncouragePriests.org initiative was launched on Holy Thursday in 2010 by the same nonprofit Catholic media apostolate as the one that has produced Catholics Come Home. And like the Coming Home message, the EncouragePriests.org site hopes to develop and air multimedia messages that recognize the heroic nature of the priesthood. Visitors to the website find ways to learn more about the priesthood and show gratitude to priests who have touched their lives. Lay Catholics can print and deliver cards of thanks or send short e-cards (they call them "collar-hollers") to their priests. There are also written stories and one-minute video testimonial clips from Catholics who want to share a story about a priest who has inspired them.[8]

The Fellowship of Catholic University Students

In 1998, Curtis Martin and his wife, Michaelann, founded the Fellowship of Catholic University Students (FOCUS). Inspired by the work of the evangelical group Campus Crusade for Christ, Martin recognized the need for Catholic campus missionaries to strengthen young believers in their Catholic faith and witness to those who were in search for a deeper meaning to their lives. At the invitation of Archbishop Chaput, Martin established FOCUS in Denver. Dedicated to "inviting college students into a growing relationship with Jesus Christ and his Church," FOCUS works to "inspire and equip them for a lifetime of Christ-centered evangelization, discipleship, and friendships in which they lead others to do the same."[9] A 2008 CARA study found that age twenty-one was the median age when Catholics are most prone to losing their faith. So FOCUS directly addresses this by providing reinforcement to the faith of young, college-age students within this demographic.[10] Having begun his ministry under Pope John Paul II, who advised Martin to use FOCUS to "be soldiers," Martin was invited by Pope Benedict XVI to be one of his two American advisors on the newly formed Pontifical Council for Promoting New Evangelization.

Martin, who was raised Catholic, lost his faith during his teenage years. He describes his faith during this time as not only dead but also hostile to religion. When he entered college, he began interacting with evangelical Protestants—missionaries from Campus Crusade for Christ. And it was through their ministry that Martin found a renewed interest in scripture. While he briefly considered himself Protestant, he eventually found his way back to the Church—but this time with a renewed zeal for evangelism. Realizing that the Catholic Church did not have an equivalent ministry to Campus Crusade, he decided to start FOCUS. Today the group has grown to over 260 missionaries on sixty college campuses throughout the United States—all of whom are eager to join Martin in this work of promoting the New Evangelization.

Like the early apostles who were called to bear witness to the transformative power of the life of Jesus Christ despite widespread unbelief and criticism, Curtis Martin sees a new period of transformation within the Church in the aftermath of the sexual abuse crisis: "out of the ashes of this terrible scandal that rocked the Church, men are entering seminaries who are men of faith and action, who are entering for all the right reasons. They are part of a tremendous renewal in the Church."[11]

Catholic Voices

Founded in Britain, Catholic Voices is a new organization dedicated to training lay Catholics to offer articulate and compelling arguments for an active role of the Church in the public square. During Pope Benedict's 2010 Papal Visit, journalist Austen Ivereigh found himself "troubled by the British bishops' struggle to counter partisan attacks on Church policy dealing with AIDS and condoms, same-sex marriage and abortion,"[12] and in response founded Catholic Voices to train lay Catholics to speak to the media. Since then, the work of Catholic Voices has reached the United States, Mexico, Spain, Chile, Poland, Lithuania, and Ireland. Just in time to respond to the Health and Human Services mandate, Catholic Voices USA is now operating in New York and Washington, D.C., spearheaded by Kathryn Jean Lopez. While programs like Catholic Voices are the first of their kind, they offer a promising new model to begin changing public perception of the Church. Rather than relying on Church dissidents like Gary Wills and Peter Steinfelds to serve as authorities on the Church in America, Catholic Voices aims to present real Catholics who embrace the faith and teachings of their Church.

Potential Priests and Sisters

In October 2012, a study from CARA found that there are an abundance of potential priests, deacons, and religious brothers and sisters —by their estimates, almost six hundred thousand individuals who have seriously considered a vocation. This is welcome news for a Catholic population that continues to grow and needs the support of religious life. Among the report's findings is the "correlation between various practices, such as weekly Mass attendance, participation in Bible study, retreats, prayer groups or Eucharistic adoration, those who pray the Rosary or whom have a devotion to Mary, those who participate in parish ministry and those who regularly read the Bible or pray with scripture, with those who are especially likely to have considered a vocation. For male respondents, those who attended World Youth Day or a National Catholic Youth Conference were more than four times more likely than those who had not to consider becoming a priest or brother."[13]

This is only further proof that renewal is, in fact, taking place within the Church. While the study indicates that there is a large number of individuals who are considering religious life, they remain untapped. While they must first be guided by the call of the Holy Spirit, their vocations can and should be encouraged by parents, family members, and current members already in religious life. In June 2012 at a conference at St. Charles Borromeo Seminary in Philadelphia, Los Angeles archbishop Jose Gomez encouraged seminarians and potential seminarians to take culture seriously. "Culture is crucial to the new evangelization. . . the first Catholic missionaries in America were serious students of the indigenous cultures." In the same way that these missionaries understood their culture, Gomez encouraged his audience to study and understand American culture in order to transform it.[14] When seminarians—and the Church, at large—accept this challenge, they will find that more and more people respond to the call of religious life as something they want to be a part of.

A United Hierarchy

In April 2012, the Committee on Evangelization and Catechesis of the USCCB issued their manifesto *Disciples Called to Witness: The New Evangelization*. This plan of action is meant to capitalize on the current momentum of groups like FOCUS and Catholics Come Home, with a special focus on revitalized parish life. While this is already happening through various high school catechetical programs and youth groups, there remains work to be done in providing strong marriage training for new couples so that they can later establish strong Catholic families that will ultimately be what sustains Catholic parish life. Ultimately, however, strong participation in the liturgical life of the Church will yield a stronger commitment to parish life. As *Disciples Called to Witness* states, "the active participation and practice of the liturgy, prayers, devotions, and popular piety of the Church provide a powerful witness to the faith."[15]

Whereas the leadership of the USCCB may have been plagued by partisan politics and infighting, recent years have seen shown a commitment to the truths of Catholicism that must begin with a call to holiness. In a November 2012 address to the conference, President Timothy Cardinal Dolan urged his brother bishops to first examine their own hearts as a first and necessary step to bring about cultural renewal. "That's the way we become channels of a truly effective transformation of the world, through our own witness of a repentant heart. . . . The premier answer to the question 'What's wrong with the world?' is not politics, the economy, sectarianism, globalization, or global warming." Instead Dolan offered the words of Catholic convert G. K. Chesterton as his answer: "I am."[16]

Needed Reform

Yet, while these are real road markers for the renewal of the Church, there are still some serious threats ahead that must be reckoned with in order for the Church to be the mission that she is called to be. These challenges must be confronted directly and with a bold, unwavering courage.

Catholic Higher Education

Once great Catholic institutions like Georgetown, Fordham, Boston College, Notre Dame, and many others remain trapped in the 1960s and 1970s era progressivism that dominated the academy and are sustained under the banner of academic freedom and the tenure system. Most recently, in a 2008 study of students at Catholic colleges and universities 57 percent of the respondents said "the experience of attending a Catholic college or university had no effect on their participation in Mass and the sacrament of reconciliation," and 54 percent of respondents said that "their experience of attending a Catholic college or university had no effect on their support for the teachings of the Catholic Church." Another 56 percent said "their experience had no effect on their respect for the Pope and bishops."[17] If the anecdotal evidence provided in the previous chapters aren't enough, then surely these numbers are the telltale sign that something is clearly wrong. If Catholic administrators on these campuses desire authentic Catholic renewal, we maintain that the only means to beginning this process is through a full and complete implementation of *Ex Corde Ecclesiae*. This will require shake-ups within most departments of most Catholic institutions, and they will likely need to begin with the theology departments, where dissident faculty members are busy training their replacements, who will be future impediments to the success of the New Evangelization on these campuses.

This will require bold and courageous leadership by Catholic presidents and administrators, and they will need to receive the vocal support and political willpower of the remnant of faithful Catholic faculty members who remain on these campuses. They should also expect support from their bishops—a support that evidences real teeth and determination and does not shy away from hard truths, unlike the most recent USCCB ten-year review of *Ex Corde*. The USCCB should give serious consideration to launching a full audit review of Catholic colleges and universities throughout the country. Such a review would require thorough recommendations on necessary changes with real penalties for those institutions that do not fall in line—including the possibility of the stripping away of their Catholic title. These may appear to be radical proposals, but they are the only necessary response to the radical state of affairs at most Catholic institutions. Getting Catholic education right is essential for passing along the faith to future generations of Catholic families. Simply put, the work of evangelization cannot be fully realized until this reform begins to take place.

Reproductive Technologies

While a widespread embrace of contraception has become common among Catholics and non-Catholics alike, the past decade has given witness to a rapid increase in and reliance on reproductive technologies—namely, through *in vitro* fertilization, sperm and egg donor conceived children, and surrogacy. As such, some commentators have described the twenty-first century as "the biotech century." The Church must know how to respond to this growing phenomenon.

While television shows are quick to offer an optimistic message that this is, indeed, "The New Normal" and we must adapt to the "Modern Family," social science research indicates that children are not benefiting from this morphing of family life. Given this, we must begin to ask the question, are we willing to give a full-throttled endorsement of the idea that sex—and hence the institution of marriage, traditionally understood—can be divorced from children? Can the very act that has defined marriage be replaced by reproductive technologies? The Church's answer has always been no, but too often it has come at the expense of isolating those individuals within the Church who are suffering from infertility.

A 2010 report from the Institute for American Values found that the majority of sperm donor conceived children were born into Catholic households.[18] Similarly, there are several reports of pro-life groups encouraging college-age men and women to donate their sperm and eggs because it helps give the gift of life. This is only further evidence of a generation of parents and children suffering from poor catechesis. In 1987, the Congregation for the Doctrine of the Faith issued *Donum Vitae* (Instruction on Respect for Human Life), in which the Church officially forbade the use of in vitro fertilization (IVF), stating: "the child has the right to be conceived, carried in the womb, brought into the world and brought up within marriage. The good of society requires that children come into the world within a family and that the family be based on marriage, the only setting worthy of truly responsible procreation." Most recently, in his 2012 book *True Freedom: On Protecting Human Dignity and Religious Liberty*, Cardinal Dolan noted this is "another example of what I want, when I want, because I want. We can read articles about couples who want to design their own baby, essentially ordering one from a catalog. . . . Many people have babies, if at all, to satisfy their own desires, not to sacrifice for the child's."[19] This misguided understanding of freedom and personal autonomy drives the industry of reproductive technology, and unfortunately Catholics are falling into this trap at the same rate as non-Catholics. A Catholic response requires the Church to deal with the issue of infertility—providing more thoughtful counseling and guidance to couples seeking a child and wanting to contribute to the culture of life that the Church promotes. As technologies become more available—and acceptable—Catholic priests and bishops need to be better informed and willing to speak with grace, charity, and truth.

Learning Lessons from Europe

The future of the Church in Europe is bleak. In his 2002 apostolic letter *Ecclesia in Europa,* Pope John Paul II lamented the situation in Europe, describing "the loss of Europe's Christian memory and heritage, accompanied by a kind of practical agnosticism and religious indifference whereby many Europeans give the impression of living without spiritual roots and somewhat like heirs who have squandered a patrimony entrusted to them by history. It is no real surprise, then, that there are efforts to create a vision of Europe that ignores its religious heritage, and in particular, its profound Christian soul, asserting the rights of the peoples who make up Europe without grafting those rights on to the trunk which is enlivened by the sap of Christianity."[20] Joseph Ratzinger had these same concerns in mind when he chose the title Benedict, drawing on the order of Benedictine monks who educated and evangelized Europe during the Dark Ages in hopes that his papacy could do the same. Today, the Church in Europe remains flanked with all sorts of problems—the looming threat of Islam, a demographic winter, negligible Mass attendance, and society that openly rejects Church teaching on almost every matter of social policy in favor of a "dictatorship of relativism."

Unlike the Church in Europe, the Church in America continues to grow in membership and through its religious life. Yet as the Health and Human Services mandate evidences, Catholics are now having to learn how to practice their faith in an environment that is increasingly hostile to its teachings. For Catholics to truly practice faithful citizenship in America, this requires a first and prior commitment to personal holiness. As individual Catholics learn to live lives that are distinctly Catholic, this will have a reverberating effect in their families, parishes, communities, and so forth. This is the type of Catholicism that is able to combat the dictatorship of relativism so as to prevent it from plaguing America—indeed, it is the only type of Catholicism for the twenty-first-century Church.

A Public Proposal

John Paul II taught that the Church is not here to impose her beliefs or teachings, but rather to propose a better way that promotes the human flourishing of all people. Part of this requires that Church leaders and laity alike make arguments that appeal to reason, rather than faith alone. During the last decades of the twentieth century, Italy approved new laws on abortion and divorce that are contrary to the Church's teaching. Church leaders made their arguments in opposition to these laws simply by appealing to religious authority, and as a result, they lost. In 2005, however, the Italian Church leaders tried a new approach while debating a referendum on reproductive technology. As George Weigel notes in *The Cube and the Cathedral*, "the Church's leaders made a different kind of argument, a genuinely public argument, to the effect that turning human reproduction into a technological process and declaring open season on human embryos would be very bad for Italian democracy.... The authority of the Church was not invoked; the authority of genuinely public moral argument was effectively deployed." Using such language, the Church persuaded minds and hearts, and won the referendum. In recent years, similar approaches have been used in the abortion debates—and so far, it appears to be working. In May 2012, Gallup released the results of its most recent data that found only "41 percent of Americans now identify themselves as 'pro-choice.' This is down from 47 percent last July and is one percentage point below the previous record low in Gallup trends. Fifty percent now call themselves 'pro-life,' one point shy of the record high." Indeed, being pro-life is considered the new normal for Americans today, and this has been achieved by appeals to science and medicine—not simply by quoting scripture. This is the type of model that must be employed as the Church continues to engage in cultural and political debates on gay marriage and religious freedom.

Renewal

In an interview published in *Time* in 2008 titled "Is Liberal Catholicism Dead?," Terrence Tilley, chairman of Fordham University's Theology Department, lamented: "for a couple of generations, progressivism was an important way to be Catholic . . . but I think the end of an era is here."[21] Tilley points out that the millennial generation of Catholics—like the young coauthor of this book—born in the 1980s or later, share greater concern for social justice issues and may differ from their parents' generation on some issues. But, unlike the earlier generation of progressive Catholics, this generation is not looking for a fight with their bishops. They do not seek to change the Church's teachings on reproductive rights, marriage, or women's ordination. This generation is attracted to the Church because of the timelessness of these teachings. They are attracted to the ability of the Church to answer many of the much bigger questions about their lives. They accept the teachings of the Church, as an overwhelming majority of them are pro-life and respect the Church as the only major institution left that will stand up for life.

These millennial Catholics have been shaped by the events of September 11, 2001, the wars in Afghanistan and Iraq, the devastating effects of natural disasters such as Katrina and the 2004 tsunami that wreaked havoc on Thailand and Indonesia, and the awful acts of violence witnessed in Columbine, Aurora, Newtown, and elsewhere. Yet unlike their parents, who suffered from a Church reeling from the aftereffects of a poor implementation of Vatican II and still trying to make sense of its role in the world, these young Catholics understood early that the Church was a place where they could find meaning—a place that transcended their everyday lives. Seeking some stability in a society that seemed to be changing so dramatically, many of them—some of them young converts to the faith—are finding these answers in the Church and her teachings. They are not anxious to change those teachings, and they are not involved in a power struggle with their priests and bishops. As the massive crowds at World Youth Day every two to three years suggest, this is a generation that is proud to be referred to as "the John Paul II or Pope Benedict XVI generation." As Tilley suggested, we have a new generation of priests, bishops, and laity that "has neither the baggage nor the ballast of mine. . . . Theirs is the future."[22]

Theirs is the future, indeed, but in order to bring about authentic Catholic renewal, the Church must continue in her task of teaching and proposing hard truths when it comes to protecting the unborn, protecting marriage, and fighting for religious freedom. A faithful Catholic college or a faithful Catholic hospital is qualitatively different from a secular one because its Catholicism should permeate its very core. In contrast, progressive Catholics often deny this need for distinction. And those who will at least acknowledge that there are divisions in the Church suggest that the orthodox Catholics are the ones who create such polarization. In fact, there are many progressives who maintain that if the orthodox Catholic movement did not exist, there would be no polarization in the Church. They may be right. Perhaps we would all get along—and we would become the "welcoming" Church with female and openly gay priests that so many progressives dream of. Perhaps they prefer a model like that of the Episcopal Church, though this embrace of everything and nothing has not worked out especially well for them.

Unlike the dark days following Vatican II, when it appeared to the faithful that the Church they knew was disappearing, there is great hope that the bishops have joined the fight in defending the nonnegotiable teachings of the Church. As the previous chapters have pointed out, there is a growing number of courageously outspoken bishops unafraid to publicly confront some of the most powerful progressives. The bishops' strong protest against Notre Dame's honoring of President Obama and their unanimity in the face of the Health and Human Services contraceptive mandate is a hopeful sign of things to come on Catholic campuses and elsewhere.

As we conclude, many readers might be wondering if we are sending a mixed message—perhaps some may think that we've described more areas of conflict than we have renewal. Indeed, we have described the contentiousness surrounding reproductive rights and women's ordination. We have explored the assault by the state on religious liberty and the current battles over traditional marriage. We have described the current battlegrounds—the Catholic college campuses that continue to give aid and comfort to those determined to change essential Church teachings to conform to the secular zeitgeist. We admit there are challenges that exist and that there are probably even greater challenges ahead. But our focus throughout has been on the priests and bishops who have fought and continue to fight so boldly to maintain these essential teachings. These courageous men will continue to fight because they know that they have to—they know that these teachings are essential to the faith—they are part of being "simply Catholic" as Cardinal George so succinctly said.

We know that there will always be battles within our culture and within our Church because we live in a fallen world. Since the time of the fall of Adam and Eve, we have been faced with the task of reconciling our broken human condition, and a world marred by sin, with our understanding and hope of the world that is to come. We remain Walker Percy's pilgrims—his strangers in a strange land—realizing that our true home lies elsewhere. In this lifetime, the only way we hope to get a glimpse of perfection, of full healing, and of the divine, is through the sacraments. The sacrament of Reconciliation restores us to full communion with the Church, the sacrament of Baptism gives us new life and the hope of life eternal, the sacrament of Marriage reflects the unity of the Holy Trinity, and most important, the sacrament of Holy Communion allows us to physically taste and see Christ made present for us in a physical, real way.

None of these sacraments can happen without priests. Christ has promised us priests because he knew that we cannot be without them—they are the earthly instruments of our renewal. The sacramental life of the Church depends on priests. It is the priest, through the sacrament of Holy Orders, who receives the power to bestow onto us a means to see and experience life beyond the culture wars because the priest, and only the priest, provides to us an understanding of our real home—even if limited—on earth, as it is in heaven.

Appendices

Ordinations By Diocese from 2003-2011

Diocese	2003	2004	2005	2006	2007	2008	2009	2010	2011
Albany, NY	1	3	2	0	3	0	1	5	1
Alexandria, LA	4	0	3	1	3	1	0	2	0
Allentown, PA	2	5	0	1	1	1	3	1	1
Altoona-Johnstown, PA	1	0	0	4	1	0	3	1	1
Amarillo, TX	0	1	0	0	0	2	1	1	1
Anchorage, AK	0	0	1	0	0	0	0	0	0
Arlington, VA	3	1	4	7	0	3	3	3	3
Atlanta, GA	3	3	1	3	2	8	8	6	7
Austin, TX	2	3	0	2	3	5	5	7	2
Baker, OR	0	0	1	3	0	0	1	1	0
Baltimore, MD	7	3	2	7	4	1	4	1	1
Baton Rouge, LA	2	0	1	0	5	3	2	0	2
Beaumont, TX	2	0	3	1	0	1	0	0	0
Belleville, IL	1	0	2	1	2	1	0	4	1
Biloxi, MS	0	0	1	2	2	0	1	0	3
Birmingham, AL	3	3	1	0	4	2	0	2	1
Bismarck, ND	0	0	2	1	1	1	3	1	2
Boise, ID	2	2	1	4	0	6	2	5	0
Boston, MA	5	7	8	5	5	9	6	3	6
Bridgeport, CT	6	4	2	1	4	2	6	4	1
Brooklyn, NY	2	2	6	2	10	2	3	3	3
Brownsville, TX	2	3	0	4	4	1	2	1	3
Buffalo, NY	2	5	4	2	2	4	2	2	2

Diocese	2003	2004	2005	2006	2007	2008	2009	2010	2011
Burlington, VT	0	2	1	1	2	0	4	1	1
Camden, NJ	4	2	1	3	4	5	1	2	3
Charleston, SC	0	N/A	3	2	7	0	1	3	3
Charlotte, NC	3	3	1	1	6	1	1	4	4
Cheyenne, WY	2	0	2	2	0	1	1	1	0
Chicago, IL	16	16	17	12	14	13	9	14	10
Cincinnati, OH	6	8	3	5	3	3	7	2	3
Cleveland, OH	9	3	1	6	4	5	5	2	5
Colorado Springs, CO	0	0	1	0	1	2	0	1	4
Columbus, OH	1	6	2	1	2	1	1	3	2
Corpus Christi, TX	4	1	1	2	0	1	1	1	3
Covington, KY	0	1	1	2	0	2	4	2	1
Crookston, MN	0	0	0	1	0	1	1	1	0
Dallas, TX	0	2	0	3	1	1	1	0	3
Davenport, IA	3	1	1	1	0	2	0	1	0
Denver, CO	4	5	7	11	4	3	4	5	8
Des Moines, IA	1	2	0	2	1	0	2	1	0
Detroit, MI	6	9	3	3	1	5	5	6	3
Dodge City, KS	0	0	0	0	0	0	0	0	1
Dubuque, IA	2	4	1	1	2	1	2	0	2
Duluth, MN	1	0	4	0	3	1	2	0	1
El Paso, TX	0	0	0	0	1	0	0	2	2
Erie, PA	2	0	3	3	2	2	2	5	1
Evansville, IN	0	3	2	1	1	1	1	0	0
Fairbanks, AK	0	1	0	0	1	0	1	0	1
Fall River, MA	1	1	2	0	1	2	2	0	1
Fargo, ND	3	3	5	2	0	1	1	0	2
Ft. Wayne-South Bend, IN	0	1	1	1	2	12	2	1	2
Ft. Worth, TX	0	1	1	1	5	1	2	3	3
Fresno, CA	3	4	1	3	1	1	3	3	2
Gallup, NM	0	0	0	0	1	0	0	0	0
Galveston-Houston, TX	0	3	0	0	2	3	4	1	4
Gary, IN	0	1	1	1	0	3	0	1	0
Gaylord, MI	1	2	2	1	1	1	1	2	1

Diocese	2003	2004	2005	2006	2007	2008	2009	2010	2011
Grand Island, NE	0	1	0	0	0	0	3	2	1
Grand Rapids, MI	3	1	1	0	3	1	2	1	1
Great Falls-Billings, MT	0	0	1	1	0	1	1	1	0
Green Bay, WI	0	2	2	3	3	1	2	2	2
Greensburg, PA	0	0	0	0	2	0	0	0	0
Harrisburg, PA	2	3	1	3	1	1	4	2	1
Hartford, CT	3	2	0	6	2	2	2	5	5
Helena, MT	2	0	0	1	2	0	0	1	1
Honolulu, HI	0	0	0	0	3	0	1	0	4
Houma Thibodaux, LA	1	1	0	0	0	1	0	0	1
Indianapolis, IN	2	2	2	1	3	2	5	0	1
Jackson, MS	2	0	0	3	0	1	0	1	0
Jefferson City, MO	1	1	1	1	0	0	0	2	1
Joliet, IL	1	6	2	1	2	3	3	5	1
Juneau, AK	0	0	0	0	0	0	0	0	0
Kalamazoo, MI	2	1	3	5	0	1	4	0	1
Kansas City, KS	5	4	1	2	3	1	3	1	7
Kansas City-St. Joseph, MO	0	2	0	3	0	1	2	4	2
Knoxville, TN	0	0	3	1	3	1	2	1	1
LaCrosse, WI	3	0	0	0	0	0	0	0	0
Lafayette, LA	1	3	2	3	4	3	3	3	4
Lafayette, IN	0	0	0	0	0	1	1	4	4
Lake Charles, LA	N/A	0	0	0	1	2	0	1	2
Lansing, MI	3	3	5	0	1	0	1	4	3
Laredo, TX	0	0	0	0	2	0	0	0	0
Las Cruces, NM	0	0	3	0	1	0	2	1	0
Las Vegas, NV	0	1	2	0	0	0	1	0	0
Lexington, KY	0	1	1	0	3	3	1	2	2
Lincoln, NE	3	4	3	3	2	1	4	4	3
Little Rock, AR	1	1	2	0	1	0	2	5	0
Los Angeles, CA	4	6	5	4	5	12	6	3	6
Louisville, KY	1	4	0	3	0	1	0	2	2
Lubbock, TX	1	1	1	3	0	0	1	1	1
Madison, WI	3	0	0	0	0	4	3	4	2
Manchester, NH	5	1	2	3	1	0	2	0	1

Diocese	2003	2004	2005	2006	2007	2008	2009	2010	2011
Marquette, MI	1	2	0	1	2	3	2	0	0
Memphis, TN	0	1	2	1	2	1	6	2	3
Meteuchen, NJ	1	3	0	1	1	1	3	2	3
Miami, FL	6	4	3	5	4	6	3	4	0
Milwaukee, WI	2	2	3	5	3	1	6	5	6
Mobile, AL	0	2	1	0	0	0	0	4	2
Monterey, CA	0	1	2	2	0	0	2	2	0
Nashville, TN	0	0	0	1	1	3	1	1	1
Newark, NJ	9	14	12	17	13	9	13	12	18
New Orleans, LA	3	1	N/A	1	1	1	3	1	2
New Ulm, MN	0	1	0	1	1	0	0	0	1
New York, NY	4	13	7	5	7	6	3	7	4
Norwich, CT	4	0	2	2	0	3	1	1	1
Oakland, CA	1	4	4	3	2	3	1	1	4
Ogdensburg, NY	2	0	2	0	1	0	0	0	0
Oklahoma City, OK	1	2	1	1	0	3	2	0	1
Omaha, NE	4	2	5	4	3	3	0	1	4
Orange, CA	6	3	7	3	2	3	6	1	6
Orlando, FL	1	0	0	3	2	2	1	1	1
Owensboro, KY	2	0	0	0	0	0	2	3	1
Palm Beach, FL	4	3	1	1	0	2	2	1	2
Paterson, NJ	3	2	3	3	5	3	8	6	9
Pensacola-Tallahassee, FL	1	0	3	1	1	1	0	3	3
Peoria, IL	7	1	4	1	3	1	2	2	0
Philadelphia, PA	9	4	5	3	7	3	6	6	3
Phoenix, AZ	3	0	1	2	6	3	3	4	0
Pittsburgh, PA	1	4	2	1	3	3	4	3	4
Portland, ME	3	1	1	0	5	2	1	0	1
Portland, OR	0	2	3	2	3	2	6	·4	3
Providence, RI	4	7	1	3	4	5	3	3	2
Pueblo, CO	1	0	1	1	1	2	0	0	1
Raleigh, NC	3	1	0	0	2	2	0	1	1
Rapid City, SD	1	1	0	1	0	0	1	0	1
Reno, NV	1	2	1	0	1	0	0	0	0
Richmond, VA	1	0	1	4	2	0	1	2	2
Rochester, NY	1	1	1	0	2	1	1	0	1

Diocese	2003	2004	2005	2006	2007	2008	2009	2010	2011
Rockford, IL	12	2	4	9	7	7	2	3	7
Rockville Centre, NY	3	4	1	2	3	9	4	3	4
Sacramento, CA	8	2	1	4	9	3	2	3	4
Saginaw, MI	1	0	0	0	2	5	3	2	4
St. Augustine, FL	0	2	1	1	3	5	0	0	0
St. Cloud, MN	2	0	1	1	3	0	1	3	2
St. Louis, MO	8	1	1	4	4	9	4	8	4
St. Paul and Minneapolis, MN	7	6	15	5	8	6	3	7	5
St. Petersburg, FL	1	2	2	2	0	2	2	2	0
Salina, KS	1	1	1	0	0	0	1	2	1
Salt Lake City, UT	1	1	0	4	2	0	0	2	0
San Angelo, TX	2	0	0	3	0	0	0	0	2
San Antonio, TX	2	3	1	1	1	5	9	1	0
San Bernardino, CA	0	0	1	2	2	6	2	2	5
San Diego, CA	0	2	5	4	1	1	0	3	0
San Francisco, CA	2	4	2	6	3	2	3	2	1
San Jose, CA	3	1	5	2	2	1	7	3	3
Santa Fe, NM	5	4	2	0	1	3	2	3	0
Santa Rosa, CA	0	0	0	0	1	0	0	3	0
Savannah, GA	2	4	5	1	4	1	4	0	2
Scranton, PA	5	2	3	2	2	3	2	0	1
Seattle, WA	5	4	1	7	2	3	6	4	5
Shreveport, LA	0	0	0	0	0	0	1	0	0
Sioux City, IA	1	1	1	0	2	2	0	0	0
Sioux Falls, SD	2	2	2	2	4	2	2	3	5
Spokane, WA	1	1	0	3	4	1	0	1	4
Springfield-Cape Girardeau, MO	1	1	3	2	2	2	0	0	0
Springfield, IL	0	0	7	1	1	1	1	2	1
Springfield, MA	2	1	3	0	1	3	0	3	3
Steubenville, OH	1	3	3	0	1	0	2	0	1
Stockton, CA	0	0	1	0	3	2	0	1	2
Superior, WI	1	0	1	2	1	2	2	2	2
Syracuse, NY	1	2	3	0	2	1	1	1	1
Toledo, OH	2	1	1	4	1	2	5	1	3

Diocese	2003	2004	2005	2006	2007	2008	2009	2010	2011
Trenton, NJ	1	4	4	3	5	2	3	5	6
Tucson, AZ	5	0	0	2	1	4	1	0	0
Tulsa, OK	3	2	1	1	3	1	0	2	2
Tyler, TX	3	0	0	3	1	2	3	2	6
Venice, FL	2	4	3	3	0	0	3	2	2
Victoria, TX	0	1	0	1	2	1	1	0	0
Washington, DC	9	8	5	12	5	7	8	8	5
Wheeling-Charleston, WV	1	2	3	3	4	0	3	1	2
Wichita, KS	3	4	1	1	4	3	1	5	4
Wilmington, DE	3	3	2	2	3	1	2	2	3
Winnoa, MN	0	0	0	2	1	4	1	1	0
Worcester, MA	1	4	4	2	0	1	1	2	7
Yakima, WA	3	3	0	1	1	1	4	0	0
Youngstown, OH	1	0	2	1	1	1	0	3	4

Data from P. J. Kennedy and Sons, *Official Catholic Directory* (Providence, N.J.: National Register)

Bishops Opposing the Notre Dame Invitation and Award to President Obama

Bishop	Diocese (as of 2008)
Edward Cullen	Allentown, PA
Joseph V. Adamec	Altoona-Johnston, PA
John Yanta	Amarillo, TX
Paul Loverde	Arlington, VA
Gregory Aymond	Austin, TX
Robert Vasa	Baker, OR
Edwin O'Brien	Baltimore, MD
Robert Baker	Birmingham, AL
William E. Lori	Bridgeport, CT
Nicholas DiMarzio	Brooklyn, NY
Reymundo Pena	Brownsville, TX
Joseph Galante	Camden, NJ
Peter Jugis	Charlotte, NC
Francis George	Chicago, IL
Daniel E. Pilarczyk	Cincinnati, OH
Roger Gries	Cleveland, OH
Michael Sheridan	Colorado Springs, CO
Roger Foys	Covington, KY
Charles Chaput	Denver, CO
James Conley	Denver, CO
Allen Vigneron	Detroit, MI
Donald Trautman	Erie, PA
Gerald Gettelfinger	Evansville, IN
Samuel Aquila	Fargo, ND

Bishop	Diocese (as of 2008)
John D'Arcy	Fort Wayne-South Bend, IN
Dale Melczek	Gary, IN
Michael Warfel	Great Falls-Billings, MT
David Ricken	Green Bay, WI
Lawrence Brandt	Greensburg, PA
Kevin Rhoades	Harrisburg, PA
George Thomas	Helena, MT
Sam Jacobs	Houma-Thibodaux, LA
Daniel DiNardo	Houston, TX
Daniel Buechlein	Indianapolis, IN
Joseph Latino	Jackson, MS
John Gaydos	Jefferson City, MO
Joseph Naumann	Kansas City, KS
Robert Finn	Kansas City-St. Joseph, MO
Richard Stika	Knoxville, TN
Jerome Listecki	La Crosse, WI
William Higi	Lafayette, IN
Glen Provost	Lake Charles, LA
Fabian Bruskewitz	Lincoln, NE
Anthony Taylor	Little Rock, AR
Robert Morlino	Madison, WI
John McCormack	Manchester, NH
Alexander Sample	Marquette, MI
Alfred Hughes	New Orleans, LA
John LeVoir	New Ulm, MN
Timothy Dolan	New York, NY
John Myers	Newark, NJ
Eusebius Beltran	Oklahoma City, OK
Thomas Wenski	Orlando, FL
Gerald Barbarito	Palm Beach, FL
Anthony Bevilacqua (emeritus)	Philadelphia, PA
Justin Rigali	Philadelphia, PA
Thomas Olmsted	Phoenix, AZ
David Zubick	Pittsburgh, PA
Thomas Doran	Rockford, IL
William Murphy	Rockville Centre, NY
Paul Coakley	Salina, KS

Bishop	Diocese (as of 2008)
Michael Pfiefer	San Angelo, TX
Oscar Cantu	San Antonio, TX
Jose Gomez	San Antonio, TX
John Doughtery	Scranton, PA
Joseph Martino	Scranton, PA
R. Walker Nickless	Sioux City, IA
George Lucas	Springfield, IL
James V. Johnston	Springfield-Cape Girardeau, MO
Victor Galeone	St. Augustine, FL
Robert Carlson	St. Louis, MO
Robert Hermann	St. Louis, MO
John C. Nienstedt	St. Paul-Minneapolis, MN
Robert Lynch	St. Petersburg, FL
Leonard Blair	Toledo, OH
John Smith	Trenton, NJ
Edward J. Slattery	Tulsa, OK
Frank Dewane	Venice, CA
Donald Wuerl	Washington, DC
Michael O. Jackels	Wichita, KS
Bernard Harrington	Winona, MN
George Murry	Youngstown, OH

Notes

Introduction

1. Address of the Holy Father, Pope Francis, "Audience with the College of Cardinals," March 15, 2013, available at www.vatican.va/holy_father/francesco/speeches/2013/march/documents/papa-francesco_20130315_cardinali_en.html, accessed May 20, 2013.

2. Pope Benedict XVI, "Proclaiming a Year of Priests," June 16, 2009, available at www.vatican.va/holy_father/benedict_xvi/letters/2009/documents/hf_ben-xvi_let_20090616_anno-sacerdotale_en.html, accessed May 14, 2013.

3. Alan Holdren, "Number of Priests Growing Worldwide, Vatican Reports," *Catholic News Agency*, February 11, 2011, available at www.catholicnewsagency.com/news/number-of-priests-growing-worldwide-vatican-reports/, accessed May 15, 2013.

4. Joan Frawley Desmond, "Rebuilding from the Ruins: Cardinal O'Malley on the 2002 Boston Sex-Abuse Scandal and Aftermath," *National Catholic Register*, January 2, 2012, available at www.ncregister.com/daily-news/rebuilding-from-the-ruins-cardinal-omalley-on-the-2002-boston-sex-abuse-sca, accessed May 15, 2013.

5. See appendix for ordination rates in the dioceses of Albany and Buffalo.

6. Center for Applied Research in the Apostolate (CARA), at Georgetown University, "The Class of 2012: Survey of Ordinands to the Priesthood," April 2012, available at www.usccb.org/beliefs-and-teachings/vocations/ordination-class/upload/Ordination-Class-of-2012-Report-FINAL.pdf.

7. "Grassroots Movement of Catholics Declares Catholic Bill of Rights and Responsibilities," press release, June 5, 2011, available at http://americancatholiccouncil.org/more-about-acc/news-releases/, accessed May 16, 2013.

8. Paul Lakeland, *Catholicism at the Crossroads: How the Laity Can Save the Church* (New York: Continuum Press, 2008), 5.

9. Paul Lakeland, *The Liberation of the Laity: In Search of an Accountable Church* (New York: Continuum Press, 2004), 208.

10. Gary Wills, *Why Priests? A Failed Tradition* (New York: Viking Press, 2013), 80.

11. Most Rev. Elden Curtiss, "The Future of Priestly and Religious Vocations," *Origins* 25: 167–168.

12. James D. Hunter, *Culture Wars: The Struggle to Define America* (New York: Basic Books, 1991), 44.

13. Dean R. Hoge, *The First Five Years of the Priesthood* (Collegeville, Minn.: Liturgical Press, 2002).

14. Stephen Rossetti, *The Joy of Priesthood* (Notre Dame, Ind.: Ave Maria Press, 2005); *Why Priests Are Happy* (Notre Dame, Ind.: Ave Maria Press, 2011).

Chapter One

1. Cardinal Francis George, "How Liberalism Fails the Church," portions of the text of homily given to the assembly of the National Center for the Laity in Chicago, January 17, 1998, published in *Commonweal* as "How Liberalism Fails the Church: The Cardinal Explains," November 19, 1999, http://commonwealmagazine.org/how-liberalism-fails-church-0.

2. Ibid.

3. George Weigel, *Evangelical Catholicism: Deep Reform in the 21st Century Church* (New York: Basic Books, 2013).

4. Philip Rieff, *Sacred Order/Social Order: My Life amid the Deathworks* (Charlottesville: University of Virginia Press, 2006), 1.

5. Rieff, *Sacred Order/Social Order*, 15.

6. Pope Paul VI, *Humanae Vitae*, 1968 available at www.vatican.va/holy_father/paul_vi/encyclicals/documents/hf_p-vi_enc_25071968_humanae-vitae_en.html. Also, for more on this, see Mary Eberstadt, *Adam and Eve after the Pill: Paradoxes of the Sexual Revolution* (San Francisco: Ignatius Press, 2012).

7. George Dennis O'Brien, *The Idea of a Catholic University* (Chicago, 2002).

8. George Dennis O'Brien, *The Church and Abortion: A Catholic Dissent* (Lanham, Md.: Rowman and Littlefield, 2010).

9. Ibid., x–xi.

10. Most Rev. Elden Curtiss, "The Future of Priestly and Religious Vocations," *Origins* 25, 167–168.

11. Richard Schoenherr and Lawrence A. Young, *Full Pews and Empty Altars* (Madison: University of Wisconsin Press, 1993).

12. Bernard Cooke, *The Future of the Eucharist* (Mahwah, N.J.: Paulist Press, 1997), 32. See also lecture by Bernard Cooke, May 7, 1998, *San Diego News Notes*, June 1998.

13. Ibid.

14. Most Rev. Howard J. Hubbard, "We Are His People," pastoral letter from the bishop of Albany, September 21, 1978.

15. John Gehring, "Communion Denial and the Culture Wars,"

Faith and Public Life, March 2, 2012, www.faithinpubliclife.org/blog/communion-denial-and-culture-wars/.

16. Ibid.

17. Kennedy and Sons, *Official Catholic Directory* (Providence, N.J.: National Register), data recovered from 2005, 2006, 2007, 2008, 2009, 2010, 2011.

18. Rodney Stark and James C. McCann, "Market Forces and Catholic Commitment: Exploring the New Paradigm," *Journal for the Scientific Study of Religion* 32: 111–124.

19. Roger Finke and Rodney Stark, *The Churching of America, 1776–2005: Winners and Losers in Our Religious Economy* (Piscataway, N.J.: Rutgers University Press, 2005).

20. Most Rev. Elden Curtiss, "The Future of Priestly and Religious Vocations," *Origins* 25: 167–168.

21. Andrew Yuengert, "Do Bishops Matter? A Cross-sectional Study of Ordinations to the U.S. Catholic Diocesan Priesthood," *Review of Religious Research* (Spring 2001).

22. Walker Percy, "A Cranky Novelist Reflects on the Church," in Percy, *Signposts in a Strange Land* (New York: Picador, 1991), 316–325.

23. Ibid., 325.

Chapter Two

1, "Washington, D.C., to Open New Seminary," *Zenit*, October 20, 2010, available at www.zenit.org/en/articles/washington-d-c-to-open-new-seminary, accessed May 16, 2013.

2. "Rector's Welcome," available at the website of Theological College, http://theologicalcollege.org/published/about_us/index.html, accessed May 20, 2013.

3. "Rebuilding from the Ruins: Cardinal O'Malley on the 2002 Sex-Abuse Scandal and Aftermath," *National Catholic Register,* www.ncregister.com/daily-news/rebuilding-from-the-ruins-cardinal-omalley-on-the-2002-boston-sex-abuse-sca/, accessed May 20, 2013.

4. Available at www.catholicnewsagency.com/news/southern-catholic-boom-advances-plans-for-seminary/, accessed May 20, 2013.

5. "Southern Catholic Boom Advances Plans for Seminary, Monastery," *Catholic News Agency,* www.catholicnews.com/data/stories/cns/1104663.htm, accessed May 20, 2013.

6. "Defending the Faith on the Plains," *National Catholic Register,* www.ncregister.com/site/article/defending-the-faith-on-the-plains/#ixzz1ojMx6869, accessed May 20, 2013.

7. Michael Rose, *Goodbye Good Men*, 244.

8. Ibid., 243.

9. Jeff Ziegler, "Priestly Vocations in America: A Look at the Numbers," *Catholic World Report*, July 2005.

10. Ibid.

11. Ibid.

12. *Apostolorum Successores*, Congregation for Bishops, February 22, 2004.

13. "A 'Culture of Vocations' Brings Vitality to Saginaw," *National Catholic Register,* www.ncregister.com/site/article/a_culture_of_vocations_brings_ vitality_to_saginaw_diocese/#ixzz1snyvWLGA, accessed May 20, 2013.

14. Personal interview with coauthor Christopher White, February 2012.

15. Claudia McDonnell, "Priests Needed," *Catholic New York*, January 12, 2012.

16. Personal interview with coauthor Christopher White, January 2012.

17. Apostolic Visitation Report, 7.

18. Apostolic Visitation Report, 14.

19. *Instruction concerning the Criteria for the Discernment of Vocations with Regard to Persons with Homosexual Tendencies in View of Their Admission to the Seminary and to Holy Order*, 2005, www.vatican.va/roman_curia/ congregations/ccatheduc/documents/rc_con_ccatheduc_doc_20051104_ istruzione_en.html, accessed May 20, 2013.

20. John Burger, "The Clergy Abuse Scandal: What Is Going on in the U.S.?," www.staycatholic.com/the_seminaries.htm, accessed May 20, 2013.

21. Newman, "The Infidelity of the Future," delivered October 2, 1873, available at www.newmanreader.org/works/ninesermons/sermon9.html, accessed May 20, 2013.

22. Ibid.

23. Ibid.

24. *Pastores Dabo Vobis*, www.vatican.va/holy_father/john_paul_ii/ apost_exhortations/documents/hf_jp-ii_exh_25031992_pastores-dabo-vobis_en.html, accessed May 20, 2013.

25. Text of address to young people and seminarians at St. Joseph Seminary, www.osv.com/PapalVisitNav/NewsfromNewYorkWashington/ TextofPopesspeechatStJosephsSeminary/tabid/5889/Default.aspx, accessed May 20, 2013.

Chapter Three

1. Tom Roberts, *The Emerging Catholic Church: A Community's Search for Itself* (Maryknoll, N.Y.: Orbis Books, 2011), 85.

2. Ibid.

3. Ibid., 83.

4. Ibid., 74.

5. Ibid., 83.

6. Ibid., 84.

7. Eugene Kennedy cited by Roberts, ibid., 84.

8. Ronald Knox, *The Church on Earth: The Nature and Authority of the Catholic Church and the Place of the Pope within It* (Manchester, N.H.: Sophia Institute Press, 2003) (originally published 1929), 49.

9. Paul Lakeland, *The Liberation of the Laity: In Search of an Accountable Church* (New York: Continuum, 2004), 211.

10. David J. O'Brien, *From the Heart of the American Church* (Maryknoll, N.Y.: Orbis, 1994), 148. Also Paul Lakeland, *Catholicism at the Crossroads: How the Laity Can Save the Church* (New York: Continuum, 2008), 1.

11. Ibid., 148.

12. Ibid.

13. Paul Lakeland, *Liberation of the Laity*, 205.

14. Paul Lakeland, address to the 2007 CORPUS Conference "Prophecies, Dreams and Visions: Keeping Hope Alive," audiofile available at the website of CORPUS, www.corpus.org.

15. David J. O'Brien, *From the Heart of the American Church* (Maryknoll, N.Y.: Orbis, 1994), 148.

16. Michael J. Lacey and Francis Oakley, *The Crisis of Authority in Catholic Modernity* (New York: Oxford University Press, 2011), back cover.

17. Michael J. Lacey, "Prologue: The Problem of Authority and Its Limits," in Lacey and Oakley, *Crisis of Authority in Catholic Modernity*, 4.

18. Ibid., 10.

19. Francis Oakley, "History and the Return of the Repressed in Catholic Modernity: The Dilemma Posed by Constance," in Lacey and Oakley, *Crisis of Authority in Catholic Modernity*, 29.

20. Charles Taylor, "Magisterial Authority," in Lacey and Oakley, *Crisis of Authority in Catholic Modernity*, 259.

21. Ibid., 260.

22. Ibid., 262.

23. John P. Beal, "Something There Is That Doesn't Love a Law: Canon Law and Its Discontents," in Lacey and Oakley, *Crisis of Authority in Catholic Modernity*, 145.

24. Gerard Mannion, "A Teaching Church That Learns," in Lacey and Oakley, *Crisis of Authority in Catholic Modernity,* 170, 181.

25. Francis Oakley, "Epilogue: The Matter of Unity," in Lacey and Oakley, *Crisis of Authority in Catholic Modernity*, 350, 352.

26. American Catholic Council, www.americancatholiccouncil.org, accessed May 22, 2013.

27. Archbishop Allen Vigneron, "Archdiocese of Detroit Statement on the American Catholic Council," issued and posted October 12, 2010, website of the American Catholic Council, www.aodonline.org.

28. Joseph Bottum, "When the Swallows Come Back to Capistrano: Catholic Culture in America," *First Things,* October 2006.

29. American Catholic Council, www.americancatholiccouncil.org, accessed May 22, 2013.

30. Ibid.

31. Voice of the Faithful, www.votf.org, accessed May 20, 2013.

32. CT Bill No. 1098, Connecticut General Assembly: An Act Modifying Corporate Laws Relating to Certain Religious Corporations, available

at the website of the state of Connecticut, www.cga.ct.gov/2009/TOB/
S/2009SB-01098-ROO-SB.htm, accessed May 22, 2013.

33. Tom McFeely, "Voice of the Un-Faithful: Lay Group under Renewed Fire for Promoting Dissent, *National Catholic Register,* September 19, 2006.

34. Lisa Sowle Cahill, "A Crisis of Clergy, Not of Faith," *New York Times,* March 6, 2002.

35. "Voice of the Faithful in the Diocese of Bridgeport," Annual Report, July 2004 to July 2005, available at www.votfbpt.org/2005_VOTF_Annual_Report.pdf, accessed May 20, 2013.

36. "Connecticut Bishops Reverse Stand on Plan B," *Catholic World News,* September 28, 2007, www.catholicculture.org/news/fatures/index.cfm?recnum=53823.

37. Ken Dixon, "Bishop Scolds Lawmakers: Lori Calls Proposed Legislation an Attempt to Silence Roman Catholic Church," *Connecticut Post,* March 10, 2009, 1. See also Chaz Muth, "Bishops Urge Catholics to Reject Bill Giving Laity Parish Fiscal Rule," March 9, 2009, Catholic News Service, www.catholicnews.com/data/stories/cns/0901086.htm, accessed May 22, 2013.

38. Ken Dixon, "Catholics Protest, Celebrate Victory," *Connecticut Post,* March 12, 2009, A1, A7.

39. "Vatican Approves Excommunication of Liberal Catholic Group, Call to Action," December 8, 2006, *Lifesite News,* www.lifesitenews.com.

40. Peter Steinfels, "Liberal Catholicism Reexamined," in *Believing Scholars: Catholic Intellectuals,* edited by James L. Heft, S.M. (New York: Fordham University Press, 2005), 140.

41. Archbishop John R. Quinn, *The Reform of the Papacy* (New York: Crossroads, 1999).

42. Archbishop John R. Quinn, speech delivered at Campion Hall, Oxford University, June 29, 1996. Archbishop Quinn (retired) asked whether the Holy See had engaged in appropriate dialogue before making decisions regarding a great variety of matters, including contraception, the appointment of bishops, the approval of the Catechism of the Catholic Church, clerical celibacy, and the ordination of women.

43. "With Friends Like These," editorial, *Catholic World Report,* November 2010, 48.

44. Bishop Robert Francis Vasa, "Sacred Duties, Episcopal Ministry," address delivered at 2010 Inside Catholic Partnership Award Dinner, September 16, 2010.

45. Committee on Doctrine, United States Conference of Catholic Bishops, "Inadequacies in the Theological Methodology and Conclusions of *The Sexual Person: Toward a Renewed Catholic Anthropology* by Todd A. Salzman and Michael G. Lawler," issued September 15, 2010.

46. Statement Defending Sr. Elizabeth Johnson's 2007 book *Quest for the Living God,* issued by the Board of the Catholic Theological Society of America, April 9, 2011. See also response from Cardinal Donald Wuerl,

"Bishop as Teachers: A Resource for Bishops," United States Conference of Catholic Bishops, April 18, 2010.

47. Pope Benedict XVI in his interview book *The Ratzinger Report* (Ignatius Press, 1986), notes that "Bishops, the successors of the Apostles holding the fullness of the Sacrament of Holy Orders, are the authentic, autonomous and immediate authority in the Dioceses entrusted to them, of which they are the principle and foundation of unity. United in the Episcopal college with their head, the Pope, they act in the Person of Christ in order to govern the Universal Church. All these definitions are specific to the perennial Catholic doctrine on the episcopate and they have been vigorously reaffirmed by the Second Vatican Council." Of Episcopal conferences, Pope Benedict also wrote: "We must not forget the Episcopal conferences have no theological basis. They do not belong to the structure of the Church as willed by Christ as structures that cannot be eliminated. Those conferences have only a practical and concrete function. The new Code of Canon Law prescribes the extent of the authority of the conferences which cannot validly act in the name of all Bishops unless each and every Bishop has given his consent. . . . No Episcopal conference as such has a teaching mission. Its documents have no weight of their own save that of the consent given to them by individual Bishops."

48. Decree Revoking Episcopal Consent to Claim the "Catholic" Name according to Canon 216 for St. Joseph's Hospital and Medical Center, Phoenix, Arizona, by Bishop Thomas J. Olmsted, December 21, 2010, at the Chancery of the Diocese of Phoenix.

49. Bishop Thomas Olmsted, "Letter to Catholic Healthcare West President Lloyd Dean," November 22, 2010. See also Denys Powlett-Jones, "Bishops Letter to Catholic Healthcare West Leaked: Hospital to Lose Catholic Status," December 15, 2010, *Catholic Phoenix*, www.catholicphoenix.com, accessed May 22, 2013.

50. Thomas J. Olmsted, bishop of Phoenix, to Lloyd H. Dean, November 22, 2010, available at www.azcentral.com/ic/community/pdf/bishopletter.pdf, accessed May 20, 2013.

51. "Sr. Keehan Receives Presidential Pen for Supporting Health Care despite Bishops' Objections," Catholic News Agency, March 24, 2010.

52. Nicholas M. Healy, "By the Working of the Holy Spirit: The Crisis of Authority in the Christian Churches," *Anglican Theological Review* (Winter 2006).

53. Bishop Thomas Olmsted, "Letter to Catholic Healthcare West President Lloyd Dean," November 22, 2010.

54. Kevin O'Rourke, "Rights of Conscience," *America,* August 1, 2011, available at http://americamagazine.org/issue/783/article/rights-conscience, accessed May 22, 2013.

55. Bishop Thomas Olmsted, "Letter to Catholic Healthcare West President Lloyd Dean," November 22, 2010.

Chapter Four

1. Richard A. Schoenherr and Lawrence A. Young, *Full Pews and Empty Altars: Demographics of the Priest Shortage in the United States Catholic Dioceses* (Madison: University of Wisconsin Press, 1993).

2. Richard A. Schoenherr, "Numbers Don't Lie: A Priesthood in Irreversible Decline," *Commonweal,* April 7, 1995, 11–14.

3. Lawrence A. Young, "Assessing and Updating the Schoenherr-Young Projections of a Clergy Decline in the United States Roman Catholic Church," *Sociology of Religion* 59 (1) (1998): 7–23.

4. Gustav Niebuhr, "Richard Schoenherr, 60, Scholar Who Showed a Decline of Priests," *New York Times,* January 11, 1996.

5. Ibid.

6. Schoenherr and Young, *Full Pews and Empty Altars,* 7.

7. Roger Mahony, "The Good News about Priestly Vocations," *Our Sunday Visitor* (Huntington, Ind.), November 18, 1993, 3, cited by Schoenherr and Young, *Full Pews and Empty Altars,* 351.

8. Pope John Paul I, *Pastores Dabo Vobis,* 1992.

9. "Priest Shortage Leaves Faithful Alone on Sickbeds," Associated Press, January 27, 2010.

10. Ibid.

11. Roger Finke and Rodney Starke, *Churching of America, 1776–2005: Winners and Losers in Our Religious Economy* (Piscataway, N.J.: Rutgers University Press, 2005).

12. Archbishop Elden Curtiss, "Future of Priestly and Religious Vocations," 167.

13. Peter G. Northouse, *Leadership: Theory and Practice,* 4th ed. (Thousand Oaks, Calif.: Sage, 2007), 176.

14. J. V. Downton, *Rebel Leadership: Commitment and Charisma in a Revolutionary Process* (New York: Free Press, 1973).

15. James MacGregor Burns, *Leadership* (New York: Harper and Row, 1978), 18.

16. Northhouse, *Leadership,* 179.

17. Curtiss, "Future of Priestly and Religious Vocations," 168.

18. R. J. House, "A 1976 Theory of Charismatic Leadership," in *Leadership: The Cutting Edge,* edited by N. J. G. Hunt and L. L. Larson (Carbondale: Southern Illinois University Press, 1976), 189–207.

19. Philip Rieff, *Charisma: The Gift of Grace and How It Has Been Taken Away from Us* (New York: Pantheon Books, 2007), 6.

20. Ibid., 5.

21. Maureen Dowd, "The Archbishop vs. the Governor: Gay Sera, Sera," *New York Times,* June 18, 2011.

22. Ibid.

23. Marian Ronan, "US Catholic Bishops Elect a Culture Warrior," November 16, 2010, *Religion Dispatches,* www.religiondispatches.org.

24. B. M. Bass, *Leadership and Performance beyond Expectations* (New York: Free Press, 1985), 20.

25. Cited by Anne Hendershott, "Catholic Hospitals vs. the Bishops," *Wall Street Journal*, December 31, 2010.

26. Rieff, *Charisma*, 82.

27. "Pope Names New York's Catholic Rock Star Archbishop Timothy Dolan a Cardinal," *New York Daily News,* February 21, 2012. See also "Cardinal Timothy Dolan as Pope Not Likely According to Paddy Power Bookmakers Who Quote 80/1," *Irish Central*, February 19, 2012.

28. Robert Kolker, "The Archbishop of Charm," *New York*, September 20, 2009.

29. Ibid.

30. Timothy M. Dolan, *Priests for the Third Millennium* (Huntington, Ind.: Our Sunday Visitor, 2000), 19.

31. Ibid., 22.

32. Clara Smith, "Religious Group Poll: 70 Percent of NY Thinks Abortion Proposal Goes Too Far," *Legislative Gazette*, February 14, 2013.

33. Michael Barbaro, "Behind New York Gay Marriage, an Unlikely Mix of Forces," *New York Times*, June 25, 2011.

34. Ibid.

35. Timothy M. Dolan, "Some Afterthoughts," July 7, 2011, blog entry, http://blog.archny.org/?p=1349, accessed May 22, 2013.

36. Sue Ellin Browder, California's Marriage Lessons: Behind the Scenes on Proposition 8," *National Catholic Register*, June 7, 2009, 1.

37. Ibid., 9.

38. Ibid.

39. "Catholic Bishops Fight Contraception Rule at House Hearing," *Wall Street Journal*, February 16, 2012.

40. "Portrayal of the Church Causes Unease," *New York Times,* March 19, 2002, www.nytimes.com/2002/05/04nuregion/portrayal-of-the-church-causes-unease.html, accessed May 22, 2013.

41. Janice D'Arcy, "Bishop Law and Order Lori Takes the Point," *Hartford Courant*, November 13, 2002.

42. Charles J. Chaput, C.F.M., preface to *Living Miracles: The Spiritual Sons of John Paul the Great,* by Randall J. Meisssen, L.C. (Alpharetta, Ga.: Mission Network, 2011), 6.

43. Chaput, preface, 6–7.

44. Charles J. Chaput, "A Bad Bill and How We Got It," March 22, 2010, columns posted on the website of the Archdiocese of Denver, www.archden.org/index.cfm/ID/3631, accessed May 22, 2013.

45. Charles J. Chaput, "Little Murders," address, October 18, 2008, published online in "Public Discourse: Ethics, Law and the Common Good," www.publicdiscourse.com, accessed May 20, 2013.

46. Charles J. Chaput, *Render unto Caesar: Serving the Nation by Living Our Catholic Beliefs in Political Life* (New York: Image Books, 2008), 7.

47. Ibid., 207.

48. Chaput, "Little Murders."

49. Chaput, *Render unto Caesar*, 207.

50. David J. O'Brien, "For Archbishop's Camp, the Church Is the Hierarchy, *Philadelphia Inquirer*, July 26, 2011, available at http://articles.philly .com/2011-07-26/news/29816769_1_female-priests-catholic-church-bishops, accessed May 22, 2013.

51. Cathleen Kaveny, *Commonweal*.

52. Charles Chaput, "Converting the Culture," address at Assumption College, Worcester, Mass., November 10, 2011, text included in Benjamin Mann, "Archbishop Chaput Challenges Catholic Educators to Convert the Culture," www.catholicnewsagency.com/utles/, accessed May 22, 2013.

53. "Archbishop Chaput: Effective Church Reform Demands Repentance, Faith," address to the Annual Convention of the Knights of Columbus, August 3, 2011, EWTN News.

54. Ibid.

55. John Allen, "Cardinal George's Plan to Evangelize America," interview with Cardinal Francis George, *National Catholic Reporter*, http:// ncronline.org/print/15222., accessed May 22, 2013.

56. Francis George, *God in Action: How Faith in God Can Address the Challenges of the World* (New York: Doubleday, 2011), 214.

57. Ibid., 18.

58. Cited by Chaput, "Little Murders."

59. Daniel Burke, "Catholic Bishops Warn against Abortion Rights Expansion," November 30, 2008, Religion News Service, www .districtchronicles.com/home/index.cfm?event=displayArticlePrinter Friendly/, accessed May 22, 2013.

60. Francis Cardinal George, "Dear Brother Bishops," farewell address, November 15, 2010, available at http://whispersinthloggia.blogspot .com/2010/11/dear-brother-bishops-chiefs-farewell.html, accessed May 22, 2013.

61. Jim Graves, "Lost Generations: Bishop Alexander Sample on the Need for a Renewal of Orthodoxy," *Catholic World Report*, November 1, 2011.

Chapter Five

1. Michael S. Rose, "Killing the Messenger," *New Oxford Review*, March 2005.

2. Peter W. Miller, "Archbishop Weakland's Legacy," *Seattle Catholic*, June 7, 2002.

3. Ibid.

4. Ibid.

5. Michael H. Crosby, "Is Celibacy a Main Reason for the Lack of Vocations?," *Human Development* 32 (2) (Summer 2011): 30–33.

6. Michael H. Crosby, "Beyond the Notre Dame Brouhaha: How U.S. Catholics Are Tuning Out Their Bishops," Fr. Crosby's personal website.

7. Pope John Paul II, *Veritatis Splendor* [The splendor of truth], encyclical published by the Vatican (1993), no. 84.

8. Ibid., introduction.

9. Ibid., no. 30.

10. Ibid., no. 29.

11. Ibid., no. 29.

12. George Weigel, *Evangelical Catholicism: Deep Reform in the 21st Century Church* (New York: Basic Books, 2013).

13. *Veritatis Splendor,* no. 4.

14. Ibid., no. 84.

15. Pope John Paul II, *Ex Corde Ecclesiae* (Rome: Vatican, 1990).

16, "New Norms for Catholic Higher Education: Unworkable and Dangerous," *America,* November 14, 1998, 3–4.

17. Jon Nilson, "The Impending Death of Catholic Higher Education," May 28, 2001, *America,* http://americamagazine.org/content/article.cfm?article_id=927, accessed May 22, 2013.

18. Ibid.

19. Burton Bollag, "Mourning a Pope Who Stressed Orthodoxy," *Chronicle of Higher Education,* April 15, 2005, A-1.

20. Ralph McInerny, "Picking and Choosing Church Doctrines," Beliefnet, www.beliefnet.com/story/17/story_1729.html.

21. Gerard V. Bradley, "Looking Ahead at Catholic Higher Education," *Fellowship of Catholic Scholars Quarterly* (Spring 2002): 16.

22. Richard Byrne, "Pope Benedict Thanks Educators and Addresses Academic Freedom in Talk at Catholic University, April 18, 2008, *Chronicle of Higher Education,* http://chronicle.com/article/Pope-Sees-Academic-Freedom-and/707, accessed May 22, 2013.

23. "Bishop Curry Announces the 10 Year Review of *The Application of Ex Corde Ecclesiae for the United States,*" January 20, 2011, available at http://old.usccb.org/comm/archives/2011/11-017.shtml, accessed May 20, 2013.

24. "Final Report for the Ten Year Review of *The Application of Ex Corde Ecclesiae for the United States,*" June 11, 2012, available at www.usccb.org/beliefs-and-teachings/how-we-teach/catholic-education/higher-education/, accessed May 20, 2013.

25. Ibid.

26. Ibid.

27. Rev. Wilson Miscamble, "The Faculty Problem," September 10, 2007, *America,* www.americamagazine.org/content/article.cfm?article_id=10176, accessed May 22, 2013.

28. Ibid.

29. Michael Rose, *Benedict XVI: The Man Who Was Ratzinger* (Dallas: Spence, 2005).

30. Michele Dillon, *Catholic Identity: Balancing Reason, Faith, and Power* (New York: Cambridge University Press, 1999), 10.

31. Ibid., book jacket.

32. Ibid., 4.

33. Ibid., 88.

34. Ibid., book jacket.

35. Hilary White, "Catholic St. Thomas University Votes to Sever Historic Ties with St. Paul Archdiocese," November 21, 2007, *Lifesite News*, www .lifesite.net/ldn/200/nov/07/12103.html, accessed May 22, 2013.

36. Ibid.

37. Michelle Dillon, *Catholic Identity: Balancing Reason, Faith and Power* (New York: Cambridge University Press, 1999), 2.

38. Ibid., 24.

39. Ibid.

40. Barbara E. Wall, "Mission and Ministry," in *Women in Catholic Higher Education,* edited by Sharlene Nagy Hesse-Biber and Denise Leckenby (Lanham, Md.: Lexington Books, 2003), 146.

41. David O'Brien, *From the Heart of the American Church: Catholic Higher Education and American Culture* (Maryknoll, N.Y.: Orbis Books, 1994), 148.

42. Ibid.

43. Ibid.

44. Richard John Neuhaus, "A University of a Particular Kind," *First Things*, April 2007, 32.

45. T. S. Eliot, *The Cocktail Party* (Orlando, Fla.: Harcourt Brace Jovanovich, 1950), 156.

46. Margaret Anderson and Howard Taylor, *Sociology* (Belmont, Calif.: Wadsworth, 2000), 504–506.

47. Travis Hirschi, *Causes of Delinquency* (Berkeley: University of California Press, 1969).

48. Maria Cortes Gonzalez, "El Paso Bishop Armando X. Ochoa Files Lawsuit against Reverend Michael Rodriguez," *El Paso Times*, January 13, 2012.

49. Michael Rodriguez, "Every Catholic Must Oppose Certain Things," *El Paso Times*, August 3, 2010, available at www.elpasotimes.com/ci_15649815, accessed May 22, 2013.

50. "El Paso Bishop Halts Priest's Anti-gay, Political Discourse," ABC-7, www.kvia.com/news/29257419/detail.html, accessed May 22, 2013.

51. Philip Rieff, *The Triumph of the Therapeutic: The Uses of Faith after Freud* (Washington, D.C.: ISI Books, 2006) (originally published by Harper and Row, 1966).

52. Ibid., 205.

53. Ibid., 20.

54. Philip Rieff, *Fellow Teachers* (New York, 1973) 39.

55. Philip Rieff, *Sacred Order/Social Order: My Life among the Deathworks* (Charlottesville: University of Virginia Press, 2006).

56. Ibid., xxii.

57. Rieff, *Sacred Order/Social Order*, 59.

58. Rieff, *Fellow Teachers*, 107.

59. Ibid., 42.

60. R. R. Reno, "Philip Rieff's Charisma," *First Things*, April 25, 2007.

61. Philip Rieff, *Charisma: The Gift of Grace and How It Has Been Taken Away from Us* (New York: Pantheon, 2007), 6.

Chapter Six

1. "Some Priests May Choose Not to Become Pastors," *California Catholic Daily*, August 22, 2011, http://calcatholic.com/news/newsArticle .aspx?id=30c13aef-83a6-4993-a7de-89d37b181f8f, accessed May 22, 2013.

2. Paul Likoudis, "For Bishop Clark . . . Women-Run Church Is Becoming a Reality," *Wanderer*, May 19, 2011.

3. Ibid.

4. Ibid.

5. Matthew H. Clark, *Forward in Hope: Saying Amen to Lay Ecclesial Ministry* (Notre Dame, Ind.: Ave Maria Press, 2009), 29.

6. Ibid., 3.

7. Ibid., 81.

8. Ibid., 82.

9. Constitution on the Church, Vatican II.

10. Paul Lakeland, *The Liberation of the Laity: In Search of an Accountable Church* (New York: Continuum Press, 2004), 205.

11. Most Rev. Howard J. Hubbard, "We Are His People," pastoral letter from the bishop of Albany, September 21, 1978.

12. Ibid.

13. Mark M. Gray and Mary L. *Gautier*, "Understanding the Experience: A Profile of Lay Ecclesial Ministers Serving as Parish Life Coordinators," Center for Applied Research in the Apostolate, Georgetown University, Washington, D.C., May 2004.

14. Ibid.

15. Anne-Marie Brogan, "Voices from the Vineyard," in Clark, *Forward in Hope,* 89.

16. Ibid., 90.

17. Ibid., 99.

18. Ibid., 101.

19. Cited by Paul Likoudis, "For Bishop Clark . . . Women-Run Church Is Becoming a Reality," *Wanderer*, May 19, 2011.

20. Ibid.

21. Women for Faith and Family, "Bishop Matthew Clark of Rochester Imposes Severe Restrictions on the Catholic Physicians Guild and the Catholic Lawyers Guild," www.wf-f.org/othervoices97.html, accessed May 22, 2013.

22. Tim Louis Macaluso, "Religion Interview: Bishop Matthew Clark and a Changing Church, *Rochester City (New York) Newspaper*, March 2, 2011

23. Ibid.

24. Ibid.

25. Tricia Wittman-Todd (pastoral life coordinator, St. Mary's Parish, Seattle), "Dear People of St. Mary's."

26. Robert Kinast, "How Much Is Lay Ministry Worth?," *Origins* 23 (1992): 289.

27. Dean Hoge and Mari R. Jewell, *The Next Generation of Pastoral Leaders: What the Church Needs to Know* (Chicago: Loyola Press, 2010).

28. Ibid.

29. Michael Novak and William E. Simon, Jr., *Living the Call: An Introduction to the Lay Vocation* (New York: Encounter Books, 2012), 59.

30. Ibid., 65.

31. Ibid.

32. Howard J. Hubbard, "Failings of the Church," Bishops Column, *Evangelist*, November 3, 2011.

33. Richard McBrien, "Bishop Ponders Reasons Americans Leave the Catholic Church," *National Catholic Reporter*, January 2, 2012.

34. Shelby Steele, cited by William Murchison, *Mortal Follies: Episcopalians and the Crisis of Mainline Christianity* (New York: Encounter Books, 2009), 29.

35. Ibid., 28.

36. Alexander K. Sample, "The Deacon: Icon of Jesus Christ the Servant," pastoral letter, from Chancery of the Diocese of Marquette, June 9, 2011.

37. Ibid.

38. David N. Power, "The Basis for Official Ministry in the Church," *Jurist* 41 (1982): 336.

39. Priestly Life and Ministry Committee of the National Conference of Catholic Bishops, *As One Who Serves: Reflections of the Pastoral Ministry on Priests in the United States* (Washington, D.C.: United States Catholic Conference, 1977), 10. See also Bishop's Committee on Priestly Life and Ministry, *A Shepherd's Care: Reflections on the Changing Role of Pastor* (National Conference of Catholic Bishops, 1987).

40. Clark, *Forward in Hope*, 6.

41. Peter Hebblethwaite, "Pope Draws Sharp Distinction between Priests, Lay Ministers," *National Catholic Reporter*, May 6, 1994, 5.

42. Pope John Paul II, "Do Laity Share in the Priest's Pastoral Ministry?," *Origins* 24 (1994): 42.

43. Pope John Paul II, "Do Laity Share in the Priest's Pastoral Ministry?," cited by Sharon Henderson Callahan and James Eblen, "Roman Catholic Polity and Leadership," *Journal of Religious Leadership* 5 (1 and 2) (Spring and Fall 2006).

44. Ibid.

45. Ibid.

Chapter Seven

1. David J. O'Brien, *From the Heart of the American Church: Catholic Higher Education and American Culture* (Maryknoll, N.Y.: Orbis Books, 1994), 21.

2. Philip Gleason, *Contending with Modernity: Catholic Higher Education in the Twentieth Century* (New York: Oxford University Press, 1995), 5.

3. James Turnstead Burtchaell, *The Dying of the Light* (Grand Rapids, Mich.: Eerdmans, 1998), 569.

4. Theodore M. Hesburgh, ed., *The Challenge and Promise of a Catholic University* (Notre Dame, Ind.: University of Notre Dame Press, 1994) 1–2.

5. Ibid., 2.

6. Ibid., 5.

7. The Rockefeller Foundation remains one of the top ten U.S. funders of population, reproductive health, and reproductive rights work throughout the world. Concentrating on international initiatives that focus on contraception, abortifacients, sterilization, and abortion legalization, all counter to the teachings of the Catholic Church, the Rockefeller Foundation, under the leadership of Fr. Hesburgh and beyond, has attempted to change the moral and religious values and practices of people, especially Catholic people, throughout the world.

8. Hesburgh biography, University of Notre Dame website, www.nd.edu/ aboutnd/about/history/hesburgh_bio.shtml, accessed May 22, 2013.

9. 261.

10. John Tracy Ellis, "American Catholics and the Intellectual Life," *Thought* 30 (Autumn 1955): 351–388.

11. Gleason, *Contending with Modernity*, 290.

12. Burtchaell, *Dying of the Light*, 576.

13. Gleason, *Contending with Modernity*, 298.

14. Ibid., 298.

15. Burtchaell, *Dying of the Light*, 578.

16. Andrew Greeley and Peter Rossi, *The Education of Catholic Americans* (Chicago: Aldine, 1966), 28.

17. Christopher Jencks and David Riesman, *The Academic Revolution* (New Brunswick, N.J.: Transaction, 1968), 338.

18. Ibid.

19. Ibid.

20. *National Catholic Reporter*, "Scholar Traces History of Catholic Identity of Universities," Catholic News Service, 2005, www.findarticles.com/p/ articles/mi_m1141/is_2_42_/ai_n15954415/print, accessed May 22, 2013.

21. Gleason, *Contending with Modernity*, 317.

22. O'Brien, *From the Heart of the American Church*, 58; also Gleason, *Contending with Modernity*, 317.

23. Gleason, *Contending with Modernity*, 317.

24. Ibid., 317. See also Jencks and Riesman, *Academic Revolution*, 346.

25. Philip Gleason, "What Made Identity a Problem?," in Hesburgh, *Challenge and Promise of a Catholic University*, 96.

26. Barack Obama, "Open Hearts, Open Minds, and Fair Minded Words," text of President Obama's Notre Dame speech, May 17, 2009, *Guardian*, www.guardian.co.uk/world/feedarticle/8512245/print.

27. United States Conference of Catholic Bishops, "Catholics in Political Life," June 2004.

28. Steven Ertelt, "Georgetown University to Honor Pro-abortion Vice President Joe Biden with Award," April 21, 2009, Lifenews.com, accessed May 22, 2013.

29. Felicia Lee, "Bishop Protests Notre Dame Films," *New York Times*, February 12, 2007.

30. "Formerly Catholic Notre Dame Runs Second Annual Queer Film Fest," February 14, 2005, *LifeSite News*, www.lifesite.net/ldn/2005/feb/05021406.html, accessed May 22, 2013.

31. Lively, "U. S. Bishops Endorse Papal Statement on Catholic Colleges."

32. "Catholic Bishops Issue Statement on McBrien's Work," editorial, *Angelus* 7 (8) (August 1985).

33. Janice D'Arcy, "Cardinal Says New Policy Led to Loyola Boycott," *Baltimore Sun*, May 20, 2005.

34. Peter Steinfels, "Roman Catholics' War over Abortion," *New York Times*, May 9, 2009.

35. Karen Travers, "Notre Dame Not Budging on Obama Invite," March 26, 2009, ABCNews.com. http://abcnews.go.com/print?id+717810, accessed May 22, 2013.

36. Kathleen Gilbert, "Notre Dame President Jenkins: We Are Tremendously Proud to Honor Obama at Notre Dame," April 21, 2009, LifeSiteNews.com, www.lifesitenews.com/ldn/printerfriendly.html?articleid+0942104, accessed May 22, 2013.

37. Ibid.

38. Dan Gilgoff, "Catholics Who Back Obama's Visit Raise Voices with Newspaper Ad," May 14, 2009, USNews.com, www.usnews.com/blogs/god-and-country/2009/05/14/catholics-who-back-obama-visit-raise-voices, accessed May 22, 2013.

39. "Survey Finds Church-Going Catholics More Likely to Disapprove of Notre Dame Obama Invite," Catholic News Agency, May 1, 2009, www.catholicnewsagency.com/utiles/myprint/print.php, accessed May 22, 2013.

40. Steven Ertelt, "Pew Poll Finds Catholics Support Notre Dame's Decision to Invite President Obama," May 1, 2009, LifeNews.com, www.lifenews.com/state4106.html, accessed May 22, 2013, and Jaweed Kaleem, "Religious Vote Data Show Shifts in Obama's Faith Based Support," November 8, 2012, *Huffington Post*, www.huffingtonpost.com/2012/11/07/obama-religion-voters-2012_n_2090258.html, accessed May 22, 2013.

41. Cardinal Joseph Ratzinger, "Worthiness to Receive Holy Communion: General Principles," letter to Cardinal McCarrick, leader of the U.S. Conference of Catholic Bishops, June 2004, www.priestsforlife.org/magisterium/bishops/04-07ratzingerommunion.htm, accessed May 22, 2013.

42. Ibid.

43. Cindy Wooden, "Church Must Better Explain Teaching on Sexuality, Pope Tells US Bishops," March 9, 2012, Catholic News Service, www.catholicnews.com/data/stories/cns/12--971.htm, accessed May 22, 2013.

44. Ralph McInerny, "A House Divided," May 17, 2009, *Catholic Thing*, www.thecatholicthing.or/content/view/1602/2/, accessed May 22, 2013.

45. Bishop John D'Arcy, "Statement to the Faithful," April 22, 2009, www.indiananewscenter.com/news/local/4327367.html, accessed www.elpasotimes.com/ci_15649815.

46. Dexter Duggan, "Sees a Darkening of Conscience at Notre Dame," *Wanderer*, April 23, 2009.

47. Ibid.

48. Kathleen Gilbert, "More Bishops Protest Notre Dame's Invitation to President Obama, *Wanderer*, April 16, 2009.

49. Ibid.

50. Kathleen Gilbert, "One of Five U. S. Bishops Protested Notre Dame's Honoring of Obama," *Wanderer,* May 14, 2009.

51. "Bishop Wenski Offers Mass of Reparation for Notre Dame Scandal," editorial, *Wanderer*, May 14, 2009.

52. Archbishop Charles Chaput, "Statement on Notre Dame Commencement," May 18, 2009, http://catholickey.blogspot.com/2009/05/archbishop-chaput-obama-honor-fitting.html, accessed May 22, 2013.

53. Ralph McInerny, "Is Obama Worth a Mass?," March 22, 2009, *Catholic Thing,* www.thecatholicthing.org/columns/2009/is-obama-worth-a-mass.html, accessed May 22, 2013.

54. Ralph McInerny, "A House Divided," *Catholic Thing,* May 17, 2009, www.thecatholicthing.or/content/view/1602/2/, accessed May 22, 2013.

55. Tim Drake, "Catholic University of America Phases Out Coed Dorms," *National Catholic Register,* July 1, 2011.

56. Nathan Koppel, "Justice Scalia Takes Sides in Same Sex Dorm Dispute," *Wall Street Journal*, September 26, 2011.

57. Wayne Laugesen, "ACCU Falls Short on Ex Corde Ecclesiae," June 20, 1999, *National Catholic Register,* www.ncregister.com/site/print_article/8980/, accessed May 22, 2013.

58. Ibid.

59. Becket Fund for Religious Liberty, www.becketfund.org/hhs/, accessed May 22, 2013.

60. Ben Johnson, "Franciscan University of Steubenville Drops Student Health Plan over HHS Mandate," May 16, 2012, LifeSiteNews, www.lifesitenews.com/home/print_article/news/3549/, accessed May 22, 2013.

61. Philip Ryken and John Garvey, "Ryken and Garvey: An Evangelical-Catholic Stand on Liberty," *Wall Street Journal,* July 18, 2012.

62. 2013 Commencement Address at Notre Dame, delivered by Timothy Cardinal Dolan, available at http://blog.archny.org/images/2013/05/

CardinalDolan_CommencementAddress_NotreDame.pdf, accessed May 20, 2013.

Chapter Eight

1. Charles J. Chaput, *A Heart on Fire: Catholic Witness and the Next America* (New York: Image, 2011).

2. Cardinal Donald Wuerl, statement on New Ways Ministry.

3. "Catholic Attitudes on Gay and Lesbian Issues: A Comprehensive Portrait from Recent Research," March 22, 2011, Public Religion Research Institute, http://publicreligion.org/research/2011/03/for-catholics-open-attitudes-on-gay-issues/, accessed May 22, 2013.

4. "Opposition to Same-Sex Marriage Dropping in United States, among Catholics," April 26, 2012, *Catholic World News*, www.catholiculture.org/news/headlines/index.cfm?storyid=14136.

5. http://articles.cnn.com/2008-05-15/us/same.sex.marriage_1_lesbian-couples-marriage-licenses-shannon-minter?_s=PM:US, accessed May 22, 2013.

6. Available at www.ruthinstitute.org/articles/underfire.html, accessed May 22, 2013.

7. Available at www.cacatholic.org/old/index.php?option=com_content&view=article&id=191:a-statement-of-the-catholic-bishops-of-california-in-support-of-proposition-8-&catid=30:california-bishops-statements&Itemid=83, accessed May 22, 2013.

8. Available at www.christiannewswire.com/news/863947548.html, accessed May 22, 2013.

9. Available at http://latimesblogs.latimes.com/lanow/2008/12/prop-8-poll-eva.html, accessed May 22, 2013.

10 . Available at www.sfgate.com/cgi-bin/article.cgi?f=/c/a/2008/11/09/MNU1140AQQ.DTL, accessed May 22, 2013.

11. Available at http://manhattandeclaration.org/resources/faqs.aspx#a3ba0b1f-256d-470e-8f10-c77e895d8c1d, accessed May 22, 2013.

12 . Available at www.ncregister.com/site/article/manhattan_declaration/, accessed May 22, 2013.

13. Available at www.catholicnewsagency.com/news/archbishop_chaput_manhattan_declaration_will_galvanize_christians_in_difficult_times/, accessed May 22, 2013.

14. Available at www.ncregister.com/site/article/manhattan_declaration/#ixzz1sgetB8Cz, accessed May 22, 2013.

15. Available at http://manhattandeclaration.org/home.aspx; 525,225 signatures as of April 20, 2012.

16. Ibid., 16.

17. United States Conference of Catholic Bishops, *Forming Consciences for Faithful Citizenship: A Call to Political Responsibility from the Catholic Bishops of the United States* (Washington, D.C.).

18. Catechism of the Catholic Church, 1778.

19. Ibid., 13.

20. United States Conference of Catholic Bishops, "Six Things Everyone Should Know about the HHS Mandate."

21. EWTN News, "160-Plus Bishops Speak Out against HHS Mandate," *National Catholic Register*, February 6, 2012.

22. Ibid.

23. "Policy, Not Liberty," editorial, *America*, March 5, 2012.

24. Ibid.

25. Cardinal Dolan.

26. Tim Riedy, "Bishop Lori Responds to *America*," editorial, March 2012, *America* website.

27. "United for Religious Freedom: A Statement of the Administrative Committee of the USCCB," March 14, 2012, www.usccb.org/issues-and-action/religious-liberty/upload/admin-religious-freedom.pdf, accessed May 22, 2013.

28. Cardinal Francis George, "Address to His Brother Bishops," November 15, 2010.

Chapter Nine

1. Inside the Vatican Staff, "Pope Declares Year of the Priest to Inspire Spiritual Perfection inside the Vatican," April 2009.

2. "Orthodox Catholics More Hopeful about Future of the Church, Poll Finds," Catholic News Agency, April 15, 2009, www.catholicnewsagency.com/news/orthodox_catholics_more_hopeful_about_future_of_church_poll_finds/, accessed May 22, 2013.

3. Avery Dulles, *The Priestly Office*, 2.

4. Bernard Cooke, *The Future of the Eucharist* (Paulist Press, 1997), 32.

5. LeMoyne-Zogby Contemporary Catholic Trends Survey, 2009, www.lemoyne.edu/academics/centersofexcellence/contemporary catholictrends/latestpoll/tabid/548/default.aspx, accessed May 22, 2013.

6. Ibid.

7. Pope Benedict XVI, *Homily Concluding the Year for Priests*, Solemnity of the Sacred Heart of Jesus, St. Peter's Square, June 11, 2010.

8. Kieran Quinlan, *Walker Percy: The Last Catholic Novelist* (Baton Rouge: Louisiana State University Press, 1996), 116.

9. Walker Percy, "Symposium on Roman Catholicism and American Exceptionalism," *New Oxford Review*, March 1987, 4.

10. Lewis A. Lawson and Victor A. Kramer, *More Conversations with Walker Percy* (Jackson: University Press of Mississippi, 1993), 185.

11. Catechism of the Catholic Church, 1536.

12. Scott Hahn, *Many Are Called*.

13. Jean Galot, *Theology of the Priesthood* (Ignatius), 254.

14. Gary Macy, *The Hidden History of Women's Ordination: Female Clergy in the Medieval West* (New York: Oxford University Press, 2007).

15. Catechism of the Catholic Church, 1584.

16. Michelle Somerville, "Catholic Bishops Endanger Church Tax Exempt Status," www.huffingtonpost.com/michele-somerville/catholic-bishops-doma_b_1001524.html, accessed May 22, 2013.

17. Maureen Dowd, "Bishops Play Church Queens as Pawns," *New York Times*, April 28, 2012.

18. Stephen Rossetti, *The Joy of Priesthood* (Notre Dame, Ind.: Ave Maria Press, 2005), 2.

19. Stephen Rossetti, *Why Priests Are Happy* (Notre Dame, Ind.: Ave Maria Press, 2011), 86–87.

20. *A Priest's Life*, 12.

21. Rossetti, *Why Priests Are Happy*, 17.

22. Rossetti, *Joy of Priesthood*, 69.

23. Ibid., 70.

24. Mary Gautier, Paul Perl, and Stephen Fichter, *Same Call, Different Men: The Evolution of the Priesthood since Vatican II* (Collegeville, Minn.: Liturgical Press, 2012), 25.

25. Ibid., 28.

26. Ibid., 29.

27. *Redemptoris Missio* 33.3.

28. Cardinal Timothy Dolan, "The Gospel in the Digital Age," http://blog.archny.org/?p-1210, accessed May 22, 2013.

Chapter Ten

1. Matthew Gamber, "An Interview with Father Robert Barron about His New TV Series on the Catholic Faith," *Catholic World Report*, September 29, 2011.

2. Ibid.

3. Ibid.

4. Ibid.

5. Ibid.

6. Catholics Come Home website, www.catholicscomehome.org, accessed May 22, 2013.

7. Peter Kreeft, endorsement, Catholics Come Home website, www.catholicscomehome.org, accessed May 22, 2013.

8. Encourage Priests website, http://encouragepriests.org/ste/home-page, accessed May 22, 2013.

9. FOCUS website, www.focus.org/about/the-main-thing.html, accessed May 22, 2013.

10 . Available at www.usccb.org/beliefs-and-teachings/how-we-teach/new-evangelization/disciples-called-witness/disciples-called-to-witness-part-i.cfm, accessed May 22, 2013.

11 . Available at www.denverpost.com/search/ci_19619647#ixzz1sme ZwSLt, accessed May 22, 2013.

12. Joan Desmond Frawley, "'Catholic Voices' Reaches America Just in

Time for a Full-Blown First Amendment Battle," *National Catholic Register*, May 25, 2012, www.ncregister.com/daily-news/catholic-voices-reaches-america-just-in-time-for-a-full-blown-first-amendme/, accessed May 22, 2013.

13. Tim Drake, "CARA Study Finds Abundance of Potential Priests and Sisters," October 9, 2012, *National Catholic Register*, www.ncregister.com/daily-news/cara-study-finds-abundance-of-potential-priests-and-sisters, accessed May 22, 2013.

14. "Archbishop Gomez: Seminary Teachers Must Be Students of American Culture," June 15, 2012, Catholic News Agency, www.catholic-newsagency.com/news/archbishop-gomez-tells-seminarians-to-be-students-of-american-culture/, accessed May 22, 2013.

15. United States Conference of Catholic Bishops, *Disciples Called to Witness: The New Evangelization* (Washington, D.C.: Committee on Evangelization and Catechesis, United States Conference of Catholic Bishops, 2012).

16. USCCB General Assembly, 2012 November, Presidential Address, November 12, 2012, available at www.usccb.org/about/leadership/usccb-general-assembly/2012-november-meeting/presidential-address-cardinal-dolan.cfm, accessed May 20, 2013.

17. Tim Drake, "Catholic Students Losing Their Religion," November 4, 2008, *National Catholic Register*, www.ncregister.com/site/article/16432/, accessed May 22, 2013.

18. "My Daddy's Name Is Donor," released May 2010, Institute for American Values, http://familyscholars.org/my-daddys-name-is-donor-2/, accessed May 22, 2013.

19. Cardinal Timothy M. Dolan, *True Freedom: On Protecting Human Dignity and Religious Liberty* (Image Books: New York, 2012).

20. John Paul II, *Ecclesia in Europa*, June 28, 2003, www.vatican.va/holy_father/john_paul_ii/apost_exhortations/documents/hf_jp-ii_exh_20030628_ecclesia-in-europa_en.html, accessed May 22, 2013.

21. David Van Biehma, "Is Liberal Catholicism Dead?," *Time*, May 3, 2008.

22. Ibid.

Index

McBride, Margaret, Sister, 60
McBrien, Richard, 124–126, 143, 144
McDonald, Andrew J., Connecticut state senator, 51, 54–55
McFadden, Joseph P., Bishop, 96–98
McGrath, Parick, Bishop, 110
McInerney, Ralph, 143, 147, 150
Meyers, John, J., Archbishop, 17, 160
Miscamble, Wilson, Reverend, 99
Moll, Ben, 30
Monan, Donald, Reverend, 94
Moriarity, Maris, 31
Mount St. Mary's Seminary, Baltimore, 26
Moynihan, Daniel Patrick, 136
Murtchison, William, 125
National Association of American Nuns, 50
National Catholic Register, 77–78, 151
National Catholic Reporter, 8, 41, 52, 74, 96, 124, 129, 150
National Catholic Youth Conference, 194
National Gay and Lesbian Task Force, 157
National Right to Life, 18
natural law, 59–60
Naumann, Joseph F., Archbishop, 160
Network, 82
Neuhaus, Richard, Reverend, 103
new evangelization, 2, 187, 196
New Ways Ministry, 49; and Grammick, Jeanine, 143, 155–157
Newman, John Henry, Cardinal, 35–36, 100
Nicene Creed, 178
Nienstedt, John C., Bishop, 160
Northhouse, Peter, 67–70
Novak, Michael, 123
O'Brien, David, 44, 45, 83–84; and Cardinal Raymond Burke, 84, 103, 132
O'Brien, Edwin, Archbishop, 148, 184
O'Brien, George Dennis, 15, 100–101
O'Callaghan, Joseph, 50
O'Connell, Jack, 140
O'Connor, John Joseph, Cardinal, 73
O'Malley, Sean Patrick Cardinal, 3
O'Rourke, Kevin, 61
Oakley, Francis, 46–48

Obama, Barack, on health care, 60, 82, 83, 86; and Notre Dame controversy, 131, 138–141, 147–150, 165–170
Obey, David, 84
Ochoa, Armando X., Bishop, 104–105
Olmsted, Thomas, J., Bishop, 17; on excommunication of hospital worker, 59–61; on social class, 21; on demographics of ordination in 1980s, 66; courage of, 71; on charisma, 72; on Notre Dame, 147, 161
Operation Andrew, 30
Ortiz, Edsil, Reverend, 110
Our Lady of Guadalupe Seminary, 27
Panke, Robert, Monsignor, 31
parish life coordinators, 117–130
Pastores Dabo Vobis ("I Will Give You Shepherds"), 37
Paul VI, Pope, 14, 181, 187
Pax Christi, 50
Pelosi, Nancy, U.S. representative, 18
Pena, Raymundo, Bishop, 149
Pendergast, Joseph, Reverend, 111
Percy, Walker, 24, 175–176, 202
Perl, Paul, 185
Peters, Thomas, 156
Pew Foundation data on Catholics, 3; Pew poll on Notre Dame controversy, 146
Plate, Brian, Reverend, 29
Pontifical Academy for Life, 53
Pontifical College Josephinum, Columbus, OH, 26
Pontifical Council for Promoting New Evangelization, 193
Pontifical Lateran University, 28
Poust, Dennis, 76
Power, David, 128
Presbyterorum Ordinis, 177, 185
priest as saving remnant, 24
priesthood of all believers, 129, 174
priesthood of all of the baptized, 45
Priestly Fraternity of St. Peter, 27
Quinn, John R., Archbishop, 57
Rainbow Sash Alliance, 101
Ratzinger, Joseph, Cardinal, 146–147
Reilly, Patrick, 150; see also Cardinal Newman Society
Reno, R. R., 107